Advance Praise

Nabaparna Ghosh's *Hygienic City-Nation* is an important and timely work, bringing the long historical project of Hindu nation formation down to the neighbourhood level. Deeply researched and lucidly presented, it shows how a regime of upper caste Bengali spatial dominance determined the urbanization process in colonial Calcutta. The work is especially commendable for moving past accounts of colonial power as totalizing—as it shows, very modern logics drove Bengali upper caste Hindus to appropriate colonial discourses of sanitation and hygiene. Ultimately, colonial discourses of sanitation were domesticated into Calcutta's neighbourhood setting for an anti-Dalit and anti-Muslim urban consolidation of local, regional, and national power.

—Sheetal Chhabria, Connecticut College

Nabaparna Ghosh's important new work is a critical study of how the Hindu elite in Calcutta responded to and qualified urban regulation by the colonial state, generating an alternative Hindu spatial and hygienic order, politicizing informal spaces like the *para* (neighbourhood). A fascinating and engaging account, this book extends the frontiers of urban and Calcutta studies in many significant ways.

—Partho Datta, Jawaharlal Nehru University

An account that weaves an extraordinary tale out of the ordinary—a dense narrative of privies, contests over land, neighbourhood clubs and community festivals—painstakingly culled from reports, law suits, photographs, memoirs and a deep understanding of the communities inhabiting Calcutta in the late 19th and early 20th centuries.

This is a conscious departure from the conventional reading of the archive that offers new perspectives on the colonial city, by shifting the focus onto its residents. By showing the intimate connection between health and sanitation and the articulation of citizenship, Ghosh enters the intense debate between the colonial imperative to introduce uniform civic regulations on the one hand and the dictates of custom and tradition for the residents on the other.

The study also offers a history from below of nation-building in the everyday spaces of *para*s or neighbourhoods. The emerging discourses of health and hygiene within middle class neighbourhoods, Ghosh argues, inscribed competing claims on citizenship and leadership for Bengalis. Hygiene, as she shows, made for hierarchies—

moral, material, and social—not only between the colonials and colonized, but also within indigenous society.

This is a new way of looking at the city, beyond town plans, built environment, maps, and statistics. It places the lived experiences of the city's residents at the heart of urbanity, defining both its possibilities and its limits.

—Anindita Ghosh, University of Manchester

This fascinating study makes an important contribution to the historiography of urban South Asia. Through a careful reading of a range of sources, Nabaparna Ghosh shows how Indians shaped urban spaces and practices in colonial Calcutta. In the process, her book offers illuminating insights into the making of India's urban modernity.

—Prashant Kidambi, University of Leicester

Nabaparna Ghosh's *A Hygienic City-Nation* is a critical addition to the literature on cities under colonialism. This fascinating book complicates ideas about the control of the British Empire over urban space and shows that city dwellers carved out autonomous spaces in Calcutta at the neighbourhood level of the *para*. Along the way, Ghosh demonstrates how the social group of the *bhadralok* began to promote specific practices of hygiene in these neighbourhoods. The author illustrates how *bhadralok* practices came to underpin ideas of a Bengali Hindu nation and presents the city as a key site of an emerging nationalism in South Asia. In this way, *A Hygienic City-Nation* offers an urban history with implications far beyond the individual case of Calcutta. Ghosh's illuminating study will resonate with historians of cities and nationalism around the world.

—Joseph Ben Prestel, author of *Emotional Cities: Debates on Urban Change in Berlin and Cairo, 1860–1910*

A groundbreaking study of colonial Calcutta from the perspective of its Indian neighbourhoods and everyday life. Ghosh delivers skilful analysis of the gritty spaces of urban modernity and resistance, and explores the colonial spatialization of hygiene and race with fresh insight. Well written and engaging, the book is a must-read for scholars of South Asian cities and global urban history in general.

—Rosemary Wakeman, Fordham University

A Hygienic City-Nation

Calcutta, the centre of British imperial power in India, figures in scholarship as the locus of colonialism and the hotbed of anti-colonial nationalist movements. Yet historians have largely ignored how the city shaped these movements. This monograph is the first academic work that examines everyday urban formations in the colonial city that informed the broad global forces of imperialism, nationalism, and urbanism, and were, in turn, shaped by them.

Drawing on previously unexplored archives of the Calcutta Improvement Trust and neighbourhood clubs, the author uncovers hidden stories of the city at the everyday level of neighbourhoods or *para*s, where kinship-like ties, caste, religion, and ethnicity constituted new urban modernity. By the early twentieth century, paras grew as microcosms of a city-nation or a city designed to unite a Hindu-Bengali nation. Ghosh focuses on an emergent discourse on Hindu spatial hygiene that powered nationalist pedagogic efforts to train city dwellers in conduct fit for the city-nation. In such pedagogic efforts, upper-caste Bengalis were pitted against the lower-caste working poor and featured as ideal inhabitants of the city: the citizen.

Nabaparna Ghosh teaches Global Studies at Babson College, USA. She has formerly been a Postdoctoral Fellow of History at The Cooper Union, New York City. Her research primarily focuses on the urban history of South Asia; some of her other interests are empire and colonialism, comparative cities, and postcolonial politics.

A Hygienic City-Nation
Space, Community, and Everyday Life in Colonial Calcutta

Nabaparna Ghosh

CAMBRIDGE
UNIVERSITY PRESS

University Printing House, Cambridge CB2 8BS, United Kingdom

One Liberty Plaza, 20th Floor, New York, NY 10006, USA

477 Williamstown Road, Port Melbourne, VIC 3207, Australia

314–321, 3rd Floor, Plot 3, Splendor Forum, Jasola District Centre, New Delhi–110025, India

79 Anson Road, #06–04/06, Singapore 079906

Cambridge University Press is part of the University of Cambridge.

It furthers the University's mission by disseminating knowledge in the pursuit of
education, learning and research at the highest international levels of excellence.

www.cambridge.org
Information on this title: www.cambridge.org/9781108489898

© Nabaparna Ghosh 2020

This publication is in copyright. Subject to statutory exception
and to the provisions of relevant collective licensing agreements,
no reproduction of any part may take place without the written
permission of Cambridge University Press.

First published 2020

Printed in India by Thomson Press India Ltd.

A catalogue record for this publication is available from the British Library

ISBN 978-1-108-48989-8 Hardback

Cambridge University Press has no responsibility for the persistence or accuracy
of URLs for external or third-party internet websites referred to in this publication,
and does not guarantee that any content on such websites is, or will remain,
accurate or appropriate.

Contents

List of Figures, Tables, and Boxes	ix
List of Abbreviations	xi
Acknowledgements	xiii
Introduction	1
1. The Black Town, Spaces of Pathology, and a Hindu Discourse of Citizenship	25
2. The Calcutta Improvement Trust: Racialized Hygiene, Expropriation, and Resistance by Religion	68
3. A City-Nation: *Para*s, Hygiene, and *Swaraj*	106
4. A New Black Town: Recolonizing Calcutta's *Bustee*s	154
Epilogue	190
Glossary	199
Bibliography	201
Index	218

Figures, Tables, and Boxes

Figures

1.1 Photograph of privy vaults and receptacles in a two-storey building. 1. Upper-storey privy. 2. Pipes to carry off soil water. 3. Receptacles to privy vault. 4. Mehtranee. 5. Ground on which a new hut is about to be erected. 6. A pole of the new hut. 7. Adjoining hut.   43

1.2 Photograph showing privies in *kutcha* and *pukka* houses. 1 and 2. Upper storeyed privies. 3. Receptacle. 4. Water pipe almost level with ground. 5. Water vessel. 6. Two-storeyed hut. 7. Hand mill for grinding corn. 8. Poles for a new hut to be erected. 9. A vessel for water.   44

1.3 Photograph of verandah privies. 1, 2, and 3. Verandahs used as privies.   45

1.4 Plan of Shama Bewah's house in Burtola Road, with the courtyard covered up.   47

1.5 An Indian neighbourhood at Machuaabazaar Street before and after demolition.   50

1.6 To the left: The Varaha Avataar in a Hindu calendar showing Lord Vishnu reborn as the Varaha or boar in his second incarnation. He lifts the earth on his tusk after rescuing it from the bottom of the ocean. To the right: A cartoon in the Bengali periodical *Basantak* showing Vishnu holding town improvements—tramways, drainage, markets (all written in Bengali), and tax—on his tusk.   57

3.1 Hindoo *mutt* (temple) in the Chitpore Bazaar. Sir Charles D'Oyly's twenty-eight 'Views of Calcutta and its Environs' [Object no. R2566-24].   115

3.2 Europeans visiting a princely home in Calcutta to witness Durga Puja. A painting by Alexis Soltykoff (1859).   122

3.3 Swarajist pamphlet on cleanliness as self-control.   131

3.4 The Balak Sangha boys practising drills in a park in Calcutta.   134

3.5 The Tarun Sangha boys practising *lathi khela* in a park in Calcutta.   136

x   Figures, Tables, and Boxes

4.1 'The leader of the famine'. The image shows a Swarajist leader picking the fruit of a Swarajist Fund from a tree.   160

4.2 'The depots of disease in the city', a pamphlet published in *Svasthya Samacara*.   162

Tables

1.1 Plague incidents in Alipore prison reported as chicken pox and general weakness. Some patients are also reported as having good health.   41

2.1 As the Calcutta Improvement Trust improved the northern parts of Calcutta, property owners were evicted and forced to move to the southern parts of the city from improvement schemes 7, 7B, 7C, and 7D in the north to 5 and 4A in the south.   78

2.2 A steep increase in land prices, calculated per *cottah* (32 cottahs make 1 acre), between May–June 1919 and January 1920.   82

2.3 The Calcutta Improvement Trust Tribunal decisions between 1922 and 1926.   87

Boxes

3.1 A neighbourhood in Simla Road, Manicktola.   130

3.2 A neighbourhood in Shombhubabur Lane, Entally.   130

3.3 A neighbourhood in Chattubabu Lane, Entally.   130

Abbreviations

CSSSC	Centre for Studies in Social Sciences, Calcutta
HSS	Harijan Sevak Sangh
HULA	Harvard University Library Archives
KCA	King's College Archives
NLA	National Library Archives, Calcutta
NYPL	New York Public Library
TBLA	The British Library Archives
UOLA	University of Oxford Library Archives

Acknowledgements

I owe a great debt of gratitude to individuals and institutions across three continents who made this book possible. Rajat Kanta Ray, Subhas Ranjan Chakraborty, and Jayasree Mukopadhyay at Presidency College sparked my love for history. At the University of Calcutta, Bhaskar Chakraborty and Samita Sen were exceptional teachers. I was fortunate to have Rajsekhar Basu as my professor at the Alipore Campus; a terrific teacher, he also fielded all of my questions as I travelled from Calcutta to Princeton for graduate studies and then back from Princeton to Calcutta for the archives. His generosity has made many distant possibilities a reality for me.

My deepest gratitude is to Gyan Prakash for supervising my dissertation, on which this book is based. With his incredible mind, Gyan taught me, among other important lessons, how important it is to understand the hidden stories of the city. His encouragement at every stage of this work gave the book its current shape. Gyan's support remains unwavering since graduate school, and his advice has always been timely. Bhavani Raman taught me that urbanization is as much a pedagogic tool, as it is spatial. Her endless knowledge and kindness towards graduate students made Princeton a rewarding experience for me. Bhavani taught me how to write and how to think. She read everything I wrote, multiple times, and offered insightful comments on each draft. I cannot thank her enough for travelling all the way from Toronto to Princeton to attend my final public oral exam—thank you. Partha Chatterjee taught me that *para*s (neighbourhood) of Calcutta do not overlap with administrative jurisdictions set by the state and, for that reason, needs attention. An extraordinary scholar, Partha-da always already knew what I established in long hours of tedious research at the archives. His knowledge is infinite and pushed my work in new directions. Benjamin Conisbee Baer shared with me fresh insights on how literature can be a source of history. His vast knowledge of the literary archives and his thoughtful comments on my work enriched my own understanding of the city.

At Princeton, a dynamic intellectual environment—the numerous seminar-lunches, the colonialism and imperialism workshops, research-talks sponsored by the Princeton Institute for International and Regional Studies (PIIRS), and writing boot-camps—nurtured a supportive academic setting to carry out research

xiv   Acknowledgements

on colonial cities. I benefitted from the wisdom of scholars like Alison Isenberg, Anson Rabinbach, Anthony Grafton, Emmanuel Kreike, Jeremy Adelman, and Bonnie Smith (at Rutgers University). I am grateful to the history department at Princeton University and PIIRS for the generous financial support that they offered as I made multiple archival trips to London and Calcutta. In 2013, PIIRS supported an entire year of my dissertation writing at Princeton. I am indebted to Michael Laffan for leading the PIIRS dissertation writing seminar that year. I am grateful to my cohorts at the seminar for listening to my work and offering detailed comments. I am thankful to Reagan Campbell, Lauren Kane, and Jaclyn Wasneski for their support in making the paperwork for these funds a breeze.

I was fortunate to have an excellent cohort at Princeton who supported my research right from when it was a dissertation prospectus to the final, revised version that I sent out as 'writing sample'. Alexander Bevilacqua, Jennifer Jones, Helen Pfeifer, Hannah Louise Clark, Seiji Shirane, and Valeria Lopez Fadul, among others offered useful comments on the prospectus. I would also like to thank Radha Kumar, Rohit De, Rotem Geva, Ninad Pandit, Nikhil Menon, Joppan George, Zack Kagan Guthrie, Ritwik Ranjan, Christina Welsch, Nimisha Barton, Ronny Regev, and Tikia Hamilton for their comments at various stages of this work and also for their friendship and support.

Thanks to the staff at the archives and libraries for their zealous efforts in tracing sources and persistence in acquiring these for me. I would like to thank the staff of the West Bengal State Archives (Calcutta), The National Library (Calcutta), Bangiya Sahitya Parishad (Calcutta), the archives of the Victoria Memorial (Calcutta), the British Library (London), SOAS libraries (London), Bodleian Libraries (Oxford), Firestone Library (Princeton), Widener Library (Cambridge), New York Public Library(New York), Alexander Library (New Brunswick), and Horn Library (Wellesley). A special thanks to Abhijit Bhattacharya at the Centre for Studies in Social Sciences, Calcutta (CSSSC), who pointed out some of the most valuable archives that I explored. The staff at the Town Hall archive in Calcutta always had reports and gazettes ready for me. Housed in a monumental building, the Town Hall archive is one of the most organized places I have worked at. Thanks to Gary Hausman (then at Princeton University) and Philip McEldowney at the University of Virginia for finding some the most significant historical sources for me.

I am grateful to Partho Datta for reading Chapter 2 and offering insightful comments. An inspiring and affable scholar, Stephen Legg, read Chapter 3 and wrote three emails full of constructive comments. Thank you, Steve. Sincere thanks to John Hutnyk for reading a chapter in its very early stage. I am also indebted to Nikhil Rao, Anindita Ghosh, Prashant Kidambi, Jawhar Sircar, Janam Mukherjee, Christine Furedy, Sandip Hazareesingh, David Boyk, Carl

Acknowledgements   xv

Nightingale, and Kristin Stapleton, who listened to my work in its various stages. I would also like to thank Qudsiya Ahmed and her team at Cambridge University Press. I am indebted to the anonymous reviewers who offered many useful edits.

I was fortunate to be a part of the NEH funded Space and Place Institute in 2017 at Northeastern University. Thanks to Tim Creswell and Elizabeth Maddock Dillon, directors of the institute, who drew my attention to global literature on urban space; the institute offered a fantastic place to engage in stimulating conversations on the meaning of place.

I am thankful to the many people of Calcutta who opened their homes, offered me tea, and shared with me both their family archives and their thoughts on the city. Devarshi Roy Choudhury at the Sabarna Sangrahashala, V. Ramaswamy, and P. T. Nair spent hours listening to my project. I am grateful to the club administrators of Badamtala Ashar Sangha and Simla Byaym Samiti who shared the histories of the clubs and relevant publications with me.

I am indebted to the Centre for Modern Indian Studies (CeMIS) at the University of Gottingen for inviting me to present my work. It was a pleasure to present my research at a centre that extended such great collegiality and warmth. Thanks to Ritajyoti Bandopadhyay for the intellectual enrichment, the superb comments, the gyros, and the Pilsners. Kaustubh Mani Sengupta is a terrific historian, who offered a significant revision to Chapter 3. Debarati Bagchi, Gayatri Jai Singh Rathore, Camille Buat, Maria-Daniela Pomohaci, Saeed Ahmad, and Anwesha Sengupta—thank you for listening to the chapters and for your comments.

My colleagues at Babson College—Marjorie Feld and Kevin Bruyneel—have been pillars of support. Stephen Deets made sure that I had the most peaceful travels to conferences and archives. Katie Platt cooked dinners and offered mentorship. Sandra Graham, Kandice Hauf, Janice Yellin, and James Bradford are extraordinarily supportive colleagues. Stephen Spiess taught me how to write a book proposal and then how to respond to reviewer comments. Xinghua Li keeps me spirited—I treasure your friendship and advice. Thanks, Xinghua, for introducing me to the city of Cambridge.

I am thankful to my parents, Narayan Chandra Ghosh and Gouri Ghosh, for teaching me to love books. Their trips to College Street on hot summer afternoons and their proud acquisition of a copy of the most recent Bengali book inspired me to start reading. Thanks to my sister, Netraparna Ghosh, who lives in the snow-capped mountains of Utah where I was fortunate to enjoy scenic breaks between writing. Arnab Sinha, Sushant Sachdeva, and Sreechakra Goparaju were like family in Princeton—they offered too many dinners and whole-milk *chai*s on cold evenings. Manasvi Nagrecha was always ready to meet up in New York City and find the best Ramen place for me.

Debanjan Ghosh has shared with me all excitements and disappointments that make this book; he has always seen purpose in the joys and hardships that coloured the decade that I took to write this book. His love has helped me sail through difficult times and get back to the routine of writing.

My mum did not live to see this book. Losing her has been critical to my understanding of Calcutta—what it offers, only to take away. I dedicate this book to her memory.

Introduction

In July 1925, the opening of a beef shop in Mudialy, in south Calcutta, led to loud protests in the neighbourhood. It was the store's location—a three-minute walk from both Hindu and Muslim houses—that triggered the protests. Sheikh Keramat Ali, a meat seller, had opened the shop after local Muslims complained that there were not enough beef stores in the region.[1] Although Muslim neighbours welcomed the store, Hindus complained that it was an affront to their religion. They grouped together, protesting that there were already enough beef stores in the city, and a new one was not needed. Two Hindu gentlemen, leaders of associations that oversaw health and hygiene in the locality, demanded that Ali close his store. They explained that the Hindus on their way to work had to pass by the store every morning, and that the sight of beef, placed on display, offended their religious sentiments. The growing, frequently violent protests forced Ali to close his store.[2]

A few years before this incident, the nationalist Swaraj party had defeated the British in the Calcutta municipal elections of 1923. When the Swarajists took over the city's administration, the Indian city dwellers hoped that after two hundred years of British colonial rule, they would enjoy equal rights to the city. The protests against Ali's beef shop, however, revealed a different reality. The protests showed that the Hindu-Bengali city dwellers exerted a powerful influence over their neighbourhoods, suspending the needs of other communities. Hindu neighbours organizing to pressure Ali into closing his store did invoke city laws to show that the beef shop was indeed outside the space assigned for such stores. Yet pointing out the violation of law was only a small part of their protests. Much of their protest centred on how a beef store was culturally inappropriate in a neighbourhood where Hindus lived.

Theorizations of the 'colonial city'—particularly those elaborated by historians and architectural historians—have discussed how race segregated the colonial city into enclaves of the European (white) town and Indian (black) town.[3] Scholars have, however, also explored whether there existed easy passages between these two zones.[4] But how was space organized *within* the black town and how did it differ from imperial urban spatial organization? Who planned space in the black town? How did religion, caste, and ethnic differences among Indians, which grew violent with colonialism, inform colonial urban configuration? This book seeks answers to these questions in the everyday culture and politics of neighbourhoods in colonial Calcutta's black town.

Offering a new perspective on South Asian cities, this book explores for the first time how colonial urban space was made, experienced, and narrated by Indian city dwellers in the shadow of colonialism. It presents the important but relatively unknown stories of Calcutta's neighbourhoods or *para*s and their centrality in resisting and reworking colonial city planning. More than planned physical spaces, paras were Bengali spatial communities that celebrated kinship-like ties between neighbours.[5] The para was not an administrative category; the state did not plan its spaces. Instead, the para's residents planned its spaces. A cluster of houses along a street where neighbours lived like an extended family, a club, a sports field, a temple, and a water-reservoir comprised the space of a para. The cultural life of the para—including festivals and informal associations—reinforced the sense of neighbourhood community.

What Henri Lefebvre called 'monumental' space—space that is sacred or belongs to authority, including religious or governmental buildings, institutions, boulevards, monuments, and landmark architectures that derive meaning both as symbolic structures and lived spaces—has dominated studies on colonial cities.[6] Going beyond the planned spaces of the city, this book fills a gap in scholarship with a detailed and multifaceted analysis of ground-level urbanization in the para. The book breaks from much of the previous scholarship on colonial cities, which has tended to treat urban space as a container for politics, economics, and culture or as spaces shaped through contests between state, planners, and the people.[7] This book, in contrast, studies how Indian city dwellers shaped spaces that did not feature in colonial city maps and were thus outside British plans for Calcutta. It engages with scholarship on neighbourhoods that explain these spaces as displays of a widely different spatial knowledge to argue that this difference was not simply critical to resistance against colonial interventions but also constitutive of a new urban modernity.

The para, I argue, was the spatial unit of the *samaj*—a pre-colonial social formation that the Hindus shaped to live together when faced with years of Muslim rule. From the thirteenth century onwards, extended Muslim rule in Bengal threatened the Hindus who feared that the Muslim rulers would either force them to convert to Islam or seize their property.[8] To protect their property, practice their religion, and resist the interventions of Muslim rulers, Hindus formed samajes in their villages, where they lived together as

Introduction 3

a community. Caste informed the space of the samaj: each caste lived in a separate neighbourhood or para. These paras were also named after the caste of its settlers.

The earliest paras of Calcutta took shape under Indian merchants who moved in the nineteenth century from their villages to live near upcoming markets; they shaped paras that resembled those in their villages and evoked nostalgia.[9] They organized these paras along caste lines; as in their villages, neighbours who belonged to the same caste lived together as a family in paras that reflected their Hindu identities. Because the para embodied their religious views, the boundaries between public and private space blurred.

In the colonial city, samajes resisted colonial town planning in the same way they resisted the earlier Muslim rule. As Swarupa Gupta's work has shown, samajes were social formations based on caste that existed in pre-colonial times and later became the foundation on which the community of the nation took shape; the samaj therefore complicates the understanding of scholarship on anti-colonial nationalism as a derivative discourse.[10] Analysing the space of the para on which the samaj was built, this book explores how caste, religion, class, and ethnicity shaped the colonial city, and was, in turn, shaped by it.

A certain imaginary of a 'city'—vastly different from pre-colonial Indian spatial forms or the industrial metropolises of Britain—steered British urbanism in India. British merchants, together with Indian traders, built urban centres that demonstrated the region's growing imperial connections. These urban centres or colonial cities were replete with ports, forts, business centres dominated by whites, and enclaves of white and black residential neighbourhoods that grafted colonial capitalism onto indigenous cultures. Whether the British worked on their own to transform the physical environment or whether Indians assisted them, however, remains a matter of debate. As William Glover has shown, for the case of colonial Lahore, the British colonizers did craft a new space, but did so by working with Indian officials.[11] Preeti Chopra has similarly described the colonial city as a 'joint enterprise' between British colonizers and Indian traders.[12] This book, on the other hand, departs from the view that colonial cities were spaces of collaboration. I argue that in colonial Calcutta, Hindu traders established business partnerships with British merchants, while crafting spaces of autonomy at the level of paras. They designed paras to preserve the social spaces of their villages in the city, deploying religion to govern these spaces and resist British town plans. After the battle of Plassey in 1757, the British were finally able to extend their financial partnership into political authority, but doing so required not further collaboration but rather brute force.

I argue that the spatial configuration of the paras changed drastically when the British introduced English education in 1835. English education shaped a new social group of *bhadraloks* (literally 'gentlemen' in Bengali), a category of propertied middle- and upper-class, upper-caste, and largely English-educated Hindu urban professionals.[13] In the early twentieth century, the bhadraloks engaged in an urban management of space that re-configured their paras as microcosms of a Hindu-Bengali nation. By taking a closer look at everyday life in the para—voluntary associations of bhadraloks at para clubs, health camps, annual festivals, and seasonal theatres—I underscore everyday processes that carved a regional Bengali identity.

Scholarship on anti-colonial nationalism and communalism have already addressed the tension between nationalism's broad homogenizing impulses and the fragmented and regional sentiments of particular communities. Gyanendra Pandey's ground-breaking work on communalism, for instance, discussed the difficulties in imagining a nation in a country that was a patchwork of communities, each proud of its own history and belief systems.[14] While Pandey argued that around 1920 India transformed from an assemblage of communities into a collection of citizens or individuals, he also warned that this did not imply that community-based nationalism waned after the 1920s—it existed and bred communalism. Scholarship on regional community-based identity construction, such as Francesca Orsini's excellent work on the crafting of a Hindi public sphere in northern India between 1920 and 1940 and Tapan Raychaudhuri's detailed analysis of how Western sensibilities transformed the mental world of Bengali intellectuals leading to stereotypes of a morally superior East and a materially sound West, have explained how growing regional sentiments contrasted with nationalist efforts to centralize and unify the nation.[15] Sabyasachi Bhattacharya wrote that in Bengal a wide spectrum of socio-political shifts in the 1920s—the vernacularizing of politics, Marathi, Tamil, and Gujarati participation in the nationalist movement that threatened Bengali pre-eminence, the rise of *mofussils* (satellite towns), the comfort that mofussil leaders felt in conversing in Bengali, and the strong nationalist belief that a Bengali consciousness produced in the realm of the nonmaterial could keep the community together even when conflicts tore apart the material world—mandated a Bengali nation.[16]

In the early twentieth century, paras offered fertile grounds for a Bengali nation to take shape. I argue that the Swarajists initiated a process called 'civicization' that tried to transform the kinship-like ties between neighbours into community bonds of a nation. While samajes fired Swarajist envisioning of

Introduction 5

a nation, civicization reconfigured paras into spatial units of a 'city nation'—a city ordered in a way that would produce a regional Bengali identity and also bring a Hindu nation into being. A 'civilizing process' reinforced the 'city nation', disciplining the body, deportment, sexuality, and speech of individuals. Bhadraloks appropriated the colonial language of urban development and led the civilizing process in their paras. They ran health camps and scout training programmes, while also encouraging theatre performances, religious festivals, musical evenings, and sit-and-draw competitions that celebrated an emergent Bengali nation. The Bengali identity that the bhadraloks advanced was far from secular: the bodily conduct they encouraged and the music and theatre they patronized, all drew on Hindu religion and were marked with exclusionary caste practices.

This book argues that the emergence of bhadraloks as leaders of their paras was closely linked to the rise of a spatializing discourse of hygiene that segregated the city along caste lines. Caste-based paras had earlier shaped a divided landscape, but while such divisions were a spatial custom, the association of hygiene with caste in the early twentieth century portrayed non-Hindu and lower caste bodies as 'diseased' and 'dirty', demanding they be excluded, through spatial segregation, from the city and its administration. This book therefore departs from a body of work that foregrounds the importance of English education and urban professions in shaping the bhadraloks as a group or sees them as leaders of a spiritual domain.[17] It also moves away from describing bhadraloks as authors of a nation that enacted the religion and science divide. Instead, it argues that bhadraloks carefully crafted a Hindu science of hygiene, thereby emerging as urban sanitarians, a posture that reinforced their dominant role in Calcutta.

Prior to the arrival of the British, practices of cleanliness and disease prevention existed among Indians, but was seldom a state concern. Indians took to customary habits of personal hygiene that they believed kept diseases away—taking a bath twice every day and not eating with the left hand—were common practices of hygiene. When unwell, they consulted Vaidyas or health workers who prescribed Ayurveda to cure ailments.[18] In sharp contrast, the British brought with them the obsession with public health that made personal hygiene a state prerogative, transforming it into a tool of governance. The bhadraloks borrowed from the British the idea that hygiene was a public concern—they took on the roles of health supervisors in their para, advising their neighbours on hygiene. But at the same time, the language of hygiene that they endorsed was not secular like the colonial discourses on health and sanitation. Instead, it

6   A Hygienic City-Nation

heavily overlapped with Hindu caste practices. Bhadraloks placed the blame of disease and dirtiness on non-Hindu and lower caste city dwellers, demanding the segregation of their neighbourhoods and shaping a language of hygiene that set Hindu practices as normative in the city.

Projit Bihari Mukharji in *Nationalizing the Body* has already explained how hygiene played a pivotal role in shaping a national culture in South Asia. Mukharji discussed the role of *daktars*—indigenous practitioners of medicine—who authored a new medical literature that inscribed hygiene with Hindu values; Hindu hygiene and accompanying sanitary practices then shaped a national culture of hygiene.[19] Mukharji explained that as part of the Hindu hygiene, daktars prescribed a national diet and national physical developments (a selection of sports) that assisted Bengalis to internalize the disciplines of a Hindu and Bengali nation. Meanwhile, concepts of racial immunity and racial pre-disposition intersected in contagion-control methods that the daktars advised to medically produce a Bengali national body.

This book builds on Mukharji's argument that practices of Hindu hygiene served to nationalize the Bengali body but moves beyond medical discourses to show how non-medical practitioners also contributed to the new language of Hindu hygiene and enforced its practices on both Hindu and non-Hindu city dwellers. Most bhadraloks were government employees, lawyers, and school teachers. They formed health associations in their paras to advise neighbours on matters of personal hygiene. The content of this instruction conflated urbanism with Hindu and Bengali nationalism, transforming paras into microcosms of the city-nation.

Kolkata/Calcutta as a Colonial City

The city now known as Kolkata was once a conglomeration of three waterfront villages. In 1698, to finance their business efforts, East India Company merchants bought *zamindari* (tax collecting) rights for the three villages from Azim-us-Shan, the grandson of the reigning Mughal Emperor Aurangzeb. The merchants decided to thread together the three villages into a 'city' to facilitate the collection of taxes and to accelerate trade. This city that the British built was a direct response to their business and administrative needs—they built a port that connected their private trade in India to global trade routes, and they cleared the area surrounding Lal Dighi, a water reservoir, transforming it into a 'city centre' that began to house European business offices and credit unions.

Introduction

At the heart of scholarship on colonial Calcutta is the segregation of urban space into racial dyads of native/ruled and white/colonizer city sections. Similar to other colonial cities like Algiers and Singapore, early histories of Calcutta described distinct racial zones where the Europeans and Bengalis lived—a spatial pattern that recent histories have questioned.[20] Historians now argue that the racial zones or the dual city model was far from rigid, as there were numerous passages between the two zones.

In South Asian urban history, the concept of a dual city became prominent in social histories that were responses to Gerald Breeze's work on Delhi. In 1974, Breeze formulated a concept of 'subsistence urbanization'.[21] Offering a linear understanding of urbanism that traced industrialization in Europe as the starting point of urban modernity, he described all other urban forms as 'subsistence'. Breeze found that in developing countries, subsistence urbanization forced individuals to live in dense conditions—worse than in rural areas—in which the available means of support could not provide more than mere survival. Of course, urban historians criticized Breeze's theory for discounting historical differences between cities. Countering Breeze, social historians highlighted colonial economic exigencies that allowed markets to expand while also attracting village, caste, and social groups to cities: in colonial cities, they argued, modernity and tradition were dichotomous and shaped each other.[22] It was also in response to Breeze that they outlined a city in which the white population lived in the white town, and the Indians lived in the black town. Racial segregation of space, however, was not the focus of their inquiry. Instead, historians studied bustling *bazaars* or indigenous markets that stood at the heart of the black town.[23] Here pre-colonial forms of economic exchanges continued amidst the colonial push for transition to capitalist forms.

Expanding on the social histories of colonial cities, cultural history approaches to the city have paid particular attention to the spatialization of race. Anthony D. King's work, for instance, highlights the colonial city as a culture contact situation that translated into dominance-dependence relations between the colonizers and the ruled.[24] This dominance-dependence relation, he explained, crafted a new language of modernity that equated modernization with Westernization. Postcolonial scholars, however, have challenged King's argument that the 'dominant culture' represented modernity in the colonial city—Jyoti Hosagrahar, William Glover, Preeti Chopra, and Swati Chattopadhyay have all pointed to constant exchanges across the racial enclaves of the colonial city that sculpted an 'indigenous modernity' manifest in translations and contestations between European modernity and indigenous customs.[25]

A similar uncertainty regarding the actuality of definite racial zones of black and white town has also informed global literature on colonial cities. Scholars like William Bissell have questioned how strictly these racial enclaves were enforced. Bissell has shown that in colonial Zanzibar, imperial policies like town planning was often asserted but rarely put to practice.[26] This book goes beyond scholarship that describes the 'black town' as actual physical space to emphasize the discursive production of the black town in colonial health reports. I argue that a discursive black town in such reports was meant to facilitate the smooth flow of civic improvements. In other words, I argue that the 'black town' was the product of a symbolic geography that represented the native space as a culture of pathology and called for it to be radically restructured in modern ways. I describe how, more than the actual implementation of the plan itself, colonialism was driven by the discourses surrounding town plans and improvement projects—the British justification for the need of a certain town plan, how they planned to implement it, who they argued it would benefit, and why.

In his pioneering work on British colonialism in Egypt, Timothy Mitchell depicted the discursive violence that 'enframes' space.[27] Mitchell combined Michel Foucault's concept of disciplinary power with the colonial tool of visual representation to show how the state became powerful by dividing and containing populations. This book builds on the idea of enframement to point to colonial textual and photographic discourses that translated Indian neighbourhoods into a symbolic geography of filth. This translation, I argue, was materialized through an 'enframement' of space—the colonial representation of space tied to the colonial production of knowledge, constituting the totality of the colonizers' attempt to control the reality of the ruled.

Additionally, I draw on Swati Chattopadhyay's argument that the power of narration was a key tool of the imperial mission in Calcutta.[28] Chattopadhyay narrowed down on strategies that the British employed in their writings, surveys, and reports that created tropes of disease-ridden Indian spaces suggesting a complete lack of sanitary awareness among Indians. The structured representations of backward spaces that advanced British colonialism as a project to civilize has also been addressed in the works of James Ryan and Christopher Pinney. They described photographs as colonial tools and argued that photographic discourses were in fact intertextual, meaning that they connected with linguistic messages and other symbolic codes to provide reasons for colonization.[29]

Introduction

To these contributions, I add the colonial strategy of selective representation of space that underpinned British charges of poor Indian sanitation. Exploring public health reports, I point to selective representations of Indian neighbourhoods that turned them into the 'other' of progress—the 'backward' and the 'uncivilized'. I describe how enframement produced binaries that pitted the colonizers against the colonized, creating rigid discursive categories of rational/irrational, modern/backward, civilized/savage, order/chaos, and, in the context of space, the racial enclaves of Indian and British parts of the city known as the black and white towns. I point to the general style of representation in the texts and photographs through which health officers framed a geography of backwardness. The health officers mapped clean and unclean spaces onto black and white towns, delivering a message that was both political and cultural and established the need for the British to civilize a backward race.

I argue that we can locate in the spatial dyad of progress/backwardness or black/white towns the early formulations of present-day developmentalism. As Arturo Escobar has contended, development is both an ideological export and an act of cultural imperialism.[30] Escobar explained that development planning was not only a problem because it failed; it was a problem also when it succeeded because it set the terms for how people in poorer countries should live and behave—the poor are made subjects of development as much as they are subjects of their own government. With its forthright deployment of norms and value judgments, development was indeed a form of cultural imperialism that poor countries had little means of declining. John Hutnyk's study of Calcutta, for instance, details the value judgment inherent in development discourses centring on the city. Exploring technologies of representation in development discourses that frame the city as crumbling, Hutnyk shows how the politics of representation reinforces, rather than solves, the conditions of contemporary cultural and economic inequality.[31]

This book therefore resonates strongly with present-day developments in urban India—where city life is marked by official efforts to create greater legibility and flow (road widening, demolitions) and by the efforts of members of the urban middle class to portray slums and poorer neighbourhoods in a light similar to colonial productions of a black town.

The Calcutta Improvement Trust

In his influential work, *Black Marxism* (1983), Cedric Robinson wrote that capitalist societies always expand in racist directions. He coined the term 'racial capitalism' to describe race-based hierarchies that trigger social, political, and economic inequalities in capitalist nations.[32] Although race informs the social architecture of capitalist economies, Robinson pointed out, received histories of capitalism barely mention race. To address this gap in scholarship, he appealed to scholars to highlight race in their inquiries into capitalist societies.

The concept of racial capitalism has informed a wide variety of disciplines including, but not limited to, legal studies, history, business, feminist studies, sociology, and so on. The intersection of race and capitalism is also of much interest to scholars studying cities. Although seminal works by urban theorists like Henri Lefebvre, David Harvey, and Neil Smith focused primarily on class, side-lining race, in recent times Liam Kennedy, Ted Rutland, and Giovanni Picker have highlighted systems of racialization in cities that lead to uneven capitalist development.[33] The works of Robert Home and Carl Nightingale further explained racialization of space as a shared, global phenomenon.[34] While Home moves away from ascribing British choices to Social Darwinist theory to argue that racial segregation had diverse purposes in different parts of the British Empire—from creating a multi-ethnic trade city in Singapore to protecting the Empire after a deadly mutiny in 1857 in India—Nightingale's work focuses on a more connected history of segregation in Western and non-Western cities. According to him, residential segregation in the United States, widespread after the Civil War, had roots in European imperial policies. Before segregation was formally initiated in the United States, segregation in the colonies provided a wealth of information on the processes of mapping race and its repercussions.

In exploring the 'black' town, I highlight the role of race in providing more than a basis for segregating space in colonial cites—it also informed discourses on public health that facilitated British attempts to control a growing market in land. British pseudo-scientific discoveries on race and surveys that revealed Calcutta's deteriorating health conditions supported their constant theorization of Indians as weak, unclean, and barbaric. Based on these discourses, the British portrayed blackness as more than skin colour: blackness symbolized an impenetrable filth from which the Indians, as a race, could not liberate themselves. The imputed Indian lack of sanitary awareness allowed the British to encroach on their lands and demolish houses and neighbourhoods.

The black town in colonial Calcutta, as a construct of symbolic geography, implied the need for it to develop—that is, to be radically restructured in modern ways. In 1911, the state commissioned the Calcutta Improvement Trust to redesign the city to improve public health. Working in the aftermath of a plague epidemic, the Trust engaged in an authoritarian language of

Introduction

development. To develop the city, trustees imported town plans from Europe, encased in their original forms, and enforced these without making necessary modifications to match Indian social and cultural preferences. Trust officials also worked with British real estate developers and land promoters to acquire as much land as they wished. Armed with an independent law court and emergency 'public purpose' clauses—allowing private land to be acquired by the state for the public good—the Trust engaged in massive demolitions of private property.[35] Trustees explained demolitions as efforts to open land to sunlight and improve ventilation; in fact, however, such demolitions actually cleared land for a growing market.

The British had commissioned similar 'improvement trusts' in all major cities of their colonies. Describing the work of the Singapore Improvement Trust, Brenda Yeoh found a similar British obsession for improving the health of the city by opening streets and houses to sunlight.[36] This 'opening of space' came at the cost of the wholesale destruction of large swaths of existing houses, shops, and businesses. In Calcutta, the Trustees auctioned and sold surplus lands to developers who built suburbs and flats (apartments) that segregated the city along lines of caste, religion, and class.

Historians studying improvement trusts in British colonies have pointed out periodic resistances: financial problems, failed rehousing schemes, the refusal of property owners to move when served with eviction notices, and customary practices of city dwellers that limited the ability of these organizations to achieve their aims.[37] In a detailed reading of the Trust's work in Calcutta, Partho Datta, however, offers a different insight about resistance. He argues that Indian city dwellers increasingly desired the amelioration of the urban environment in the nineteenth century.[38] Starting as early as the 1820s, Indian landlords wrote several petitions to town improvement committees demanding specific improvements. Almost a hundred years later, nationalist Surendranath Banerjea supported 'improvement' but was against its 'revolutionary provisions', meaning that he disapproved of the thoughtless ways in which the state carried out improvements. Datta writes that the 'nationalists felt unable to critique planning, whose sanitary precepts, they may have come to believe, were responsible for saving countless lives'.[39] What Datta argues is that the nationalists agreed that certain town improvements were necessary to fight epidemics, but they did not agree with the way in which the state carried out these improvements.

Adding to the works of Partho Datta, Brenda Yeoh, William Bissell, Prashant Kidambi, and Jiat Hwee Chang, which have described the role of colonial improvement trusts as town improvement and town planning authorities, this book also examines the Calcutta Improvement Trust's role as a court of law.[40] Existing scholarship on improvement trusts has been silent on the legal power they wielded for reshaping cities. This book discusses a series of legal trials that the Trust carried out outside of the courts in informal spaces such as the street-side, city-schools, a room in the house of an influential Indian gentleman, and so on, forcibly acquiring land for urban development. The trust had its own tribunal, which resolved land-related disputes and steered its demolitions and acquisitions of private property.

I argue that new urban identities and urban communities took shape in the movements that property owners launched against the Trust's reckless encroachments on private property. I examine petitions forwarded by Bengali property owners against the Trust's notices of eviction. Based on a close reading of these petitions, I find that as part of their everyday manoeuvring to resist the Trust, property owners reconfigured their priorities of belonging and came to identify, over and above anything else, as Hindus and Muslims. Faced with the Trust's authoritarian policies, they described their property as *debutter*—invested in the deity—thus rendering it, they argued, inalienable. They provided evidence that the debutter was in fact public, which meant that it brought together the para as a Hindu community. To avoid communal uprisings, the Trust then abstained from acquiring these properties. The now-primary Hindu and Muslim identities of the property owners and their paras protected their property from forceful acquisitions and their houses from demolition. Taking place in the private, family, and individual spheres of life, these acts were everyday tactics or strategies that they employed to resist the state. These everyday acts shaped communities based on religion but were different from nationalist projections of a Hindu community to bring together the nation.

Investing property with religious meanings, property owners transformed their dialogues with the state into negotiations between traditional customs and modern city planning. Reviewing Jyoti Hosagrahar's description of indigenous modernity—a series of contestations between the colonizer and the ruled that resisted an undisputed acceptance of European modernity—Janaki Nair raised an important question: battles between customary practices and the transformative impulses of modern regimes were fought in Western capitals, too; how much of what the colonials experienced as the un-reformable native custom was, in fact, resistance?[41] This book is an attempt to understand how upper-caste, Bengali property owners invented and foregrounded 'customary' spatial practices to create a language of resistance against state encroachments

Introduction 13

on their property. I argue that existing scholarship on improvement trusts does not capture the depth of city dwellers' unwillingness to act jointly with it. Moving beyond locating resistance in nationalist discourses, I emphasize the agency of ordinary city dwellers in selectively and creatively appropriating the Trust's improvement projects. In such efforts, this book goes beyond the discussion of planning and architectural plans usual in studies of colonial urbanism; instead, I focus on everyday life in the paras to show how people lived in and viewed their city and how that shaped their responses to colonialism.

Locality, Paras, Everyday life

In *Urban Theory Beyond the West*, Tim Edensor and Mark Jayne raise the question of whether non-Western cities should be seen as different from the West, as relational, or whether there is a need to deprovincialize space by talking about interconnections and interdependency in urban forms.[42] With the push to deprovincialize urban history, the study of the city's local spaces has become increasingly important. The local is where the global is *enacted*, meaning that the local is not simply a site where the global unfolds; instead, the local exercises significant agency in shaping the global. As Achille Mbembe and Sarah Nuttall have also explained in their effort to unpack the West and give credence to African spatial forms as original and singular, the local shapes a worldliness that relates to the 'capacity to generate one's own cultural forms, institutions, and lifeways, but also relates to the ability to foreground, translate, fragment, and disrupt realities and imaginaries originating elsewhere, and in the process place these forms and processes in the service of one's own making'.[43]

Similarly, my analysis of the para explores the local, ambiguous, elusive, and undocumented components of history and space: everyday practices, unwritten rules, identities, and marginalized city dwellers. This book then harks back to Michel de Certeau's *The Practice of Everyday Life*, which describes the everyday as going beyond the political, or the extraordinary, as the space of silent, mundane, and ordinary acts.[44] But at the same time, I question whether an everyday as de Certeau imagined it could exist in a colonial city riddled with discriminatory practices of caste, gender, and class hierarchies that divided Indians. For example, in the spaces of the para, I locate individuals routinely engaged in strategies to inhabit a city unresponsive to their caste and religious practices. I describe bhadralok urbanists borrowing from the British conceptual toolkit to discursively enframe *dalit* (lowest caste) neighbourhoods, rebuking them and other non-Hindu city dwellers for dirtiness and attempting to impose a regime of Hindu spatial hygiene on them, thus laying out the path on which the dalits were forced to find their way to respectability and social purity.

Calling attention to the local, Arjun Appadurai described neighbourhoods as different from 'localities'.[45] He explained that the nation-state can appropriate the locality as a site of commemoration and events and utilize it to engineer an idea that it wants to. The techniques of the nation-state, however, are weak in neighbourhoods, because these are social formations where the lifeworld of people are often at odds with the requirements of the nation state. Appadurai pointed out that each neighbourhood is different from the other and resist the nation-state's goals of standardizing space. Neighbourhoods, he argued, were stages for their own self reproduction, a process fundamentally opposed to the nation state's ambitions of eliminating difference and producing a regulated public.

My investigation into the para, however, departs from Appadurai's argument that the disciplines of the nation-state remain suspended in these spaces. I argue that in colonial cities, it is impossible to locate in neighbourhoods an everydayness free from external control. The processes of standardizing space and regulating communities were at the heart of bhadralok efforts to transform paras into microcosms of a Hindu-Bengali nation. In such arguments, this book also goes beyond existing global scholarship on neighbourhoods—Cem Behar's work on *mahalle*s in Istanbul and Jim Masselos and Prashant Kidambi's description of *moholla*s in Bombay—that celebrate its everydayness to argue that paras were in fact much-regulated spaces.[46]

My understanding of the para follows Ranajit Guha's argument that in the colonial city, the everyday was in fact a 'truncated everyday'.[47] Guha explained the everyday in a colonial city as 'split in the middle', with one part attached to official time and alienated from civil society. He gave the example of 'ophish para' [office-para] or the office district of Calcutta where the English suffix 'office' added to the word 'para' showed that as Bengalis compared their office district to the community of the para, colonial time-discipline encroached on the everyday. Expanding on this idea of a truncated everyday, my analysis of the para also builds on the more recent and fascinating work of Kaustubh Mani Sengupta that describes paras as exclusionary and patriarchal.[48] Adding to Sengupta's work, I argue that paras, far from autonomous communities, were co-opted in nation-building processes under the Swarajist municipal rule and were re-spatialized into units of the Bengali nation.

Introduction 15

The para nevertheless enjoyed significant autonomy from British control. Resisting British efforts to 'plan' Calcutta, paras preserved the intersections of the village and the city.

An activist, Jai Sen once wrote that if not entirely rural, Calcutta was indeed an 'overgrown village' and 'certainly has rural aspects to it'.[49] Sen's argument was that in a city where rural-minded people lived, the language of urban development had to respond to the hybrid, rural–urban nature of urban space. Any model for urban growth that did not consider the rural component of the city could not be effective. This is similar to Ashis Nandy's observations on the intersections of the city and village in modern urban India.[50] Nandy argues that the split between these two spaces is not too wide—physically, culturally, and politically the two remain separate, but the village and the city constantly inform each other in the realm of the imagination.[51] I argue that the village has not simply merged with the city in the space of the imagination, but this imagination, rather nostalgia, has also shaped the physical space of the city.

This book extends its intervention beyond Calcutta, arguing that the spatial formation of the para complicates the meaning of public and private spaces in South Asian cities generally. It builds on the argument that, in contrast to the Habermasian public sphere that facilitated democratic transitions in Europe, the public sphere in South Asian cities was much more regulated.[52] Given the colonial histories of these cities, the nationalists controlled all debates in the public realm with the ultimate goal of producing a homogenous community of the nation. This produced public 'arenas' that were different from the public sphere.[53] In pointing to the kinship-like ties that held together the para and to active community participation in para festivals, and in arguing that the para was an extension of the private, family life of the city dwellers, this book offers a new understanding of public spaces in urban South Asia.

Hygiene and Urban Modernity

Surveying nineteenth- and twentieth-century town improvements, this book builds on the growing scholarship on hygiene as a tool of empire to argue that while colonizers mobilized hygiene concerns to justify their land acquisitions, hygiene also segregated the black town from within. The conceptual weight of this book lies in its ability to highlight urbanism as a cultural process set in motion by the colonial state and later appropriated by the ruled for very different purposes. Labelling marginalized city dwellers—the poor, lower caste, and non-Hindu groups—as inherently unsanitary, Indian elites forced them to adopt Hindu practices. The language of hygiene that the British deployed to keep Indians away from white neighbourhoods ultimately became part of a racialized language of colonial modernity embedded in regional and global relationships of inequality. This new language of modernity ordered space in colonial cities, fracturing city space along multiple axes of race, caste, class, and religion.

David Arnold observed, while analysing the 'colonization of bodies', that the Indian appropriation of Western ideas of health and hygiene was more layered and complicated than simple rejection. There were groups who appropriated Western categories of hygiene to link it with their own sense of prestige.[54] In a similar way, I argue that bhadraloks borrowed the colonial categories of hygiene and sanitation, but their versions were entwined in religion and caste practices. My argument can, in fact, be aligned with Ruth Rogaski's detailed account of how a single Chinese concept, *weisheng* (hygiene), came to acquire several meanings with the shaping of Chinese modernity in the nineteenth and twentieth centuries.[55] Weisheng, in the late nineteenth century, represented diverse regimens of diet, meditation, and self-medication. With imperialism, the meaning of weisheng shifted to encompass ideas such as national sovereignty, laboratory knowledge, the cleanliness of bodies, and the fitness of races: categories that foreign observers and Chinese elites thought the Chinese lacked. In this book, I have pointed out that a similar shift took place in bhadralok discourses on hygiene; in Calcutta, however, the shift was more towards inscribing hygiene with an invented tradition articulated in the language of religion, a need that the bhadraloks felt they had to meet to resist ideas of British sanitation.

In addition, this book argues that bhadraloks took to hygiene as a form of self-distinction in a city that was increasingly segregated by race, class, and caste. The segregation involved the real estate market, forcing the lower castes to relocate to the city's fringes, along with the colonial state's efforts to zone the city by dismantling spaces of Indian business, dislocating and resettling non-white populations into the suburbs. Meanwhile, Calcutta experienced an unprecedented migration of lower-caste, non-Hindu, and non-Bengali villagers in the early twentieth century. Famines had forced them to leave their villages and move to the city. While some migrants searched for work in factories, others took up work as domestic helps, street-vendors, cooks, and day-labourers. When the state failed to house them, they erected informal settlements or *bustee*s where they found empty plots of land. Often their bustees bordered the middle-class paras.

Introduction

A focus on hygiene, I argue, allowed bhadralok reformers to claim that migrant workers lacked awareness of sanitation and their bustees required close supervision. Appropriating colonial figurations of subaltern native developments as inscrutable 'black towns', bhadralok urbanists used similar tropes to describe the bustees. In other words, they viewed the bustee in much the same way as the white ruling class of the city viewed the black town. This mimetic projection, I argue, served a dual purpose: first, as filth-ridden spaces, bustees provided an 'other' against which the para could be defined. Conversely, this projection of a class and caste-marked socio-spatial entity as 'inscrutable' was possible only as a counterpoint to the classic construction of modern space as easy to plan. With the filth-ridden bustee resembling colonial descriptions of a black town, bhadraloks expressed the need to reorder the bustee to make them resemble their paras.

By making a case for bhadralok improvements targeting both spaces and bodies, what I suggest is a more complex dynamics of a society both undergoing and resisting change. I argue that the bhadralok led a 'civilizing process' driven by a certain idea of refinement. Refinement meant the suppression of intimate functions and desires related to the body. Bhadraloks clearly laid out the manners, etiquette, and self-control required for refinement. To civilize their fellow para dwellers, they tried to introduce Hindu diet and fitness. While recasting their paras as modern, these interventions also marked their difference from the lower castes and non-Hindu city dwellers. Bhadraloks now employed the colonial construct of 'black town' to describe the bustees. These descriptions reaffirmed their difference from the lower castes and also challenged the colonial portrayal of all Indian neighbourhoods as 'black towns'.

My discussion of bhadralok supervision of hygiene in the city builds on Ishita Pande's fantastic work on medicine and liberalism in colonial India, in which she explains that 'a particular political rationality—liberalism—was articulated as a government of the biosocial body to be realized not through coercive public health measures alone, but also through an everyday and intimate control of hygienic behavior'.[56]

Pande argues that Bengalis seized the conduct of hygienic behaviour as a form of modern self-expression. In the sanitary city (which embodied British liberalism in the colonies), the elite helped secure the promise of sanitary citizenship; they wrote books that educated citizens on proper conduct and hygienic practices. To this argument, I add that the tutoring that bhadraloks offered was also manifest in health and fitness programmes in their paras and crossed over to the bustees. I explore bhadralok-led processes of 'spatial *shuddhi* (purification)', sanitary campaigns that forced their manners, customs, tastes, and language on the working poor living in the bustees. These efforts, however, were status-affirming: they preserved differences between the bhadraloks and the poor, rather than improving the conditions of the poor. To this end, the bhadraloks borrowed colonial productions of the black town not simply to show filth accumulating in the lower-caste and poor bustees, but to also produce the filth. In sum, this book explains urbanism—commonly understood as the theory and practice of the built urban environment—as a series of spatial shifts deployed to shape discrete bodies and spaces.

Chapter Descriptions

Chapter 1 examines the discursive figuration of Indian neighbourhoods as 'black towns' in colonial health reports and the work of town improvement committees in early nineteenth-century Calcutta. These committees imported town improvements from Europe and attempted to apply them on Indian soil. I argue that Calcutta's diverse cultural geography presented an obstacle to these town plans. When the British introduced scientific water filtration and subterranean sewers in Calcutta, for instance, they were incompatible with the caste practices of the Hindus. The upper castes refused to drink water that had passed through conduits running below the lower-caste houses. They complained about the new sewer system for the same reason. To overcome resistance, the British initiated a process of 'grafting', which involved coercively homogenizing space by eliminating cultural differences that informed space. The notion of the 'black town', which emerged in colonial health surveys, was meant to facilitate improvements by generalizing Indians as a culture unaware of hygiene. Detailing the representational strategies that the British employed to portray Indian (Bengali and Marwari) neighbourhoods as 'black town'— as seen in the texts, surveys, statistics, and photographs included in health reports—I argue that the black town was a discursive formation more than a physical space. It was the product of a symbolic geography that represented native space as a culture of pathology.

Chapter 2 examines the land speculation of the Calcutta Improvement Trust, an urban development committee the state commissioned in 1911 to improve the health of the 'black town'. It carried out a radical restructuration of Bengali neighbourhoods, evicting them from the city centre, building suburbs to house them and eventually selling plots of lands in the suburbs to wealthy, upper-caste Bengalis. A series of 'small dispensations', legal proceedings that

Introduction 19

took place outside the court, freed land for urban development and assisted the colonial project of improvement. I show that Bengali property owners invented new strategies to resist the Trust's acquisitions of private property. They inscribed their properties with religious meanings and wrote petitions referring to their rights as Hindus and Muslims. This reconstituted their identities as religious over and above all other defining qualities. In writing the petitions, the property owners banded together as members of their para, which they defined as a space constituted by shared religious beliefs. In such assertions, the para became more than a neighbourhood: it represented a community of Hindus and Muslims.

Chapter 3 argues that as the property owners explained their para as Hindu, the nationalist Swarajists appropriated the idea in their municipal administration. They worked with middle-class, propertied, Hindu-Bengali bhadraloks, to transform their paras into microcosms of a Hindu-Bengali nation. The chapter starts with the history of the para, tracing it to a class of Indian merchants who worked with the English East India Company. They invested their profits in buying and distributing plots of land. In distributing plots of land, they preserved the social space of the village in the city, assigning land according to the caste of the settlers who purchased plots. This shaped caste-based paras where the settlers lived like an extended family. The introduction of English education in 1835, however, marked a radical shift as a new urban professional group of bhadraloks took shape and transformed the para. I argue that in the early twentieth century, the bhadraloks—propertied and salaried—were significantly affected by the Trust's acquisitions of private property. They worked with the Swarajists to tighten the Hindu identity of their paras. Together with the Swarajists, they crafted a new language of hygiene and supervised the health and cleanliness of their para. Their health campaigns wove together hygiene with Hindu and Bengali nationalism. Under their supervision, paras expressed values embedded in a Hindu-Bengali nation.

Chapter 4 studies how bhadralok sanitarians crafted binaries of 'sanitary paras' and 'insanitary bustees' to inflict the practices of Hindu hygiene on dalit, Muslim, and non-Bengali city dwellers. A steady influx of migrant workers had resulted in a housing crisis in Calcutta in 1920. Bustees went up in all parts of the city, including the outer edges of upper caste paras. These undomesticated spaces, adjoining the paras, contrasted with their spatial order. Threatened by the growing waves of the working poor, bhadraloks in their writings discursively remade the colonial notions of the black town. I argue that a shift in political ideologies, from the Swarajist to the Communist at the time of the World War II, did little to change bhadralok attitudes towards the working poor. The same notions of unhygiene and threat that were common in Swarajist campaigns in the bustees pervaded the work of the Communist minded bhadraloks in the bustees. Both groups of bhadraloks launched campaigns to sanitize bustees. In these campaigns, they used infrastructure to initiate a bargain—they promised better streets, water supply, sewer systems in return for the bustee dwellers willingness to give up beef and alcohol, and adapt to the practices of a Hindu-Bengali nation.

Notes

1. Chief Executive Officer, *Chairman's (Chief Executive Officer's) Report on the Municipal Administration of Calcutta for the Year 1925* (Calcutta, 1925) [NYPL].
2. Ibid.
3. See Anthony D. King, *Colonial Urban Development: Culture, Social Power and Environment* (London: Routledge, 2010), 283.
4. See Swati Chattopadhyay, *Representing Calcutta : Modernity, Nationalism, and the Colonial Uncanny* (London; New York: Routledge, 2005); William J. Glover, *Making Lahore Modern: Constructing and Imagining a Colonial City* (Karachi: Oxford University Press, 2011).
5. Community sentiments shape neighbourhoods not only in Calcutta, but in other Indian cities as well. In Bombay, for instance, scholars have described tightly knit neighbourhood communities called *mohollas*, where shared social and religious lives, together with annual festivals, tighten family-like ties between neighbours. The elders who live in the moholla exercise a state-like power over residents, resolving disputes and supervising their everyday life. See Jim Masselos, *The City in Action: Bombay Struggles for Power* (New Delhi: Oxford University Press, 2007), 18; Rajnarayan Chandavarkar, *The Origins of Industrial Capitalism in India: Business Strategies and the Working Classes in Bombay, 1900–1940* (Cambridge: Cambridge University Press, 2003), 193; Prashant Kidambi, *The Making of an Indian Metropolis: Colonial Governance and Public Culture in Bombay, 1890–1920* (Burlington, VT: Ashgate Publishing Company, 2007), 122. Veena Talwar Oldenburg has also shown how caste guilds migrated to similar localities in colonial Lucknow, shaping neighbourhoods named after the caste. In these neighbourhoods, caste-based familiarity shaped close-knit neighbourhoods. See Veena Talwar Oldenburg, *The Making of Colonial Lucknow, 1856–1877* (Princeton; Princeton University Press, 2014), 14.
6. Henri Lefebvre, *The Production of Space* (Oxford, UK; Cambridge, MA, USA: Blackwell, 1991), 220. For scholarship on cities as monumental spaces see G. A. Bremner, *Architecture and Urbanism in the British Empire* (Oxford,

Introduction 21

New York: Oxford University Press, 2016); Ambe J. Njoh, *Planning Power: Town Planning and Social Control in Colonial Africa* (London: UCL Press, 2007); Zeynep Çelik, *Urban Forms and Colonial Confrontations: Algiers Under French Rule* (Berkeley; Los Angeles; London: University of California Press, 1997); Preeti Chopra, *A Joint Enterprise: Indian Elites and the Making of British Bombay* (Minneapolis; London: University of Minnesota Press, 2011). The only exception to this scholarship is a recent work by Anindita Ghosh, *Claiming the City: Protest, Crime, and Scandals in Colonial Calcutta, c. 1860–1920* (New Delhi: Oxford University Press, 2016). Ghosh offers a fascinating history of the city beyond its planned spaces, uncovering voices from the streets and reconstructing the experiences of subaltern city dwellers.

7. See Fassil Demissie, *Colonial Architecture and Urbanism in Africa: Intertwined and Contested Histories* (Surrey: Ashgate, 2012); Chattopadhyay, *Representing Calcutta*; Jyoti Hosagrahar, *Indigenous Modernities: Negotiating Architecture and Urbanism* (London: Routledge, 2009); Brenda S. A. Yeoh, *Contesting Space in Colonial Singapore: Power Relations and the Urban Built Environment* (Singapore: Singapore University Press, 2003).

8. Bhabānī Rāya Caudhurī, *Baṅgīẏa Sābarṇa Kathā, Kālikshetra Kalikātā: Ekaṭi Itibṛtta* (Kalakātā: Mānnā Pābalikeśana, 2006), 16.

9. Nagendranath Sett, *Kalikatastha Tantu Banik Jatir Itihas* (Calcutta: A. K. Basaka, 1950), 36.

10. Swarupa Gupta, *Notions of Nationhood in Bengal: Perspectives on Samaj, c. 1867–1905* (Leiden: Brill, 2009). Gupta departs from scholarship that describes anti-colonial nationalism as a derivative discourse, such as Partha Chatterjee, *Nationalist Thought and the Colonial World: A Derivative Discourse* (Delhi: Oxford University Press, 1986). Gupta points to the precolonial society of samaj as the precursor of the twentieth century nation.

11. Glover, *Making Lahore Modern*, 60.

12. Chopra, *A Joint Enterprise*, 30.

13. There exists no one definition for the bhadralok; scholars are divided over defining the group. J. H. Broomfield first engaged in a Weberian analysis to describe bhadraloks as a status group that shared similar social and cultural values. See J. H. Broomfield, *Elite Conflict in a Plural Society: Twentieth-Century Bengal* (Berkeley; Los Angeles: University of California Press, 1968). Cambridge school historians described bhadraloks as a group of upper class Bengali men who collaborated with the British and when their collaboration failed, drafted anti-colonial nationalist sentiments in their writings. See Anil Seal, *The Emergence of Indian Nationalism: Competition and Collaboration in the later Nineteenth Century* (Cambridge: Cambridge University Press, 1968). Marxist historiography has emphasized the role of English education in shaping bhadraloks. See Asok Sen, *Iswar Chandra Vidyasagar and His Elusive Milestones* (Calcutta: Riddhi-India, 1977). Sumit Sarkar has pointed to

wealth-based divides that split the bhadralok group from within. See Sumit Sarkar, *Writing Social History* (New Delhi: Oxford University Press, 1997). Tithi Bhattacharya, *The Sentinels of Culture: Class, Education, and the Colonial Intellectual in Bengal* (New Delhi; Oxford; New York: Oxford University Press, 2005) argued that education and culture were the two pillars of bhadralok identity. Subaltern studies historiography separated political from cultural nationalism arguing that although bhadraloks worked for the British, they resisted British intervention in the spiritual realm of their home. The spiritual world was where they crafted the language of anticolonial nationalism. See Partha Chatterjee, *The Nation and Its Fragments: Colonial and Postcolonial Histories* (Princeton: Princeton University Press, 1993), 120.

14. Gyanendra Pandey, *The Construction of Communalism in Colonial North India* (Delhi; New York: Oxford University Press, 1990).

15. Francesca Orsini, *The Hindi Public Sphere 1920–1940: Language and Literature in the Age of Nationalism* (Delhi; Oxford: Oxford University Press, 2000); Tapan Raychaudhuri, *Europe Reconsidered: Perceptions of the West in Nineteenth-Century Bengal* (Delhi: Oxford University Press, 1998).

16. Sabyasachi Bhattacharya, *The Defining Moments in Bengal, 1920–1947* (New Delhi: Oxford University Press, 2014).

17. Sarkar, *Writing Social History*; Chatterjee, *Nationalist Thought and the Colonial World*.

18. Chittabrata Palit and Tinni Goswami, 'Sanitation, Empire, Environment: Bengal (1880–1920)', *Proceedings of the Indian History Congress* 68 (2007): 731–44.

19. Projit Bihari Mukharji, *Nationalizing the Body: The Medical Market, Print, and Daktari Medicine* (London; New York: Anthem Press, 2009).

20. For racial segregation in colonial Algiers and Singapore see Zeynep Çelik, *Urban Forms and Colonial Confrontations: Algiers under French Rule* (Berkeley and Los Angeles; University of California Press, 1997). Yeoh, *Contesting Space in Colonial Singapore*. For early scholarship on the dual city in Calcutta, see Pradip Sinha, *Calcutta in Urban History* (Calcutta: Firma KLM, 1978) and S. N Mukherjee, *Calcutta: Myths and History* (Calcutta: Subarnarekha, 1977). For black/white towns as spaces that embodied technology-driven colonizing society and the agrarian society of the ruled, see King, *Colonial Urban Development*. Postcolonial scholars have questioned the rigidity of the boundary between the black and white towns. See Chattopadhyay, *Representing Calcutta*, and Glover, *Making Lahore Modern*.

21. Gerald Breeze, *Urbanization in Newly Developing Countries* (New Delhi: Prentice-Hall of India, 1969).

22. Sinha, *Calcutta in Urban History*; Mukherjee, *Calcutta: Myths and History*.

23. Mukherjee, *Calcutta: Myths and History*.

Introduction

24. King, *Colonial Urban Development*, 39.

25. Hosagrahar, *Indigenous Modernities*; Chattopadhyay, *Representing Calcutta*; Glover, *Making Lahore Modern*; Chopra, *A Joint Enterprise*.

26. William Cunningham Bissell, *Urban Design, Chaos, and Colonial Power in Zanzibar* (Bloomington: Indiana University Press, 2011), 217.

27. Timothy Mitchell, *Colonising Egypt* (Cambridge: Cambridge University Press, 2007), 34.

28. Chattopadhyay, *Representing Calcutta*, 68.

29. James R. Ryan, *Picturing Empire: Photography and the Visualization of the British Empire* (London: Reaktion: 1997); Christopher Pinney, *Camera Indica: The Social Life of Indian Photographs* (London: Reaktion, 1997).

30. Arturo Escobar, *Encountering Development: The Making and Unmaking of the Third World* (Princeton; Oxford: Princeton University Press, 2012), 14.

31. John Hutnyk, *The Rumour of Calcutta: Tourism, Charity, and the Poverty of Representation* (London; New Jersey: Zed Books, 1996).

32. Cedric J. Robinson and Robin D. G. Kelley, *Black Marxism: The Making of the Black Radical Tradition* (Chapel Hill, NC: The University of North Carolina Press, 2000), 308.

33. Lefebvre, *The Production of Space*; David Harvey, *Social Justice and the City* (Baltimore: The Johns Hopkins University Press, 1973); Neil Smith, *Uneven Development: Nature, Capital and the Production of Space* (Oxford: Blackwell, 1984); Liam Kennedy, *Race and Urban Space in Contemporary American Culture* (Edinburgh: Edinburgh University Press, 2000); Giovanni Picker, *Racial Cities: Governance and the Segregation of Romani People in Urban Europe* (London; New York: Routledge, 2019).

34. Robert K. Home, *Of Planting and Planning: The Making of British Colonial Cities* (London: Spon, 1997). Carl H. Nightingale, *Segregation: A Global History of Divided Cities* (Chicago; London: University Of Chicago Press, 2012).

35. Public purpose feeds state rhetoric of development while dispossessing citizens and sidelining their rights of basic housing. Rupal Oza shows that the postcolonial Indian government has engaged in neo-colonial methods of land grab, deploying the vague clause of public purpose, a tool of colonial oppression to justify their acquisitions in land. See Rupal Oza, 'Special Economic Zones: Space, Law, and Dispossession', in *India's New Economic Policy: A Critical Analysis*, ed. Waquar Ahmed, Amitabh Kundu, and Richard Peet (New York; London: Routledge, 2010), 241.

36. Yeoh, *Contesting Space in Colonial Singapore*, 96.

37. Kidambi, *The Making of an Indian Metropolis*, 103; Bissell, *Urban Design, Chaos, and Colonial Power in Zanzibar*, 148; John Drysdale, *Singapore: Struggle for Success* (Singapore: Times Book International, 1984), 59; Gyan Prakash, *Mumbai Fables* (Princeton; Oxford: Princeton University Press, 2011), 82.

38. Partho Datta, *Planning the City: Urbanization and Reform in Calcutta; c.1800–c.1940* (New Delhi: Tulika Books, 2012), 226.
39. Ibid., 291.
40. Yeoh, *Contesting Space*; Bissell, *Urban Design, Chaos, and Colonial Power in Zanzibar*; Kidambi, *The Making of an Indian Metropolis*; Jiat-Hwee Chang, *A Genealogy of Tropical Architecture: Colonial Networks, Nature and Technoscience* (London; New York: Routledge, 2016); Datta, *Planning the City*.
41. Janaki Nair, 'Beyond Nationalism: Modernity, Governance and a New Urban History for India', *Urban History* 36, no. 2 (August 2009): 327–41.
42. Tim Edensor and Mark Jayne, *Urban Theory beyond the West: A World of Cities* (London: Routledge, 2012), 5.
43. Sarah Nuttall and Achille Mbembe, *Johannesburg: The Elusive Metropolis* (Durham and London: Duke University Press, 2008), 15.
44. Michel de Certeau, *The Practice of Everyday Life* (Berkeley: University of California Press, 2008).
45. Arjun Appadurai, *Modernity at Large: Cultural Dimensions of Globalization* (Minneapolis: University of Minnesota Press, 1996), 183.
46. Cem Behar, *A Neighborhood in Ottoman Istanbul: Fruit Vendors and Civil Servants in the Kasap İlyas Mahalle* (Albany: State University of New York Press, 2003); Masselos, *The City in Action*; Kidambi, *The Making of an Indian Metropolis*.
47. Ranajit Guha, 'A Colonial City and Its Time(s)', *The Indian Economic and Social History Review* 45, no. 3 (September 2008): 329–51.
48. Sengupta, 'Community and Neighbourhood in a Colonial City'.
49. Jai Sen, 'The Unintended City', in 'Life and Living', *Seminar* 200, 1976.
50. Ashis Nandy, *An Ambiguous Journey to the City: The Village and Other Odd Ruins of the Self in the Indian Imagination* (New Delhi: Oxford University Press, 2007).
51. Ibid., 73.
52. Neeladri Bhattacharya, 'Notes towards a Conception of the Colonial Public', in *Civil Society, Public Sphere, and Citizenship: Dialogues and Perceptions* (New Delhi: Sage Publications, 2005), 130–56.
53. Sandria B. Freitag, *Collective Action and Community: Public Arenas and the Emergence of Communalism in North India* (Berkeley: University of California Press, 1989), 292.
54. David Arnold, *Colonizing the Body: State Medicine and Epidemic Disease in Nineteenth-Century India* (Berkeley: University of California Press, 1993), 288.
55. Ruth Rogaski, *Hygienic Modernity* (Berkeley, California: University of California Press, 2014).
56. Ishita Pande, *Medicine, Race and Liberalism in British Bengal: Symptoms of Empire* (London: Routledge, 2012).

1 The Black Town, Spaces of Pathology, and a Hindu Discourse of Citizenship

Koriya buddhir koushol
Pultah theke anle jol
Nikaash hochche moyla jol, koreche prostut drainage *kol,*
Dhulo thame dile jol. swatontro ek kol ...
Machine *te dile dom, korey jhomjhom, teje beroy* water.

—Rupchand Pakshi[1]

(With cleverness immense/Water from Pultah commence/Dirty water runs out, that's what this drainage contraption is about/With water settles dust, a unique device to trust/Rev up the machine, hear it gurgle, as water gushes out.)

The British in 1869 inaugurated a brand-new machine to filter water at Pultah, a small town near Calcutta. A few years later, the urban poet Rupchand Pakshi wrote the poem 'Dhonyo Sohor Kolkata', an excerpt of which is cited above. The poem chronicles the wonder that the waterworks produced among Calcuttans as they watched machines sifting dirt and pumping filtered water into conduits that then supplied city-houses with clean water. Pakshi described the filtration process as *buddhir koushol*: a demonstration of human intelligence. But at the same time, he employed the English words 'drainage', 'machine', and 'water' to argue that the science of filtration was incompatible to the city's cultural geography.[2] The three English words signalled that the filtration processes were indeed part of a larger colonizing culture.

Given clean water is a basic human necessity, why did Pakshi describe the filtration paraphernalia as a tool of colonialism? Pakshi's concern, I argue, fitted well within a broader climate of resistance that British civic improvements had shaped in nineteenth-century Calcutta. The British imported town improvements—both their plans and the apparatus—from Europe and enforced these on the city, without tailoring these to meet Calcutta's diverse cultural needs. For example, the British introduced subterranean sewers that required Indians to forego their caste and religious practices. Indian city dwellers,

26   A Hygienic City-Nation

however, refused to give up their caste practices; Calcutta's cultural geography resisted the new improvements. To overcome resistance, the British initiated a process of 'grafting' that involved a brute force to homogenize space by eliminating cultural differences.

A British corporation, James Watt & Company, that designed and sold steam engines used the plans of William Clark, an English civil engineer, to construct the Pultah waterworks. With the paraphernalia imported from London, the waterworks were a technological and visual wonder. Two enormous iron pipes supplied the water, and machines pumped it into six settling tanks where, thanks to Clark's design, the sediment was filtered. Adding to these new techniques were the subterranean conduits: scientific marvels that ran beneath the streets and houses supplying Calcutta with water. City dwellers collected filtered water from stand posts (public faucets or hydrants) that the British built along the city's main thoroughfares. As work for the waterworks progressed, John Strachey, a sanitary commissioner, cautioned the British that the waterworks would not improve Calcutta's health unless the city had a system of modern sewers. He described the existing sewer system as 'open', or uncovered, that dumped enormous amounts of filth on the street sides.[3] Following Strachey's advice, improvement commissioners planned for a network of subterranean sewers.

Unprecedented in their technical capacities, the waterworks and the sewers, nevertheless, contrasted with the spatial customs of the Bengalis and failed to improve their health. The Bengalis simply refused to drink water that passed through conduits running below houses of city dwellers who had different castes and religions. Besides, a subterranean network of sewers violated the basic custom of the Bengalis' management of filth: keeping out the sewage and preventing it from coming in contact with the house. They believed that sewage and filth were part of the world outside their houses; that was why Bengali houses were spotless while the adjoining streets remained dirty.[4] That was also why the Bengalis built their privies away from the residential quarters. According to Clark's plan, the new sewers ran indiscriminately, and the possibilities that sewage would flow below the residential quarters were high. This infuriated the Bengalis, and they refused to connect their houses to the labyrinth of underground channels.

The resistance of Bengali city dwellers to the waterworks gathered steam when the stand posts failed to deliver the promised water. Even if the posts ran the entire day with their engines at full pressure, these could supply no more than two million gallons of water in half a day. The British passed an act in

The Black Town, Spaces of Pathology, and a Hindu Discourse of Citizenship 27

1863 that made provision for levying rates and taxes to enhance conservancy and carry out improvements. This meant that although the Bengalis paid taxes for civic improvements, they did not enjoy its benefits.[5]

In this chapter, I argue that in the late nineteenth century, the British, faced with resistance to their civic improvements, retaliated by shaping a discursive 'black town' in health reports. As Anthony D. King has explained, in a colonial city, the black town was a native space moulded by indigenous, craft-based societies that contrasted with the 'white town' built by the colonizing industrial society.[6] King's argument has faced criticism, particularly from postcolonial scholars, who hold that routine exchanges between the colonizer and the ruled made it difficult to enforce any strict boundary between black and white towns.[7] Departing from such understandings of colonial space, I argue that the black town signified more than the actual physical space: while the native town was inhabited and moulded by Indians, the black town was produced in colonial health discourses and was a product of symbolic geography that shaped native space as a culture of pathology. The black town embodied discursive violence: it served as a tool of colonialism. British health officers crafted the black town by employing selective textual and visual pieces of evidence that produced images of Indian neighbourhoods simmering in filth.

Selective representation was the discursive tool that the state employed to craft a black town. Selective representation meant that health officers seized on occasional instances of filth to claim that it was usual. British health reports asserted that Indians assigned a low priority to sanitation. Health officers took to selective representation to describe the filthiest of Indian houses as typical; they claimed that Indian streets and privies *always* overflowed with human and animal excreta. Creating a certain image of the Indian neighbourhood, selective representation adds to what Timothy Mitchell has described, in the context of colonial Egypt, an enframement of space: strategies that the British deployed to control societies through a control of space.[8] In Calcutta, the health officers' observations of how filth covered Indian streets, their frustrations as they groped their way through this filth, their efforts to initiate town improvements, and the resistance they encountered in carrying out these improvements transformed the native town into a black town.

The importance of the black town, however, lies not simply in underscoring the discursive violence of colonialism. Early formulations of citizenship in India can also be traced to a critique of the black town produced in late nineteenth-century Indian writings. The most powerful resistance to the black town took shape in the writings of educated Hindu men who identified themselves as *nagorik*s or citizens. They wrote for Bengali health periodicals, where they discussed the need for town improvements while also deploying Hindu religion to decide which improvements were necessary. In Europe, the history of citizenship is intertwined with the rise of individual rights and secular-democratic transitions from kingdoms to nation-states. In colonial India, the public sphere was not democratic and did not allow for rights-bearing citizens. Nonetheless, a new discourse on citizenship took shape in the nagorik critique of town improvements that tied the private world of religion to the public sphere of individual rights.

Colonial Landscapes

Writing to a certain Miss Dodd in 1830, Reginald Heber, the bishop of Calcutta, described the streets of the city as dark and dense. Vast crowds, the size of the entire population of London, gathered on the streets at all times.[9] The monotonous drone of their voices, their incessant festivals and music, and the stink of fermented coconut and garlic that ascended from their food rendered the streets revolting to Heber's senses. At the time he was describing Indian streets as so noxious, the East India Company had already embarked on a mission to sanitize the region by opening new streets.

Merchants of the British East India Company first arrived in Bengal as early as 1680 to take part in its rich cotton trade. Calcutta in those days was a small eastern Indian village located next to the river Hooghly and between the low-lying districts of Govindapur and Sutanuti. The Company merchants described the region as a pestilential swamp. They argued that the Indians lived in the middle of dense forests and enormous saltwater lakes where the moist air deteriorated their health.[10] Such descriptions, however, were far from true. Before the British arrived, the riverbank was home to lively markets called *bazaar*s. As early as the sixteenth century, the Portuguese carried out an active trade with Indian merchants at these bazaars.[11] The Indian merchants, in turn, spread their trade networks to China, the Middle East, and Africa.[12] When the British described Calcutta as a wild and pestilential riverbank, they overlooked these trade networks in order to justify their agenda of reordering local Indian space to serve their business interests.

The Mughal emperor Farrukhsiyar granted the Company a *farman* (a royal order) in 1717 that exempted it from paying customs duties in return for an annual payment. Company merchants eventually decided to establish a base in the region. They appointed town improvement committees that carried out extensive surveys of the region. These surveys reported the presence of deadly diseases, which the committees traced to marshy spaces and unsanitary neighbourhood conditions. They made various small efforts—widening streets, cleansing water tanks, and sanitizing the riverbank—to improve the health of the region.

As the Company merchants explained, the utilitarian principle of ensuring the greatest happiness of the greatest number motivated these projects. British philosopher John Stuart Mill had shaped the basic principle of utilitarianism in the nineteenth century as actions measured by the happiness they promote; this became a justification for imperialism as an action that improved and fostered happiness in the less civilized worlds of Britain's colonies.[13] Although embedded in the language of utilitarianism, town improvements did little to improve health in Indian neighbourhoods. The new improvements simply served to open Indian houses to colonial surveillance, cementing British hold over the city.

As early as 1803, the Company had formally announced its plans to carry out improvements alongside the banks of the river Hooghly. Governor General Wellesley had solved the question of funds by issuing a minute that endorsed lotteries to subsidize town improvements.[14] Lotteries had funded public works in Britain as early as the seventeenth century. Gavin Weightman has shown that in the mid-eighteenth century, the British Parliament decided to raise six thousand pounds from state lotteries to build the Westminster Bridge.[15] Sale of lottery tickets also funded basic infrastructure like the water supply system of London.[16] The British had introduced similar lotteries in Calcutta in the late eighteenth century. Expensive paintings, books, statues, and plots of land (including the structures on them) were offered as prizes, while the lottery proceeds funded the region's basic physical structures.[17] For example, in the *Early History and Growth of Calcutta*, Binay Krishna Deb describes that as early as 1794 a town improvement committee advertised a lottery of ten thousand tickets at thirty-two rupees each, the proceeds of which funded the building of streets and churches.[18] Between 1805 and 1817, lotteries financed town improvements that included new water reservoirs in Short's Bazaar, the building of the Town Hall, and the excavation of the Beliaghata canal.[19]

With lotteries funding public works, the Company convened a much bigger town improvement committee called the Lottery Committee in 1817. The Committee planned on opening new streets to improve the city's health and reduce epidemics. It constructed a network of geometric and well-lit arterial streets—Elliot Road, Strand Road, Cornwallis Street, College Street,

Wellington Street, Amherst Street, and Wellesley Street—all named after British officers. The streets had an impeccably straight north–south orientation and opened inaccessible alleyways into broad, straight streets, easily accessible for the public.

The new streets were conduits for cultural changes. They engraved on the soil of Calcutta a new colonial culture that prioritized standardized structures of straight boulevards and open spaces over organic and winding streets.[20] The Lottery Committee described the existing streets as tortuous and overcrowded. Describing themselves as 'enlightened', the commissioners then took recourse to space to amplify the difference and the inferiority of the Bengalis. Prior to the arrival of the British, the Bengalis actively managed the landscape of the region, and it was integral to their culture. As the British began to settle in the area, they found the forests too wild, the rivers unclean, and the tidal flats too tempting not to fill in. They strongly believed that they carried the white man's burden of transforming villages into cities.

The streets that the Lottery Committee built provided the infrastructural backbone that supported colonial claims of scientific and racial supremacy. Wide and gas lit, some of these streets, such as the Strand Road, were actually widened at the cost of the river Hooghly.[21] The Strand Road had a tremendous impact on the river, blocking its natural flow. Ignoring the environmental hazards that the new streets brought with them, the Lottery Committee described these as their 'gifts' to Calcutta. They devised new ways to wash the streets every morning. New commercial enterprises, warehouses, and banks flanked the street sides. Magnificent public squares, also named after the British bureaucrats, interspersed these streets. Living within the spectacle, the Bengalis were expected to comply with the directives of the Company.

The new streets passed through the heart of Calcutta, leaving the interiors still congested. Mr Fairplay, a regular reader of the English periodical *Calcutta Journal*, who lived in the northern parts of the city, wrote that there the interior streets had deep hollows.[22] Another reader, who called herself 'an inhabitant', described how sewers along Moorghyhatta Road, also in north Calcutta, had widened from constant breakages on their sides, which made the road dangerous for horse-drawn carriages.[23] Added to this, Reginald Heber's description of dark and reeking city streets, described at the beginning of this section, calls into question the quality and extent of the renovations that the Lottery Committee implemented.

Within a few years from when the Lottery Committee started work, it faced charges of forceful acquisitions of land.[24] In 1818, two property owners,

The Black Town, Spaces of Pathology, and a Hindu Discourse of Citizenship   31

Madubram Mullick and Ramchunder Mullick, alleged that the Committee had seized nearly twenty-two *cottah*s (thirty-two cottahs make one acre) of their land to widen roads.[25] The ground acquired was their patrimonial inheritance that they rented monthly at rupees forty. This meant that the loss of land was also a loss of family history for the Mullicks. They wrote three petitions to the Lottery Committee that failed to bring justice. Finally, Mr Trotter, Secretary to the Lottery Committee, took up their case. Within a few days, he declared that the Committee did not acquire any land from the Mullicks.[26]

In August 1822, Bholanath Mitter and Chandra Shekher Mitter lodged a similar complaint of land grab against the Lottery Committee. This time the Lottery Committee had acquired a family-owned water reservoir by force.[27] When the Mitters resisted, the Committee, however, refused to listen to them. The commissioners simply proceeded to fill up the water body. In 1824, a case was filed against the Lottery Committee for forceful acquisition and destruction of *ghat*s (embankments where pilgrims gathered to take a holy dip in the river) to build public roads. A wealthy local resident, Gopee Mohun Deb, owner of a ghat, brought charges against the Committee for trespassing on it.[28] He demanded a decree against the Committee for damages that it had caused at the ghat. After sixteen years of deliberation, Justices Edward Ryan, Seton, and Grant of the lower courts finally delivered judgment by dismissing the unresolved case.

Justices of the Peace, commissioners appointed by the Company to oversee both law and town improvements in the early nineteenth century, dismissed all accusations brought against the work of the Lottery Committee. On one occasion, the treasurer of the Lottery Committee, however, confessed, in testimony to an inquiry committee that the Lottery Committee had indeed engaged in numerous instances of forceful land acquisitions.[29] Although the official reason for all land acquisitions was to improve the health of city dwellers, the treasurer described that in reality, land speculation drove most of the Committee's work. He explained, for instance, that the Committee had purchased land between Strand Road and Clive Street for eight hundred to sixteen hundred rupees per cottah and had filled in a branch of the Hooghly River and sold the land for sixteen hundred rupees per cottah.

Rather than any genuine desire to improve the city, it was land speculation on a grand scale that really motivated the Lottery Committee's improvements. The commissioners argued that their project was based on the utilitarian principles of ensuring the maximum happiness of the people, yet they engaged in forceful acquisitions of private property that left many homeless. This dichotomy was in tune with the particular variant of liberalism that the British practiced in India. The British endorsed the utilitarian principles of Jeremy Bentham and John Stuart Mill to introduce liberal ideals of Enlightenment—democracy, individual rights, and secularism—to India. They introduced liberal ideas not because they viewed Indians as equals but as part of their 'civilizing' mission in India. They explained that these liberal ideals would civilize and set India in the path of progress. Likewise, the Lottery commissioners masked their massive land speculations as projects to civilize the Indian masses by making their neighbourhoods sanitary.

By the late eighteenth century, a strong public outcry against lotteries as the reason for moral corruption in Britain had forced the state to act against these. While the state considered banning lotteries, British periodicals like the *Asiatic Journal and Monthly Register* described the public outcry as 'far in advance of the government, both in virtue and in good sense'.[30] In Calcutta, the Lottery Committee ran out of funds even before its work could generate a moral outcry like in Britain. When residents of Boithhokkhana petitioned the Committee for a public tank in 1833, the petition was turned down, as the Committee no longer had money to excavate.[31] The commissioners declared that 'lottery funds may now be declared to be extinct for all purposes of improvement in Calcutta'.[32] In place of the Lottery Committee, small town improvement committees were set up that pledged to end pestilence—but carried on with land speculations. They differed from the Lottery Committee in that local taxes funded their work.

The Company's town improvements, however, faced a temporary setback when an armed revolt of Indian soldiers in 1857 shook the foundations of its rule. The revolt led to a handoff of control of the subcontinent from the Company to Queen Victoria in Britain. Just as the Company had, the new British government carried out extensive town improvements. In the aftermath of the revolt, their improvements were planned interventions that aimed to quell future uprisings against the state. Discussing town planning in Calcutta, Partho Datta argued that unlike Delhi, town improvements in Calcutta were not responses to the revolt of 1857; the British had already started planning Calcutta, the centre of their imperial mission in India, from before the mutiny.[33] Yet what I propose is that the transfer of power, from the Company to the Queen, marked a massive shift in British attitudes towards town improvements. Utilitarianism still remained the official reason for initiating town improvements, but, unlike the Company, the new British government did not limit itself to small, piecemeal improvements. Instead, it

The Black Town, Spaces of Pathology, and a Hindu Discourse of Citizenship 33

planned urban renovations with an eye to opening the most intimate of Indian spaces to colonial surveillance.[34]

The waterworks at Pultah was among the earliest improvements the new colonial state initiated immediately after the transfer of power. As mentioned earlier in this chapter, James Watt & Company built a spectacular filtration plant at Pultah. The history of James Watt & Company can be traced back to 1795 when English entrepreneur Matthew Boulton established a foundry where steam engines were designed according to the designs of James Watt.[35] At first, the company manufactured engines for mills and factories. With Britain expanding its colonial mission to new territories, the company received major contracts for mechanical parts. In Calcutta, the excavation work for the underground pipe network required additional funds. To pay for it, the state contracted new works to James Watt & Company, which discovered new geographies on which to experiment and control.[36] While the state became an agent of improvement, designing and planning urban renovations, James Watt & Company met the necessary expenses, transferred materials, and implemented public works projects in return for a lump sum that was raised from local taxes.

The British supplemented the new waterworks with a network of underground sewers. As early as 1855, town improvement commissioners had observed that faulty local sewers were causing fatal diseases that were otherwise preventable.[37] In 1864, the sanitary commissioner of Bengal drafted a report explaining that unsanitary sewers were making the northern parts of the city too squalid for civilized people and that open sewers 'of the most abominable kind' had turned the main thoroughfares in the northern parts of the city into 'public latrines'.[38] To remedy this, Clark once again designed a plan for a network of sewers to drain sewage into nearby saltwater lakes.[39] The administration forwarded the plan to Messrs M. and G. Rendel, engineers in England, who declared the scheme scientifically accurate.[40]

Although technically precise, the subterranean conduits were incompatible with the structure of Bengali houses. Because of scorching summers, the Bengalis built their houses low and did not leave much space between them. While many Bengalis lived in *pukka* or brick-built houses, many also lived in *kutcha* huts built of mud. These kutcha huts met the needs of a tropical climate, keeping the houses cool, but were incompatible with the working of subterranean conduits. The pressure of water in these houses was insufficient to push it along the conduits.

Added to the problem of kutcha houses, the system of ventilation in both kutcha and pukka houses proved difficult for excavating the subterranean network. Ventilation in Bengali houses meant a customary way of bringing in the southern breeze.[41] A central courtyard, the *uthhon*, open to sunlight and fresh air ventilated the houses. There was, however, no single prototype of a courtyard. The space of the courtyard varied in different parts of the city according to the availability of land. Big houses usually had two courtyards: the inner and outer.[42] Courtyards in the southern parts of the city were usually bigger than the north. The Marwaris, a wealthy business group, on the other hand, had altogether new ways of building courtyards. Their houses followed the *chawk* system, where there was only one apartment with a quadrangle at the centre and a range of rooms on the floor above.

As the British soon realized, courtyards obstructed the successful execution of subterranean conduits. First, courtyards were private properties. While the improvement commissioners could dig up the streets and install new conduits, they could not do the same inside Bengali houses. The Bengalis used the courtyards for purposes of worship and social gatherings. They refused to set up a system that would make sewage flow underneath such spaces of gathering. When the British ordered the Bengalis to take initiative and fix the lines, they simply refused. Second, even when the homeowners agreed to install the lines, they refused to pay for repairs and maintenance of these pipes. Repair costs were high and sometimes led to disputes between neighbours where responsibilities were shared.

The biggest challenge to the subterranean channels, however, were the caste practices of Indian city dwellers. The upper castes considered pipes carrying sewage from lower caste houses that passed below their own houses to be polluting.[43] For that reason, they refused to connect their houses to the main channels. They also refused to drink the filtered water for the same reason: the pipes carried it below lower caste and non-Hindu houses. Another problem was that the commissioners did not erect enough stand posts for drawing water. They expected city dwellers to share water from the posts. When the upper castes queued up for water, they found the lower castes and Muslims drawing water from the same stand posts. Viewing this as a threat to their purity, they refused to drink water from the stand posts and continued to draw water from reservoirs in their neighbourhoods.[44]

It is worth mentioning here that colonial public works need to be seen as part of cultural imperialism, rather than a neutral form of material change. Such projects assisted global empires to enforce new cultural orders through the restructuration of space. Even outside the British empire in India, in colonial Algeria and Madagascar, for instance, the French empire's goals were to introduce European urban designs as the universal language of public works.[45] Universalism implied the power of European designs to work across landscapes, Western and non-Western alike. There were a few exceptions, however. The French left the Casbah in Algiers intact for its exotic value, as a tourist attraction.[46] Elsewhere, colonizers either disregarded diverse indigenous cultural practices or appropriated them to further segregate the city to divide groups and restrict economic exchanges.[47]

Town improvement officers in Calcutta were aware that the plan for waterworks—imported from London—did not meet the caste expectations of Indians. Yet they praised its utilitarian value and decided to expand it; the underground channels, after all, extended their authority to the hitherto unknown spaces. It reinforced the ambiguous role of modern technologies in providing an illusion of complete British control and comprehension of the Bengalis. Constructing the sewers, the British marched into the remote recesses of the Bengali neighbourhoods. Here they surveyed the streets and houses. They prepared an inventory of the Bengali houses, with detailed descriptions of its structures, floors, rooms, and also the inhabitants.

When extension work began in 1872, only a third of the six thousand Indian houses could be connected to the subterranean network.[48] The general disinterest of the Hindus and the customs they followed in building their houses proved impermeable to the hydraulics network. Improvement commissioners finally realized that Calcutta's cultural landscape was indeed a grave impediment to their renovation work—they responded by questioning the traditional building practices of Indians. They charged customary building patterns with being the cause of the incredible filth and epidemics in the city. Their reports described courtyards as receptacles of filth and kutcha huts as hotbeds of disease. Vivid descriptions of unhygienic conditions showed Indian neighbourhoods deteriorating the epidemic constitution of the city, thus transforming the native town into a 'black' town.

The discursive production of insanitary space and its savage inhabitants as a colonial tool have been addressed in studies widely, ranging from British imperialism in India to the American invasion in Philippines. Writing about American colonialism in the Philippines, Warwick Anderson has described how representations of the body were crucial in justifying the unequal relations of power that made up colonialism.[49] Health officers employed examples of excreta to argue that Filipinos were incapable of controlling their body and its orifices. Describing faecal matter as more dangerous than germs, health officers set boundaries between themselves and Filipinos. In a similar way,

David Arnold has shown how British colonial images of the pestilential tropics connected the landscape to culture as a means of buttressing colonial control.[50] The scientific discourses surrounding the tropics were meant to recast colonial domination.

In Calcutta, blackness immersed both space and its inhabitants in the darkness of filth and ignorance. It made all claims of cultural difference irrelevant and cleared the way for British civil engineering on Indian soil. Key to the processes of grafting was the discursive production of a black town in the colonial health reports. Black town entailed a certain representation of space as primitive and closed to reason and science, or enlightenment. In the health reports, space became a medium for the colonialist to articulate their imperialist rhetoric. Representing Bengali neighbourhoods as the black town served a dual purpose. First, blackness revealed the subterranean selves of Indians: the irrational, uncivilized, and savage. Second, the primitiveness of the black town contrasted the European parts of the city and recast its residents as culturally and technologically superior. The colonizers reasoned that improvements were necessary to prevent the black town from falling into further chaos and disorder. As we will see, such discursive subordination worked to extend colonial power in Calcutta but did not go uncontested.

Epidemics Shape a Black Town

A seventeen-year-old Indian boy named J. C. had moved from Bombay to Calcutta in 1896, where he succumbed to a strange disease.[51] After days of high fever, his groin enlarged and his body weakened. Physicians identified the disease as plague. J. C. was the son of an Indian merchant who had trade ties with Bombay. A health inquiry committee determined that he had brought plague with him from Bombay. A few days later, another Indian boy, Giga, the son of another Indian merchant, was discovered with the same fever.[52] The physicians determined, yet again, that it was plague. They explained that Giga had contracted plague while playing at a warehouse where his father stored mangoes and yarn that he imported from Bombay.

In the final decades of the nineteenth century, the British kept Calcutta on long-term alert against plague. They held Indian merchants responsible for importing the affliction and ordered them to shut down warehouses and cut off their trade ties with Bombay. Public opinion remained divided, however, on the incidences of plague. An author Bhubanchandra wrote in his book *Bangarahasya* in 1900 that an epidemic had indeed found its way from Bombay but that there was little to suggest it was plague.[53] The book went on to explain that physicians were unable to match the symptoms with any description in medical books and passed off all diseases as plague. Since the prognosis of plague was based on conjecture, the cure was also assumptive. In most cases, medicines failed to work, and the patients died within hours.

By the 1850s, scientists in London had proved the germ theory, the existence of pathogenic organisms that cause epidemics like cholera and plague. The observations and epidemiological studies of John Snow in London and William Budd in Bristol supported this theory.[54] These discoveries, however, did not inform the colonial theory of miasma, which held that pollution and vitiated air caused diseases. Health officers reported that Indian houses were *miasms*, or receptacles of uncleanliness.[55] They traced epidemics to the filth on the streets and in water tanks and the unwholesome living conditions in these houses.

Epidemics, however, were not typical to India in the late nineteenth century. Scholars have shown the trans-local nature of a panic centred on epidemics that gripped Britain's colonies at this time.[56] The British reacted to the threat of disease in contrasting ways; Michael Zeheter described, for instance, the different approaches that the British adopted in controlling cholera in Madras and Quebec.[57] In Madras, they initiated reforms that tried to restructure the city; in Quebec, they only disinfected the streets and the air. Colonial anxieties about disease resulted in draconian acts in India; these acts tried to control the body of Indians as a way to control epidemics.[58] Indians naturally resisted these acts. They took to local cures to fight diseases. Projit Bihari Mukharji in his study on hygiene, however, has complicated the meaning of the local. He argues that local responses to British epidemic control measures resisted it, while also accepting the science and rationality that they advanced.[59]

Moving beyond global ramifications of the disease and its local registers, I argue that in the wake of cholera and plague, the British embraced a certain narratology that shifted focus from disease and placed it on images of filth-ridden Indian spaces. British health reports routinely depicted dirt, clogged drains, refuse-filled courtyards, and excreta left unattended in Indian neighbourhoods. Health officers persistently described that the unhealthy habits of Indians, together with the growing filth in their houses, produced disease. Detailed portrayals of dirtiness in their reports also transformed feelings of panic into disgust.

As the Indian subcontinent transitioned to capitalism through colonialism, the binaries of 'waste' and 'profit' became more pronounced. British frustrations with waste piling in Indian houses and their wasteful habits called for more regulations. As Dominique Laporte wrote in *History of Shit*, capitalism deepens the association of money and faeces requiring that waste be mined for profit.[60] William Cohen, on the other hand, analysed the representation of filth/waste in the literature of London, Paris, and their colonies to argue that the idea of waste, that is, what society does not accept, reinforces relations between disease and disorder and shapes gender and race-based stereotypes.[61] In a similar way, Swati Chattopadhyay has discussed the politics of representation of waste and disease, highlighting the role of British health maps in Calcutta. These maps supported British assumptions that dirty Indian neighbourhoods produced disease, turning such assumptions into facts.[62] Once the maps showed the inherent dirtiness of Indians, Chattopadhyay describes that health officers proposed remodelling and setting new rules to make Indian neighbourhoods legible to the state and, thus, easy to control.

I argue that the failed attempts of the British to deploy civic improvements to excavate the city, and open it to colonial surveillance, informed the portrayals of Indian insanitation in the late nineteenth century. When plague broke out in 1898, the British saw it as yet another chance to intervene, control, and restructure Indian neighbourhoods. To that end, they targeted those structures—courtyards, kutcha huts, and narrow streets—that earlier stood in the way of their improvements. While emphasizing the frailty of Indian building patterns, the British engaged in a selective representation of space: a key strategy that coloured their descriptions of Indian neighbourhoods as filthy and transformed individual practices of unhygiene into a shared character of a race. Dirtiness as a racial disposition then established the lack of sanitary knowledge among Indians and dismissed their spatial customs as dangerous to public health.

Starting with cholera, and then plague, selective representation of dirtiness in colonial health reports transformed the native town into a black town. Pointing to courtyards that had earlier resisted the network of subterranean conduits the British questioned their need in Indian houses. Health officers argued that courtyards 'were nothing more than containers of shit' and that it was a common 'Indian habit' to throw shit in these spaces:

> Refuse is thrown from whatever part of the house they [Indians] occupy into the courtyard in the centre of the house, or into a passage in which neither light nor fresh air can have access, the filthy condition of Indian houses, the close proximity of Indian houses to one another and their overcrowded state combine to form conditions that render proper sanitation impossible in India.[63]

The Black Town, Spaces of Pathology, and a Hindu Discourse of Citizenship

In this health report excerpt, the careful use of 'Indians' in place of specific people who were found unclean served as a discursive tool to transform the poor sanitation of an individual into a racial characteristic shared by all Indians. Health officers used a single instance to represent the ongoing behaviour of the entire community. Likewise, when the state sent cleaning crews to force their way into Indian houses and cleanse the courtyards, the homeowners resisted the violation of their privacy—health officers reported that 'ignorant Indians' had little idea of sanitation.[64] They explained unsanitary behaviour as a 'bad habit of Indians', using the example of specific homeowners to speak for all Indians and translating the homeowners' resistance to colonial violence as 'ignorance'.[65]

The descriptions of unsanitary conditions in colonial health reports are extraordinary. On one occasion, a medical officer wrote that he had to climb a ladder to reach the top of a nine-foot-high refuse pile.[66] On another occasion, in Cotton Street, he employed workers to clean a lane where refuse had piled up for years. He wrote that the lane was so narrow that the cleaning crew had to pass through a private room and squeeze through a back window to clean its spaces. He described this extreme case as commonplace and argued that *Indian* streets were always narrow as *Indians* had little idea of conservancy.

Colonial health officers launched repeated attacks on the Marwari community describing their houses, warehouses, and neighbourhoods as woefully dirty. Nothing short of demolitions, argued the officers, could better living conditions for the Marwaris. Demolitions meant that the Marwaris would lose their residence and business, as their warehouses bordered their houses, and their offices were also at their home. The Marwari loss, however, would benefit the British by wiping out a major competition in their cotton trade. When cholera broke out in 1875, the British described that in Shama Bai lane, where many Marwaris lived, it spread like wildfire.[67] They described Marwari houses in the lane with very little space in between, arguing that such building patterns obstructed sunlight and produced epidemics.[68] Back-to-back houses, health officers explained also rendered conservancy difficult. They pointed out that it was a *Marwari habit* to throw shit in the centre of the house, the courtyard, or in small passages where neither light nor air could enter.[69] Privies in Marwari houses, they described, were mostly compartments with openings in the floor with a long shaft leading to a dark vault. Excreta, as a consequence of their long descent, splashed in every direction and formed a cesspool that was impossible to clean.

A Hygienic City-Nation

Furthermore, Dr G. Brien, a medical officer, in 1884 described Marwari privies in Jorabagaan, another Marwari neighbourhood, as radically faulty and insanitary.[70] He claimed to have inspected around twelve hundred privies. He found that the privies were all constructed on the plan of a drop through a shaft or compartment at one end of the building into a receptacle on the ground floor. In nearly 60 per cent of the houses, the receptacles were placed on the ground without protection against surface contamination. With radical faults in their construction, he explained they were a health hazard in the city and had to be demolished. When Brien wrote his report on the privies, he concluded that it was impossible to express in words the insanitary and filthy conditions of *native privies*.

Selective representation meant that the health officers argued that epidemics *always* brewed in Indian neighbourhoods. This, of course, was not true, as epidemics also often broke out in European neighbourhoods. In December 1871, a British bureaucrat, Mr Tracey, succumbed to cholera in a European boarding house in Calcutta.[71] He was visiting the city along with his wife and their Indian servant, who were all staying in a boarding house on Russel Street at the heart of the European town. Three days after they reached Calcutta, Mr Tracey was bed-ridden, his health deteriorating. In the following week, cholera spread among the residents of the boarding house. Mrs Wimberley and Archdaeon Pratt, who were rooming on the first floor, suffered severe bouts of dyspepsia.

Since Russel Street was geographically distant from any Indian neighbourhood, the outbreak of cholera at the boarding house challenged the colonial argument that epidemics always broke out among Indians. The colonial state commissioned an inquiry committee to investigate the outbreak. Finding it difficult to establish any credible points of contact between the Indian and European parts of the city, the council came up with an argument that a violent wind had transported pestilence from Indian neighbourhoods to Russel Street where it had decomposed and produced disease.

The second incident of cholera took place in Alipore prison. The prison was not only away from Indian neighbourhoods, but its spaces cordoned off from any contact with the world outside. A prisoner named Gobindo Chunder Bose was its first casualty.[72] In late March, Gobindo suffered choleric diarrhoea. Instead of treating him for cholera, the guards moved him to the general hospital. The next day, another prisoner, named Atterally, showed similar symptoms, and the guards moved him to the same hospital. He died the next afternoon.

The outbreak of cholera at the British-run prison, though its victims were Indians, once again challenged the colonial argument that epidemics originated

The Black Town, Spaces of Pathology, and a Hindu Discourse of Citizenship 41

only in Indian houses. As shown in the report (see Table 1.1), the cholera inquiry committee for Alipore prison refused to report the disease as cholera. They explained that the prison premises were clean but that the prisoners were suffering from general weakness. The officials described the dyspeptic spells as symptoms of fever and chicken pox. Their final report showed prisoners suffering from general debility, chicken pox, and phthisis. In some cases, like that of Sitto Khan and Bhundoo Kahar, they completely ignored the attack of cholera and reported that the health of the prisoners as 'good'. The committee went on to argue that epidemics like cholera could take place only in the 'filthy' and 'closely packed' Indian houses.

Table 1.1 Plague incidents in Alipore prison reported as chicken pox and general weakness. Some patients are also reported as having good health.

Patient name	Date of attack	Date of death	State of health
Gobindo Chunder Bose	18 March at 11 a.m.	21 March	Chicken pox
Atterally	20 March at 3 a.m.	20 March	General debility
Madhub Lohar	20 March at 1 p.m.	——	General debility
Shittoo Adhir	20 March at midnight	26 March	Debility
Abdool Aziz	21 March at 1 a.m.	23 March	Phthisis
Khedree Dome	22 March at 5 a.m.	21 March	Chicken pox
Sitto Khan	20 March at 1 a.m.	——	Good
Bhundoo Kahar	1 April at 11 a.m.	——	Good

Source: 'Report on Cholera in Alipore Jail, 1864', in *Measures for the Prevention of Cholera among European Troops in Northern India* (Calcutta: Printed at the Alipore Jail Press, 1864).

What health officers described as 'closely packed' was a common spatial practice among Indians. Other than providing relief from the summer sun, closely built houses were a cultural choice that Indians made. Unlike Europeans, who preferred to live away from business districts, Indians lived close to their workplaces. Business districts like Barrabazaar and Jorabagaan in north Calcutta were also popular residential neighbourhoods.[73] In these spaces, land prices were high. Indian families were large and kept growing, with distant relatives, friends, and domestic employees all living together. Big families living in expensive plots of land resulted in back-to-back houses.

Health officers disregarded the cultural practices that shaped closely built houses, describing them as visual demonstrations of the lack of sanitary awareness among Indians. This process of atomizing space by separating dwellings from their cultural meanings was yet another discursive tool to transform the native town into a black town. Photographs in health reports

42 A Hygienic City-Nation

further worked to detach space from context and inscribe it with new meanings. Photographs provided the colonial state with authentic information on the Indians.[74] The colonizers employed photographs to categorize, index, and *know* the natives. But as the health reports show, photographs did not simply assist colonizers in *knowing* native space, they also entailed a process of *producing* the knowledge of space.

Medical officer Dr G. Brien in 1884 surveyed kutcha houses that had earlier proved to be incompatible to the underground channels. He found that existing drop privies (outhouses), constructed on the plan of a drop-through shaft at one end, caused the huts to be smeared with excreta and immersed the entire neighbourhood in human waste.[75] A few years later, his observations informed health officer William John Ritchie Simpson's report on the health of Calcutta.[76] Simpson used photographs to provide evidence of poor levels of sanitation in all Indian houses, both pukka and kutcha. Zooming into Indian privies, he argued that these *pre-modern* spaces were a threat to the health of the entire city. He advised, with much concern, that the Indian privies should be replaced with modern ones and the refuse channels connected to the underground sewers. The photographs he provided of unsanitary privies, however, actually offered very little evidence of filth. The structures he calls privies do not appear unsanitary, and heavy atomization of space was part of the narrative of the black town he produced.

Figure 1.1 is an example of a photograph that Simpson used as evidence for unsanitary Indian privies. The photograph focuses on ephemeral structures: a pole left unused, an open space yet to be built, and thatched roofs and matted construction that suggest its kutcha or makeshift nature. Simpson describes how the privy in this house—and in most kutcha structures—had receptacles placed on the ground. Excreta that dropped freely from the upper stories often missed the receptacles and soiled the walls and floors. The water used for washing the privy also collected on the ground below, forming a poisonous mire.

In Figure 1.1, the window marked (1) is supposed to be the privy. We can see the room from the outside, but the inside appears dark. There is very little evidence to suggest that the structure actually is a privy. First, the room is inside the house and on an upper storey. The Indian custom, however, was to build privies outside houses. A small passage normally separated the privy from the inner quarters of the house, especially where the kitchen and bedrooms were. In this photo, the room marked as the privy is on the second floor of the house and is part of the main structure of the house. Even if the structure is a privy, it was the exception, rather than the norm.

The Black Town, Spaces of Pathology, and a Hindu Discourse of Citizenship 43

Figure 1.1 Photograph of privy vaults and receptacles in a two-storey building. 1. Upper-storey privy. 2. Pipes to carry off soil water. 3. Receptacles to privy vault. 4. Mehtranee. 5. Ground on which a new hut is about to be erected. 6. A pole of the new hut. 7. Adjoining hut.

Source: Report of the health officer of Calcutta for 1887 by W.J. Simpson. Courtesy of General Research Division, NYPL, New York.

As he did with Figure 1.1, Simpson used Figure 1.2 to explain the weak construction of privies (marked 1 and 2) in Indian houses. He described how the location of these privies, the pipes that carried soiled water, and the privy vaults were all kutcha—makeshift—and therefore improperly built. He argued that the pipes splashed dirty water on the streets below, causing a pool of stinking water and excreta to collect on the ground. This pool, however, cannot be seen in the photograph. Instead, a *mehtranee* (janitor), carrying the filth in a bucket over her head—possibly to empty it in the main sewers—can be seen, but gets no mention in Simpson's report.

Simpson also photographed verandahs, arguing that Indians used them as privies. He explained that there were openings in verandahs for faecal matter, urine, and water to pass through and fall to the ground below. A receptacle placed under the structures, he argued, collected excreta, but because the verandahs had varying heights, the filth often missed its destination, contaminating the ground below.

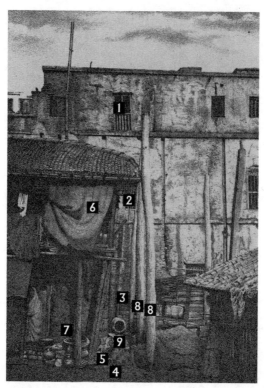

Figure 1.2 Photograph showing privies in *kutcha* and *pukka* houses. 1 and 2. Upper storeyed privies. 3. Receptacle. 4. Water pipe almost level with ground. 5. Water vessel. 6. Two-storeyed hut. 7. Hand mill for grinding corn. 8. Poles for a new hut to be erected. 9. A vessel for water.

Source: Report of the health officer of Calcutta for 1887 by W.J. Simpson. Courtesy of General Research Division, NYPL, New York.

Using Figure 1.3 as an example of a verandah-privy, Simpson wrote:

> It is hardly safe for an Inspector to go very near when the door is open; the splashes warn him to make hasty retreat. The stench issuing from the chamber is sickening, the pollution of air being intense.[77]

The photograph does not show any receptacle for collecting waste. Neither does it show filth soiling the ground below. There is, once again, very little evidence in the photo to indicate that the verandahs served as privies. The protruding structure marked (1) looks more like a window. Instead of the soiled ground, a cart can be seen restfully parked under the verandah (3).

Figure 1.3 Photograph of verandah privies. 1, 2, and 3. Verandahs used as privies.
Source: Report of the health officer of Calcutta for 1887 by W.J. Simpson. Courtesy of General Research Division, NYPL, New York.

Health officers, however, used such photographs to provide evidence of a black town riddled in waste. The photographs zoomed into courtyards and kutcha structures to argue that customary building patterns were of little use in keeping the city clean. The pictures supposedly portrayed Indian houses covered in excreta and courtyards drowned in filth.

Of course, British portrayals of filthy Bengalis were not without resistance. Simpson had handpicked health commissioners and trained them to undertake effective surveys of Indian houses, but the commissioners soon realized that Bengali houses were impossible to survey. The homeowners simply refused to open their houses to the British. Met with severe resistance, the commissioners broke into these houses. A sanitary commissioner, J. Nield Cook, for example, did not inform homeowners before entering their houses.[78] He stormed into

Indian houses and walked straight into the privies. This invasion of privacy, naturally, infuriated the homeowners. They devised new ways to stop the commissioners from marching into their homes: they hurled papers soaked in shit and pails of excreta at the commissioners to drive them away.[79]

The symbolism of hurling shit was more important than the actual physical harm it caused. The British deployed descriptions of shit and excreta to paint images of filthy Bengalis—the Bengalis, on the other hand, used shit to resist the British. The commissioners realized that the shit protests were in line with the Bengali's agenda to make their neighbourhoods ungovernable. They reacted with horror and argued that the Bengalis, primitive in their practices, should learn to hide their shit. They pointed to the dire lack of modern privies in Bengali houses that made people live like shit—packed on top of the other, enduring each other's excretions.

When cholera broke out, Simpson drafted reports on how Bengalis were living in shit. These reports carried striking portrayals of shit putrefying inside Bengali houses. This furthered colonial arguments of 'peculiar Bengalis, dirty in the extreme' and their houses as 'the reservoirs of disease'.[80] The cholera reports barely depicted germs as the specific cause of infectious diseases. Instead, health officers essentialized and pathologized the spatial environment of those diagnosed with the illness, tracing cholera to insanitary Bengali houses. Faced with such discursive violence, Bengalis used actual shit to repel the British and make their neighbourhoods unmanageable.

Finally, health officers concluded that if Indians were unable to control their habits and clean their own houses, the British had to do the work for them. Extreme filth accumulating in Indian houses called for complete demolition and rebuilding of these houses. The British convened building commissions and passed laws to replace Indian spatial customs with a more scientific use of space, similar to the West.

The Calcutta Building Commission

In 1897, armed with the discourse of a noxious black town, the state employed a building commission. The building commission worked to improve the health of the city through a close supervision of the building plans of Indian houses.[81] It functioned as a licensing body, reviewing and granting house plans. Indian property owners had to obtain permission from the commission prior to building new structures or expanding existing ones. The commission was the first official body to carry out formal inquiries into the spaces of Indian houses;

The Black Town, Spaces of Pathology, and a Hindu Discourse of Citizenship   47

it debated changes in existing building laws and placed special emphasis on maintaining the height of houses in relation to the width of adjoining streets.

Although the commission was convened for the purpose of improving sanitation, it worked to transform Indian neighbourhoods and make them amenable to town improvements.

Once the commission started work, it rejected all plans for uthhons in Indian houses. The commissioners argued that the courtyards served no purpose and only accumulated filth. In existing houses, where homeowners wanted to build additional rooms, the commission ordered them to cover courtyards and turn these into rooms. In 1897, Bama Bewah and Shama Bewah, both residents of Burtola Street in north Calcutta, submitted a plan to the building commission seeking permission to expand their house.[82] The commissioners allowed them to build new rooms only if they covered the courtyard (Figure 1.4).

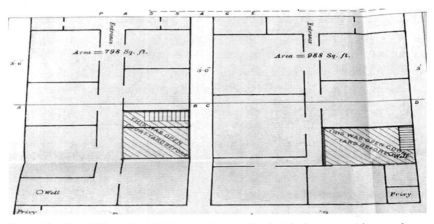

Figure 1.4 Plan of Shama Bewah's house in Burtola Road, with the courtyard covered up.
Source: Report of the Calcutta Building Commission, 1897. Courtesy of Bodleian Library Archives, Oxford.

Ultimately, however, the building commission lacked the power to eliminate courtyards from Indian houses. Property owners simply refused to follow their directives. The problem was compounded by the fact that the commission was itself divided over the building codes. The case of Abdul Gunni is a clear example of the commission's failure to reach a consensus on the law.[83] In July 1898, Abdul Gunni sought permission from the commission to rebuild two storeys of his house. The commissioners rejected his plans several times, fearing that Gunni would demolish the eastern wing of his house and open the area as a courtyard. He finally received permission after he provided written assurance that he would not open a courtyard. At the time of rebuilding, however, Gunni did exactly as the commissioners feared: he pulled down the eastern block of his house, which consisted of twelve rooms, built a single room, and opened the rest of the area as a courtyard.

When the commissioners found out about Gunni's violations of the written terms, they met to discuss whether they should go ahead and cover the courtyard. They remained deeply divided, as they did not know how to interpret the building codes: whether the courtyard should be covered or the owner let off with a fine. A member of the committee explained that if they covered the courtyard, it could lead to an injunction and a prolonged trial.[84] After the committee met several times and was still unable to reach a consensus, Gunni simply carried on with the rebuilding.

A similar case was that of Bheemraj Jhoonjhoonwala, who in April of 1898 received permission from the commission to construct a new three-storey building. In December, he submitted a proposal for adding an extra storey to the house and opening the centre as a courtyard.[85] Without waiting for permission, he proceeded to construct the courtyard. When the building commission brought a case against him, he was acquitted on the ground that the law did not provide a date, following the submission of the proposal, for when property owners could start construction.

Violations of building regulations became widespread when property owners realized that the consequences were manageable. Women who were poor and who had already been convicted once found easy acquittal.[86] Others were usually let off with a warning before they were fined.[87] In most cases, fines were low. Property owners also learned the easy process of seeking permission for a structure and then using it for some other purpose. For instance, they sought permissions for shops and warehouses and used them as houses.[88] This helped them to bypass the ventilation clauses and save on the extra expenses. When the commission found out, they sent officers to demolish the structures. The property owners bolted doors from the inside and showered the agents with brickbats, making it impossible for them to enter the houses.[89]

The building commission also launched an attack on kutcha structures that had earlier proved problematic for subterranean water channels. The commissioners argued that epidemics spread in kutcha huts and that pukka structures should replace them.[90] They described kutcha huts as 'plague spots' or 'breeding grounds for plague' and as 'crowded dwelling rooms and foul-smelling cowsheds' in need of immediate demolition.[91] The first cluster of huts they demolished was in Darmahatta Street in north Calcutta.[92] When medical officers reported plague deaths in the neighbourhood, the building

The Black Town, Spaces of Pathology, and a Hindu Discourse of Citizenship   49

commissioners forced their way into the huts.[93] They demolished the huts, isolated residents in segregation camps, and burned their belongings. The demolitions carried on for several months as the hut dwellers refused to move. Many hut dwellers had lived in these huts for generations. They had also heard that in the segregation camps they had to share space with the other castes. They feared this *mlechhachar* (practice that violates caste) of having to eat, live, and mingle with the other castes as much as they dreaded the loss of their home.[94] When they refused to move and the state could no longer tolerate the delay, the police were called in and 'the work of clearing huts was commenced' under 'lathis and bamboo *dandas* [staves]'.[95]

The building commission's findings on kutcha huts informed the demolitions of the Calcutta municipal corporation, which oversaw city administration. As Figure 1.5 shows, numerous kutcha huts were destroyed in the Machuaabazaar neighbourhood in north Calcutta in the years after the plague. The corporation made no effort to rebuild these houses in sanitary ways but simply demolished them and left the land open. In the northern half of the neighbourhood, the plague commissioners destroyed houses to build streets that were straight and allowed for the easy movement of traffic. As the two plans of the neighbourhood show, nothing much was done to improve sanitation, except leave plots of land open.

As a plague prevention measure, demolition was ineffective. In the north Calcutta neighbourhood of Jorabagaan, there was a massive fall in plague deaths, although no demolition had taken place. In sharp contrast, in Puggyaputty bustee, where the commissioners carried out massive demolitions, built new brick structures, and forced more than half of the hut dwellers to leave, plague deaths increased. The newly built brick houses abutted on each other, leaving no airspace in the back. The poor ventilation in the rooms failed to improve sanitation in the neighbourhood.

Indian property owners believed there was no plague and that the building commissioners were inventing instances of plague to demolish their houses. A rumour surfaced among them that the health officers were murdering Indians at the health camps and taking over their properties.[96] This argument became stronger in the face of drastic measures that the state introduced to control plague. For example, the state promoted a general inoculation with Haffkine's vaccine, discovered by bacteriologist Waldemar Haffkine, in a makeshift laboratory in Bombay in 1896 and used as an experiment to control epidemics in India. The vaccines led to an inoculation scare. A crowd terrified of *tickawalah*s (inoculators) broke out in violence.[97] They attacked ambulances and set them on fire.

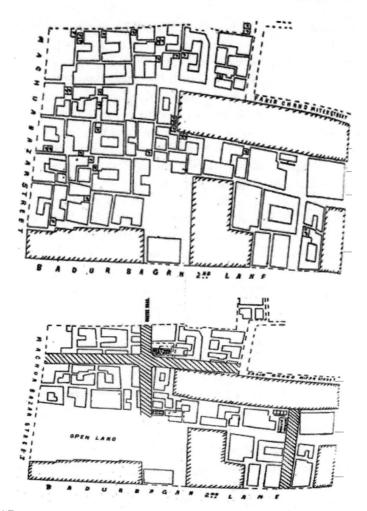

Figure 1.5 An Indian neighbourhood at Machuaabazaar Street before and after demolition.
Source: Report on the Municipal Administration of Calcutta, 1910. Courtesy of Kolkata Town Hall Archives.

Perhaps the greatest impediment to the work of the building commission was the racist outlook of its members. James Lowson, who led the commission, urged members to suggest ways to sanitize the 'Asiatic race'.[98] Writing about a law that required every native house in Hong Kong to have concrete ground floors impervious to water, he argued that a similar law would also work in Calcutta, as both were Asian cities. He explained that improvements that worked in a certain part of Asia should be effective in all cities as the city

The Black Town, Spaces of Pathology, and a Hindu Discourse of Citizenship   51

dwellers were all 'Asians' and had similar spatial practices. He thereby glossed over all customary practices that shaped Indian houses.

Mr Braunfield, who was the chief medical officer of the building commission, did not agree with Lowson. He described Indian houses as poor copies of building styles in ancient Greece.[99] In the northern parts of Calcutta, he argued, houses were built with no aesthetic sense and lacked privies. Small rooms opened to dirty lanes. With his experience of supervising building patterns in the suburbs of London and Norwood, he believed that houses in Calcutta should follow Western models conceived by the 'more advanced races'. These arguments, built on ideas of racial supremacy, did not remain uncontested for long.

Faced with the homogenizing efforts of the building commission, a new discourse on town improvements took shape in the writings of a group of educated Hindu-Bengali men who identified as nagoriks (citizens). Their use of the word 'nagorik' points to a germinating discourse on citizenship that was as an Indian response to colonial town improvements. The nagoriks wrote for Bengali health periodicals, such as *Svasthya*, offering a trenchant critique of the building commission, for multiple reasons. They felt humiliated by the commissioner's surveillance of the most intimate spaces of their home: the privies. They also believed that a uniform building code was not possible in Calcutta because the building practices of Hindus and Muslims, rich and poor, Bengalis and non-Bengalis, and the upper and lower castes were all different. But at the same time, as nagoriks of a colonial city, they described ideal spatial practices by drawing upon Hindu scriptural texts like the Shastras.

Citizenship in India is a legal status that draws upon multiple identities that Indians have inhabited from colonial times to the present. With the onset of colonial rule, the British carried out 'enumerations' that classified Indians into unfamiliar categories.[100] A good example of this was the caste system that the British made mandatory for census purposes. Indians who did not know their caste were forced to identify with one to be part of the census. Added to this were the deep racial views of British lawmakers that restricted the exercise of equal rights. Ashna Ashesh and Arjun Thiruvengadam have shown that colonial legislations did not at first clarify to whom these applied, technically making rights available to all individuals.[101] This changed with the British Nationality and Status of Aliens Act of 1914 that was heavily imbued with a racist understanding of citizenship and openly preferred the British over Indians. In a fascinating study, Niraja Gopal Jayal has differentiated between imperial (more external, between colonies and Britain) and colonial (more internal, within colonies) citizenship to show that claims for equality confronted a variety of considerations—race when it came to *imperial* citizenship, and class in debates about *colonial* citizenship.[102]

The new categories like caste and race that the British employed to understand Indian society found their way to colonial and later postcolonial understandings of citizenship. The 1950 constitution offered equal rights to all, but in practice, the exercise of equal rights was fraught with differences that were historically constructed. As Gyanendra Pandey argues, nationalism required all Indians to share a common identity, but subaltern citizenship emerged as a discourse of difference rather than equality.[103] The most unique strand in citizenship ideas in India, however, was its conflation with religious identities that still make citizenship—often interchanged with nationality—a contested terrain. The next section situates the processes of layering citizenship with religious markers as a response to civic improvements in the colonial city.

Hindu Nagoriks of a Colonial City

Broadly defined, citizenship is a system of rights that shape relations between individuals and the state, and also among individuals themselves. The history of citizenship can be traced back to ancient Greece and Rome, but historians date modern citizenship to the French Revolution of 1789. The French Revolution ended an era of feudalism. It laid the grounds for democracy by advancing a new language of human rights. Individuals were no longer 'subjects' owing allegiance to a king. Neither could divine sanction be the basis for royal power. With subjects evolving into citizens, the loyalty of individuals shifted from the king to the nation-state. Democratic political processes guaranteed equality and liberty as the nation-state preserved the citizens' right to vote, to perform military service, and to access legal resources. Different from subject hood, citizenship became a participatory process that kept the engines of democracy running.

As Frederick Cooper argues, however, individual experiences of citizenship remain vastly different. The language of rights drafted by certain groups does not apply to all.[104] In countries shaped by ethnic diversity, citizenship rights can hardly constitute a uniform code; citizenship does not bring with it a sense of belonging. While some groups are able to exercise their rights, exclusion of minority groups has become the norm.

Nor does citizenship have a shared history in Western and non-Western countries. Momentous events that unfurled in Europe—the French Revolution,

The Black Town, Spaces of Pathology, and a Hindu Discourse of Citizenship 53

Industrial Revolution, nationalism, world wars, and so on—did not occur in the non-West at the same time. When the French Revolution was transforming France, the British East India Company was colonizing natural resources and monopolizing trade networks in the Indian Ocean region. Given the colonial context, a new language of imperial citizenship took shape in Britain's colonies that was different from discourses on citizenship in Britain itself. This new language of imperial citizenship shaped a body of rights that pre-dated the emergence of a nation-state and the country's transition to democracy. Scholars have argued that imperial citizenship emerged in elite and educated circles in Britain.[105] They describe that the British authored it to justify the need for colonies. Seeing imperial citizenship as an offshoot of citizenship discourses taking shape in Britain, however, this approach overlooks all exchanges that took place between the colonizer and the ruled and which were key to colonialism. In sharp contrast, scholars like Sukanya Banerjee offers a more nuanced understanding of imperial citizenship by locating it in the realm of affective, rather than actual, enactments.[106] Citizenship features in Banerjee's work as a subject position that moderate nationalists assumed to push for their demands, while underscoring their difference from the British.

I argue that nagorik responses to colonial town improvements wove together citizenship and subject position investing the former with religious meanings. Nagoriks were urban, upper-caste, educated men who held property and paid taxes. They demanded that the British consult them because their taxes funded town improvements. Their claim that the payment of taxes qualified them to decide on improvements inscribed on them a secular character. Nonetheless, nagoriks soon departed from this secular tone to argue that their work was to preserve a Hindu spatial order in the city. In authoring new principles of urban administration and creating a new discourse on civil rights (in this case community-based rather than individual rights), they drew on Hindu scriptures, such as the Dharma Shastras that recast their role as somewhat similar to citizens. Reinventing a Hindu code from the scriptures, they posited it as essential for city administration, only to argue that English laws were incompatible with Indian cities. In other words, nagoriks drew on a secular footing—the payment of taxes—in their demand to be included in town improvement projects; however, the language they employed to negotiate these improvements—the improvements they argued Calcutta needed and the state's role in carrying these out—were informed by Hindu religion.

In Europe, citizenship was a secular idea that challenged the divine roots of an emperor's authority. Nagorik writings, on the other hand, embraced

54 A Hygienic City-Nation

Hindu religion in formulating ideas of citizenship. Unlike in Europe, where philosophers challenged the divine and absolute power of the monarch, the nagoriks proposed a new language of citizenship rights that was contingent on the king or city administrator wielding ultimate authority and ensuring peace and equality. Nagoriks explained that a *nogor-poti*—a city leader who ruled using his moral judgement—could govern the city better. Writing for the Bengali periodical *Svasthya Samacara* in 1912, author Bhabataran Bidyaratna explained that a nogor-poti had a pure heart. He writes,

> A nogor-poti has a very pure heart / he protects the city with great care/ So many anxious people live in the city with so much pain / he lets no harm happen to anyone / He cares for all living in the city / ruling righteously, he lets peace reign/ If ever harm happens to a city dweller/ he uses all his power to lessen it / so that no danger happens / Winning over evil he talks of the moral / he rears his *projas* (subjects), never failing them /ruling over time and space / he fights the worst of danger / his wealth and hard-work enhances the happiness of the city.[107]

As the passage above explains, nagoriks believed that the nogor-poti, the leader of the city, was a kind of king who had moral authority over his subjects. He had a 'pure heart' and 'talks of the moral', is committed to the work of 'rearing' projas (subjects), and his rule 'enhances happiness'. Nagoriks further explained that the work of the nogor-poti was paternal and also religiously binding (*dhormotto badhyo*).[108] The responsibility of 'rearing his projas' and the idea that kingship was dhormotto badhyo show the religious foundations of the nogor-poti's rule and imply that administering the city was his *rajdharma* or spiritual duty.

Rajdharma is a Hindu understanding of governance as a spiritual act. Ancient Hindu texts like *Manu-Samhita* and the Dharma Shastras describe the king as the father and the spiritual master, instructing subjects in spiritual liberation. The texts see Brahmins acting as advisors to the king, steering him to the path of righteousness. At the heart of rajdharma, however, were ideas of fairness that set limits to both state power and the role of the subjects. Gautam Bhadra has described rajdharma as the realm within which the power of the privileged classes operated and was also restricted.[109] In peasant–landlord relations that he discussed, Bhadra showed that landlords exercised power within the framework of fairness (*insaf*) that rajdharma approved. While the landlords were *ma-baap* (parents) who protected and punished (*dwondo*) the peasants, they had to abide by the notions of insaf that rajdharma upheld.

The Black Town, Spaces of Pathology, and a Hindu Discourse of Citizenship   55

When nagoriks described urban administration as rajdharma, they warned city dwellers that the British had little understanding of Indian religions and could not comprehend rajdharma. This helped them to define their own role in city administration. They became interpreters of rajdharma and, through it, supervisors of the state's improvement schemes. They argued that similar to the nogor-poti, their leadership also had divine origins. But unlike the state, their authority was not provisional. In the Bengali periodical, *Svasthya*, a nagorik wrote that British rule would be short-lived: god had temporarily handed over Calcutta to the British. The colonial state had to take good care, improve the health of the people, and return a better city to the Indians. The author also warned the readers that the state was not doing its work of improving the city:

> Reader! If your very close relative leaves his son with you while he goes to visit his friend, is it not your duty to take care of the son? In that way, the great lord has handed us over to the Raja. He is now a protector of our money and health. The government needs to take care of us. The improvement schemes the government is advancing is not enough.[110]

Nagoriks did not question the fact that they were 'subjects' of a king who was morally superior and the 'protector of their money and health'. They agreed that their civic knowledge could never match that of the Raja (state). But they believed that if the king was not doing his duty, they could not remain silent subjects. According to rajdharma, it was within their *spordha* (courage/dare/right) to challenge the king.

Rajdharma transformed nagoriks from subjects into citizens by setting limits on the king's power. It carved a religious-ideational sphere in which colonial subjects exercised their rights to challenge the king and appeared as citizens. Challenging the king, however, did not necessarily mean acting against him. They considered such actions beyond their spordha. Instead, they offered a detailed written critique of the state.

In their writings, nagoriks demanded that the state make its improvement schemes public. They pointed out that in Barrabazaar the doctors were not aware of as many plague deaths as the colonial health officers reported. This prompted them to ask: 'Where, then, is the plague? Who will answer this question? Is plague a reality or is it a nightmare of the plague officers? The government needs to solve this.'[111] Reviewing the state's plague prevention measures, they explained that health officers were disrupting the privacy of Indian homes and forcing open its interiors to the state. Health officers were examining Indian women and forcing them to visit plague hospitals. While in England it was normal for women to visit hospitals, in India women loathed being examined by British doctors in hospitals. Worse, health officers stormed into Indian houses, separating women from their families and segregating them in health camps.

An incident that took place in Madras at the time influenced nagorik discourse on anti-plague measures. Plague-prevention workers boarded a train near Madras and took away a woman from a compartment.[112] Her husband later heard of her plight, found her in a plague prevention camp, and killed a plague worker.

The nagoriks believed that it was against rajdharma for the king to traumatize subjects with disease-control measures. They did not, however, question the state's power to punish subjects. In fact, they believed that the punishments reinforced state authority, writing, for example:

> Those who violate the rules [of civil discipline] will first be warned and then if they still violate, the commissioners should see that they get dwondo [punishment].[113]

They argued that a religious (*dharmikprobor*) and righteous king (*nyay dorshi*) did not rule by instilling the fear of dwondo in the minds of his subjects. They insisted that if the plague was indeed a reality, the state had to work with the subjects, instead of isolating them from their families and torturing them in health camps. To begin with, the state had to provide them with the details of the incidences of plague: when, where, and who was affected, how the state was treating patients, and what policies it had adopted to fight the epidemic.

More importantly, the nagoriks explained that even if there was plague, the state's plague prevention measures should be informed by *jaat* (religion, in this context). They pointed out that Hindus were brought up to follow Hindu spatial practices and could never adapt to the science of hygiene applicable in London.[114] What was good for the British or European *jati* (race) could not be imposed on a different jati without making necessary changes. Nagoriks pointed out that different *jatigoto achaar* (racial practices) structured everyday life in the city and argued that they should also determine town improvements.

The nagoriks described that the threat to jatigoto achaar was not new to Bengal. The Muslims who preceded the British as rulers of Bengal were all *bijatoyo* (outsiders) and had refused to follow a Hindu science of hygiene.[115] According to the nagoriks, the Muslim rule saw a deterioration in the practices of sanitation; towns were built without consideration of ventilation and streets

The Black Town, Spaces of Pathology, and a Hindu Discourse of Citizenship

remained covered in filth for days. The British conquest improved hygiene by driving out Muslim rulers and planning towns in new ways. But British reliance on science and refusal to follow religious principles had failed to address local needs.

In their critique of town improvements, nagoriks demanded that a Hindu spatial order be restored. In 1874, a cartoon published in the Bengali periodical *Basantak* depicted the Hindu deity Vishnu in his Varaha Avataar (reincarnation as a boar). Vishnu can be seen carrying town improvements on his tusk (Figure 1.6).[116]

In Hindu mythology, Vishnu in his Varaha Avataar defeated the demon Hiranyaksha and rescued the earth from the bottom of an ocean. In the cartoon, Vishnu rescues town improvements from the British. In place of the earth, the cartoon shows Vishnu rescuing improvements and taxes on his tusk. Justices of the Peace and a British bureaucrat, both responsible for carrying out town improvements, stand defeated and offer their prayers to him.

Figure 1.6 To the left: The Varaha Avataar in a Hindu calendar showing Lord Vishnu reborn as the Varaha or boar in his second incarnation. He lifts the earth on his tusk after rescuing it from the bottom of the ocean.

Source: Courtesy of Victoria and Albert Museum, London. Bequeathed by Mrs Grace S. Anderson in memory of her husband John Anderson, M. D., C. E. O., F. R. S.

To the right: A cartoon in the Bengali periodical *Basantak* showing Vishnu holding town improvements—tramways, drainage, markets (all written in Bengali), and tax—on his tusk.

Source: *Basantak*, vol.1, 1874. Courtesy of CSSSC, originally from the Bangiya Sahitya Parishad, Calcutta.

58
A Hygienic City-Nation

Nagoriks explained that from their earliest days, Hindus valued sanitation and built their houses in sanitary ways. In 1898, Saratchandra Mullick wrote in the journal *Lancet* that, for the Hindus,

> [d]isinfection is an everyday practice; isolation is an ancient custom; inoculation is immemorial. So that in principle, there is nothing [the colonial state is doing for public health] that can be called an innovation.[117]

The nagoriks found in the Shastras a long history of Indian sanitation and an important Hindu building law:

Pub e hash / poschime bansh / Uttor e guya / dokkhine dhhua [118]

(To the east [of a Hindu house] is a pond where ducks swam / to the west were bamboo trees / to the north were areca-nut trees / and the south empty lands)

According to this law, Hindus had to excavate water tanks to the east of their house where ducks could wade. To the west of their house, bamboo trees shielded the heat of the setting sun from spawning disease, to the north were guya or *gubak* (areca-nut) trees to ward off northern drafts, and in the south plots of empty land brought in fresh air. These building laws were incompatible with those of the building commission. The building commission required all homeowners to leave open a third of the land on which they built houses. After keeping so much land open, it was difficult to assign additional space for ponds, bamboo trees, gubaks, and a southern field.

The nagoriks further explained that the scriptures mandated that all Hindu houses should have a courtyard. They argued that, more than providing ventilation, the courtyards held symbolic value. They traced back the history of the courtyards to sanitary laws that existed at the time of the Hindu king Vikramaditya (380–415 CE).[119] These laws made courtyards mandatory in Hindu houses and permitted them to be built only in a *suryavedi* or north–south direction; any courtyard running in the opposite (*chandravedi*) direction was condemned. The laws also did not allow southward expansion of courtyards, as this was believed to block the southern breeze and thereby deteriorate the town's health.

According to the nagoriks, Hindu laws instructed the king to build streets only in a north–south and east–west direction. Buildings had to be built to allow the inflow of air from all directions.[120] This meant that there had to be open spaces on all sides of a house. The interior of the Hindu house had to follow a distinct pattern: the front room was the *sadar* and the inner room the

The Black Town, Spaces of Pathology, and a Hindu Discourse of Citizenship 59

andar. This division of space was required for religious ceremonies. A distinct *poojah dalaan,* or space in front of the house, was required for worshiping deities and performing rituals. This space was mostly covered with a *natyamandir* or *chandnee* (a covered space for prayers) or left open as a quadrangle. The direction of the poojah dalaan had to be such that when the priest sat to perform the ceremony, he would sit facing the north or the east. The second dalaan, in contrast, was a space for family gatherings. The most approved way of constructing the inner dalaan was to place it just behind the poojah dalaan.

The building commission's refusal to allow courtyards in Indian houses and its repeated efforts to force property owners to cover existing courtyards therefore violated Hindu sanitary laws. The nagoriks explained that it was within their spordha to refuse state directives that challenged their spiritual practices. Conflating Indians with Hindus, their writings reinvented and legitimized Hindu spatial norms as acceptable customs. This systematically disempowered all other building practices prevalent in the city, for instance that of the Muslim and Christian Indians. The nagorik argument, that Indian spatial customs followed Hindu religious tenets, re-imagined the city as Hindu, an idea that gained currency, as we will see, all through the nineteenth and twentieth centuries.

Conclusion

In this chapter, I have argued that colonial town improvements went beyond restructuring city space to produce a certain kind of knowledge of that space. Actual physical processes of sanitizing and reordering the built environment entailed a discursive production of space that crafted a symbolic terrain of a black town emblematic of Indian backwardness. This symbolic geography extended colonial control not simply by restructuring Indian neighbourhoods but by inscribing both space and its inhabitants with new meanings. An idea of blackness took shape in colonial health reports and through photographs that tried to bring Indian city dwellers—their habits, sanitation, health, and so on—under British surveillance. As I will argue in the next chapter, the production of the knowledge of a black town fuelled British efforts to shape a land market in Calcutta and engage in massive land speculation in the early twentieth century.

Sanitation was at the heart of the colonial production of Indian uncleanliness but emerged as a contested terrain between the British and Indians. This contestation was not limited to the ordering of space but also impacted urban identities. Nagorik efforts to refashion their own identities were closely tied

60   A Hygienic City-Nation

to the processes of reimagining the city. Articulating a new discourse on space and sanitation, they described themselves first and foremost as Hindus. Presenting a bifurcated vision for Calcutta, they favoured colonial public works projects, demanded the state engage in more improvements, and at the same time contested and remoulded them to meet the needs of the Hindu religion. They saw in built forms the possibility of challenging colonial rule and also of keeping alive some aspects of the Hindu religion. During the twentieth century, colonial efforts to civilize the black town became even more intense. Segregation policies allowed them to open 'breathing' spaces between European and Indian properties, to clear the city centre, order demolitions, and commission a complete reordering of the city for the purposes of public health. As I will argue in the next chapter, authoritarian town improvements continued to overlay colonial citizenship with religious meanings; the vision of a Hindu city brought together property owners against the state.

Notes

1. Rupchand Pakshi, 'Dhonyo Sohor Kolkata'. Reproduced in Benoy Ghosh, ed., *Samayikpatre Banglar Samajchitra*, Vol. 4 (Calcutta: Papyrus, 1966), 957.
2. Colonial improvement commissioners described town improvements as useful tools to reconfigure Indian cities in scientific ways. They argued that town improvements would reduce filth and control epidemics. In all major cities of India, town improvements, however, shaped uneven geographies of development. See Eric Lewis Beverley, *Hyderabad, British India, and the World* (Cambridge: Cambridge University Press, 2014), 232. Vijay Prashad studied waste disposal systems in colonial Delhi and pointed to a social nexus between technology and capital that held back British promises of scientific improvements—the British implemented an up-to-date waste disposal system only in the wealthier parts of the city. See Vijay Prashad, 'The Technology of Sanitation in Colonial Delhi', *Modern Asian Studies* 35, no. 1 (2001): 113–55.
3. 'Minute by President of the Sanitary Commission for Bengal, March 5, 1864', in Bengal (India) Sanitary Commission, *First Annual Report of the Sanitary Commission for Bengal, 1864–65* (London, 1866) [TBLA].
4. See Dipesh Chakrabarty, 'Of Garbage, Modernity and the Citizen's Gaze', *Economic and Political Weekly* 27, no. 10/11 (1992): 541–7. Chakrabarty described that the gendered space of the home reinforced the divide between the inside and outside of the home. Men trusted women with the work of keeping the interiors of the home clean, while they viewed the world outside their home as the space for disease and affliction. Sudipta Kaviraj added to this argument that the outside/inside binary in South Asian cities is not the

same as public/private space. The home features in South Asian imagination of the city as the space of family and security and the outside features as wild and dangerous. See Sudipta Kaviraj, 'Filth and the Public Sphere: Concepts and Practices about Space in Calcutta', *Public Culture: Bulletin of the Project for Transnational Cultural Studies* 10, no. 1 (1997): 83.

5. 'Minute by President of the Sanitary Commission for Bengal, March 5, 1864'.

6. Anthony D. King, *Colonial Urban Development: Culture, Social Power and Environment* (London: Routledge, 2010), 283.

7. For scholarship that challenge King's dual city model, see Swati Chattopadhyay, *Representing Calcutta: Modernity, Nationalism, and the Colonial Uncanny* (London; New York: Routledge, 2005); William J. Glover, *Making Lahore Modern: Constructing and Imagining a Colonial City* (London; Minneapolis: University of Minnesota Press, 2008).

8. Timothy Mitchell, *Colonising Egypt* (Cambridge: Cambridge University Press, 2007), 35.

9. Reginald Heber, J. W. B., and Mrs Amelia Shipley Heber, *The Life and Writings of Bishop Heber the Great Missionary to Calcutta, the Scholar, the Poet, and the Christian* (Boston: Albert Colby & Company, 1861).

10. Walter Hamilton, *The East India Gazetteer; Containing Particular Descriptions of the Empires, Kingdoms, Principalities, Provinces, Cities, Towns, Districts, Fortresses, Harbours, Rivers, Lakes, &c. of Hindostan, and the Adjacent Countries, India beyond the Ganges, and the Eastern Archipelago; Together with Sketches of the Manners, Customs, Institutions, Agriculture, Commerce, Manufactures, Revenues, Population, Castes, Religion, History, &c. of Their Various Inhabitants* (London : Printed for J. Murray by Dove, 1815), 322.

11. For Portuguese trade in Bengal, see Sanjay Subrahmanyam, *Improvising Empire: Portuguese Trade and Settlement in the Bay of Bengal, 1500–1700* (Delhi; New York: Oxford University Press, 1990), 115; Abhay Kumar Singh, *Modern World System and Indian Proto-Industrialization: Bengal 1650–1800* (New Delhi: Northern Book Centre, 2006), 437. Sushil Chaudhury argued that the Portuguese engaged in both external and inland trade in Bengal. See Sushil Chaudhury, *Companies, Commerce and Merchants: Bengal in the Pre-Colonial Era* (London: Routledge, Taylor & Francis Group, 2017).

12. K. N. Chaudhuri, *Trade and Civilisation in the Indian Ocean: An Economic History from the Rise of Islam to 1750* (Cambridge: Cambridge University Press, 2008), 19.

13. Eric Stokes, *The English Utilitarians and India* (Delhi; New York: Oxford University Press, 1990). Uday Singh Mehta explained how liberalism, introduced in Indian as part of British utilitarian mission, assisted, rather than questioned, the subduing of individual rights. Uday Singh Mehta, *Liberalism and Empire: A Study in Nineteenth-Century British Liberal Thought* (Chicago: The University of Chicago Press, 1999).

14. Richard Colley, Marques of Wellesley, *The Despatches, Minutes and Correspondence during His Administration in India*, edited by Robert Montgomery Martin (London: John Murray, 1837).

15. Gavin Weightman, *London's Thames: The River That Shaped a City and Its History* (New York: St. Martin's Press, 2005), 50.

16. Jim Orford, Kerry Sproston, Bob Erens, Clarissa White, and Laura Mitchell, *Gambling and Problem Gambling in Britain* (Hove and New York: Brunner Routledge, Taylor and Francis, 2003), 27.

17. A. M. F. Abdul Ali, 'Lotteries in Calcutta in Days of John Company', *Calcutta Municipal Gazette*, January 1929, 82.

18. Binay Krishna Deb, *The Early History and Growth of Calcutta* (Calcutta: The Bengal Printing Company, 1905), 45.

19. Ibid.

20. Ambe J. Njoh described street planning as a tool of French colonialism in West Africa. See Ambe J. Njoh, *Planning Power: Town Planning and Social Control in Colonial Africa* (London; New York: UCL Press, 2007), 98. See also Brenda S. A. Yeoh, *Contesting Space in Colonial Singapore: Power Relations and the Urban Built Environment* (Singapore: Singapore University Press, 2003), 222–29. Yeoh's discussion of street planning in colonial Singapore highlights the role of the streets—their order and nomenclature—in establishing British cultural control.

21. A. Upjohn, *Calcutta in the Olden Time—Its Localities: From the Calcutta Review ... Map of Calcutta, 1792–3*, 1852, 33 [TBLA].

22. *Calcutta Journal: or, Political, Commercial and Literary Gazette*, 16 February 1821.

23. Ibid., 16 April 1821.

24. Ranjit Sen briefly mentions that the Lottery Committee's land grabs resulted in landholders' protests; he described these protests as impediments to urbanization. Sen therefore views urbanization as a state-led process, without considering that the protests were very much part of the urbanization process. Ranjit Sen, *Birth of a Colonial City: Calcutta* (New York: Routledge, Taylor & Francis, 2019), 60–1. Swati Chattopadhyay, on the other hand, has showed that the work of the Lottery Committee evicted the city's poorer residents. These evictions gave Calcutta a certain shape. See Chattopadhyay, *Representing Calcutta*, 87.

25. Letter to the Governor General in council at Fort William from H. Mackenzie, 2 April, Bengal Civil Judicial Proceedings, 1818 [TBLA].

26. Letter to W. B. Bayley, Secretary to the Government, from A. Trotter, 16 March 1822, Bengal Judicial Criminal Proceedings [TBLA].

27. Letter to Governor General in Council from Chunder Seker Mitter and Bholanauth Mitter, 6 August 1822, Bengal Judicial Criminal Proceedings [TBLA].

The Black Town, Spaces of Pathology, and a Hindu Discourse of Citizenship 63

28. *Calcutta Journal of Medicine* (Calcutta: Calcutta Medical Club, 1906) [HULA].
29. 'Letter from the Commissioners for the Improvement of Calcutta to F. J. Halliday', in Report of David Boyes Smith, *Report on the Drainage and Conservancy of Calcutta* (Bengal Secretariat Press, 1869).
30. 'Abolition of Lotteries', *The Asiatic Journal and Monthly Register for British India and Its Dependencies* 20 (1836): 22.
31. 'Letter of D. M. Farlan to Residents of Boithhokkhana', 1 December 1833, Bengal Judicial Proceedings [TBLA].
32. Ibid.
33. Partho Datta, *Planning the City: Urbanization and Reform in Calcutta, c. 1800–c. 1940* (New Delhi: Tulika Books, 2012), 5.
34. A British urgency in planning Delhi after the Revolt of 1857 resulted in large-scale demolitions and a radical restructuration of space that facilitated British surveillance of Indian city dwellers. See Jyoti Hosagrahar, *Indigenous Modernities: Negotiating Architecture, Urbanism, and Colonialism in Delhi* (London: Routledge, 2009). See also Narayani Gupta, *Delhi between Two Empires, 1803–1931: Society, Government and Urban Growth* (Delhi: Oxford University Press, 1997).
35. Nicholas J. Garber and Lester A. Hoel, *Traffic and Highway Engineering* (Stamford: Cengage Learning, 2014), 11.
36. Report of the German Cholera Commission published in the *Report on the Municipal Administration of Calcutta, 1887–1888* [TBLA].
37. 'Letter from the Commissioners for the Improvement of Calcutta to F.J. Halliday'.
38. John Strachey, 'The Second and Third Sections of the Report of the Commissioners Appointed to Inquire into the Cholera Epidemic of 1861 in Northern India', in *Report of the Commission to Inquire into the Cholera Epidemic* (Calcutta, 1864).
39. William Clark, 'A Collection of Papers Relating to the Drainage System of Calcutta Carried Out by W. Clark, 1869', Minutes of Proceedings of the Institution of Civil Engineers, Vol. 63 (London, 1869).
40. Calcutta Corporation, 'The Drainage of Calcutta [A Letter from the Commissioners for the Improvement of Calcutta on the Subject of a Proposed New System of Drainage of That City, with the Report of Messrs. M. and G. Rendel, and Observations Thereon by W. Clark and A.M. Dowleans]', Calcutta, 1859.
41. Ernest John Trevelyan, 'Answers by Babu Satish Chandra Ghosh and Okhil Chandra Ray to the Building commission', in *Calcutta Building Commission Reports*, May 1897.
42. Ernest John Trevelyan, 'Answers by Babu Dinendra Narain Roy to the Building Commission', in *Calcutta Building Commission Reports*, May 1897.

43. Bengal Drainage Committee and London School of Hygiene and Tropical Medicine, *Report of the Drainage Committee, Bengal* (Calcutta: Bengal Secretariat Press, 1907).
44. Ibid.
45. See Zeynep Çelik, *Urban Forms and Colonial Confrontations: Algiers under French Rule* (Berkeley; Los Angeles; London: University of California Press, 1997); Gwendolyn Wright, *The Politics of Design in French Colonial Urbanism* (Chicago: University of Chicago Press, 1991).
46. Çelik, *Urban Forms and Colonial Confrontations*, 36.
47. James R. Brennan, Andrew Burton, and Yusuf Lawi, eds, *Dar Es Salaam Histories from an Emerging African Metropolis* (Dar Es Salaam; Nairobi: Mkuki na Nyota Publishers; The British Institute in Eastern Africa, 2007), 42.
48. *Report on the Administration of Bengal, 1872–73*, 1873 [TBLA].
49. Warwick Anderson, 'Excremental Colonialism: Public Health and the Poetics of Pollution', *Critical Inquiry* 21, no. 3 (1995): 640–69.
50. David Arnold, *The Tropics and the Traveling Gaze: India, Landscape, and Science, 1800–1856* (London; Seattle: University of Washington Press, 2015).
51. W. J. Simpson, 'A Note on the Sanitation of Calcutta and Other Papers', 1894–1897 [KCA].
52. Ibid.
53. Bhubanchandra Mukhopadhyay, *Bangarahasya (Nutan Naksa)* (Calcutta: Upendranath Mukhopadhyay. Printed by Basumati Electro Press by Purnachandra Mukhopadhyay, 1904).
54. See Sandra Hempel, *The Medical Detective: John Snow, Cholera and the Mystery of the Broad Street Pump* (London: Granta Books, 2014).
55. Partho Datta describes that the Lottery Committee created new knowledge of space in Calcutta by using the trope of 'miasms' that employed pseudo-medical knowledge to advance imperial imperatives. See Partho Datta, 'Ranald Martin's Medical Topography', in *The Social History of Health and Medicine in Colonial India*, ed. Biswamoy Pati and Mark Harrison (Delhi: Primus Books, 2015), 22.
56. Robert Peckham, 'Introduction: Panic: Reading the Signs', in *Empires of Panic: Epidemics and Colonial Anxieties* (Hong Kong: Hong Kong University Press, 2015), 1–22.
57. Michael Zeheter, *Epidemics, Empire, and Environments: Cholera in Madras and Quebec City, 1818–1910* (Pittsburgh: University of Pittsburgh Press, 2016), 21–51, 53–98.
58. David Arnold, *Science, Technology and Medicine in Colonial India* (Cambridge: Cambridge University Press, 2000), 86.
59. Projit Bihari Mukharji, *Nationalizing the Body: The Medical Market, Print, and Daktari Medicine* (London; New York: Anthem Press, 2009), 19.

The Black Town, Spaces of Pathology, and a Hindu Discourse of Citizenship   65

60. Dominique Laporte, *History of Shit* (Cambridge, MA: MIT, 2002).
61. William A. Cohen and Ryan Johnson, *Filth: Dirt, Disgust, and Modern Life* (Minneapolis: University of Minnesota Press, 2005), 48.
62. Chattopadhyay, *Representing Calcutta*, 70.
63. Indian Plague Commission, *Minutes of Evidence Taken by the Indian Plague Commission with Appendices* (London: Printed for H.M.S.O. by Eyre and Spottiswoode, 1900–1901) [HULA].
64. T. Frederick Pearse, *Report on Plague in Calcutta for the Year Ending 30th June 1908* (Calcutta: Bengal Secretariat Press, 1908).
65. Ibid.
66. H. Beverley, *Report of the Commission Appointed under Section 28 of Act IV (B.C.) of 1876 to Enquire into Certain Matters Connected with the Sanitation of the Town of Calcutta* (Calcutta: Printed at the Bengal Secretariat Press, 1885).
67. Report on Cholera in Calcutta by Kailash Chunder Bose in the *Report on Municipal Administration of Calcutta, 1875*.
68. Ibid.
69. W. J. Simpson, *Report of the Health Officer of the Town on Calcutta, and the Resolutions of Commissioners Thereon: 1886* (Calcutta: Municipal Print Office, 1887) [TBLA].
70. Report on Jorabagaan bustee by G. Brien, 1885 in W. J. Simpson, *Report of the Health Officer of the Town on Calcutta* [TBLA].
71. H. W. Bellew, *The History of Cholera in India from 1862 to 1881: Being a Descriptive and Statistical Account of the Disease: As Derived from the Published Official Reports of the Several Provincial Governments during That Period and Mainly in Illustration of the Relation between Cholera Activity and Climatic Conditions: Together with Original Observations on the Causes and Nature of Cholera* (London: Trubner & Co., 1885).
72. Royal College of Surgeons of England, 'Report on Cholera in Alipore Jail, 1864', in *Measures for the Prevention of Cholera among European Troops in Northern India* (Calcutta: Printed at the Alipore Jail Press, 1864) [NLA].
73. *Report on the Municipal Administration of Calcutta, 1899* [TBLA].
74. Christopher Pinney, *Camera Indica: The Social Life of Indian Photographs* (Chicago: University of Chicago Press, 1997). See also Zahid R Chaudhary, *Afterimage of Empire: Photography in Nineteenth-Century India* (Minneapolis: University of Minnesota Press, 2012).
75. Report on Jorabagaan bustee by G. Brien, 1885.
76. Ibid.
77. Simpson, *Report of the Health Officer*.
78. *Svasthya Samacara*, 16 (1927): 112–13.
79. Ibid., 113.
80. W. J. Simpson, *Cholera in Calcutta in 1894 and Anti-choleraic Inoculation* (Calcutta, 1895), 26.

81. Brenda Yeoh discusses similar efforts of the colonial state in Singapore to outlaw the building of verandahs in native houses that resulted in riots, called the 'verandah riots'. See Yeoh, *Contesting Space in Colonial Singapore*, 271.
82. Ernest John Trevelyan, 'The Case of Bama Bewah and Shama Bewah', in *Report of the Calcutta Building Commission, 1897* [UOLA].
83. Ernest John Trevelyan, 'Papers Related to the Erection of a Building at 31 Dhurrumtollah Lane', in *Report of the Calcutta Building Commission, 1897* [UOLA].
84. Ernest John Trevelyan, 'Speech of Babu Priya Nath Mullick', in *Report of the Calcutta Building Commission, 1898* [UOLA].
85. Ernest John Trevelyan, 'Bheemraj Jhoonjhoonwala, 33 Ezra Street versus the Calcutta Corporation', in *Report of the Calcutta Building Commission, 1898* [UOLA].
86. Engineers Department of Calcutta Corporation, 'Aughore Moni Bewah versus Calcutta Corporation', in *Annual Report on the Municipal Administration of Calcutta, 1897* [UOLA].
87. Engineers Department Calcutta Corporation, 'Doorgah Money Bewah versus the Calcutta Corporation', in *Annual Report on the Municipal Administration of Calcutta, 1897* [UOLA].
88. Ernest John Trevelyan, 'Papers on Kali Prasad Dutt Street', in *Report of the Calcutta Building Commission, 1898* [UOLA].
89. Ernest John Trevelyan 'Papers on 1, Bysack Lane', in *Report of the Calcutta Building Commission, 1898* [UOLA].
90. H. M. Crake, *The Calcutta Plague 1896–1907* (Calcutta: Criterion Printing Works, 1908).
91. Dr E. C. Pettifer, 'A Report on Plague in Calcutta', in W. R. Bright, *Report of the Epidemics of Plague in Calcutta during the Years 1898–99, 1899–1900 and up to 30th June, 1900–1901* (Calcutta: E. D'Rozario at the Municipal Press, 1900) [NLA].
92. *Report on the Municipal Administration of Calcutta for 1901* [TBLA].
93. Calcutta (India) Plague Department, *Report on Plague in Calcutta, 1904* [NLA].
94. Amrita Krishna Basu, *Plaguetottwo* (Calcutta: Taruni Press, 1899).
95. Herbert Milverton Crake, *Report on Plague in Calcutta for the Year Ending 30th June 1910* (Calcutta: Bengal Secretariat Press, 1910) [NLA]
96. Mukhopadhyay, *Bangarahasya*, 33.
97. F. G. Clemow and W. C. Hossack, *Report upon the Sanitary Condition of Ward VII (Burra Bazaar)* (Caledonian Steam Printing Press, 1899) [NLA].
98. Ernest John Trevelyan, 'Extract of a Letter from James A. Lowson to H. H. Risley', in *Report of the Calcutta Building Commission, 1897* [UOLA].
99. Ernest John Trevelyan, 'Answers by Mr. Braunfield to James A. Lowson', in *Report of the Calcutta Building Commission, 1897* [UOLA].

The Black Town, Spaces of Pathology, and a Hindu Discourse of Citizenship 67

100. Nicholas B. Dirks, *Castes of Mind: Colonialism and the Making of Modern India* (Princeton, N.J.: Princeton University Press, 2011), 211.
101. Ashna Ashesh and Arun K. Thiruvengadam, *Report on Citizenship Law: India* (GLOBALCIT, 2017).
102. Niraja Gopal Jayal, *Citizenship and Its Discontents: An Indian History* (Cambridge, Mass.: Harvard University Press, 2013), 48.
103. Gyanendra Pandey, 'The Subaltern as Subaltern Citizen', *Economic and Political Weekly* 41, no. 46 (2006): 4735–41.
104. Frederick Cooper, *Citizenship between Empire and Nation: Remaking France and French Africa, 1945–1960* (Princeton: Princeton University Press, 2016).
105. Daniel Gorman, *Imperial Citizenship: Empire and the Question of Belonging* (Manchester; New York: Manchester University Press, 2013), 20.
106. Sukanya Banerjee, *Becoming Imperial Citizens Indians in the Late-Victorian Empire* (Durham NC: Duke University Press, 2013), 192.
107. Bhabataran Bidyaratna, 'Shastriyo Svasthya Kotha', *Svasthya Samacara* 1 (1912): 328–9.
108. 'Municipality O Tahar Kortobbo', *Svasthya* 5, no. 1 (1902).
109. Gautam Bhadra, 'The Mentality of Subalternity: Kantanama or Rajdharma', CSSSC Occasional Paper No. 104, CSSSC, Calcutta, August 1988.
110. 'Svasthyproshongo', *Svasthya* 2, no. 1 (1899).
111. Ibid.
112. *India*, 18 November 1898.
113. *Svasthya* 4, no. 2 (1901).
114. 'Prachin Hindur Chikitsagyan', *Svasthya* 3, no. 4 (1900).
115. Ibid.
116. *Basantak* 1 (1874).
117. *The Lancet*, 5 November 1898.
118. 'Hindur Baastu', *Svasthya* 5, no.1 (1902).
119. Ernest John Trevelyan, 'Answers by Babu Jadunath Sen to the Building Commission', in *Report of the Calcutta Building Commission, 1897* [UOLA].
120. Ernest John Trevelyan, 'Answers by Babu Kanayee Lall Mukherjee', in *Report of the Calcutta Building Commission, 1897* [UOLA].

2 The Calcutta Improvement Trust
Racialized Hygiene, Expropriation, and Resistance by Religion

In the last chapter, I discussed how the British tried to reduce all Indian neighbourhoods into an insanitary black town. In this chapter, I argue that the black town facilitated massive land acquisitions that powered a lucrative market in land. The British began to plan Calcutta in the wake of the plague epidemic in 1898. The plague outbreak showed that earlier town improvement committees had failed to improve the city's health. Improvement committees, such as the Lottery Committee and the Justices of Peace, had planned new streets and filled up water bodies, but these were localized projects. The ravages of the plague mandated a complete reordering of the entire city that assisted colonial land acquisitions. In 1911, the state commissioned a town planning committee—the Calcutta Improvement Trust—to draw a fresh plan for the city. The Trust's plans embraced Victorian notions of hygiene and advocated a new spatial order for Calcutta that required levelling and rebuilding Indian neighbourhoods.

In Victorian London, the state instructed citizens in hygiene. Health officers schooled city dwellers in scientific ways to dispose garbage, clean their houses, and maintain healthy bodies. But hygiene in nineteenth-century London meant more than clean spaces and bodies. It was tied to notions of respectability.[1] The obsession of wealthy Londoners with hygiene contrasted with the sweat- and dirt-covered bodies of the workers, casting the former as respectable and the latter as embodiments of shame. This divide also informed city spaces, forcing the poor to live in separate neighbourhoods away from the rich. The state was aware of the wretched living conditions in the poorer neighbourhoods but refused to extend civic amenities like modern streets or sewers. Instead, health officers labelled the poor 'inherently unhygienic', carriers of disease. This, in turn, strengthened class divides in the city.

The Calcutta Improvement Trust   69

The language of hygiene that nourished a class hierarchy in Britain, when imported to India, fuelled a hierarchy of race. Colonial health officers viewed the Indians in the same way as they viewed the urban poor in London. To that end, they employed hygiene—defined entirely according to English standards of sanitation—to condemn Indians as unhygienic by nature. Concerns about cleanliness led colonials to try to regulate the conduct of Indians by mandating routine check-ups at British clinics and by enforcing new regimes of nutrition and fitness.[2] While employing hygiene as a tool to discipline Indians, the British actually ended up shaping a new government based on a negotiation between Indian and British ideas of body and disease, which met to shape a new language of hygiene that informed colonial discourses on race and medicine.

In this chapter, I review the Trust's project and the resistance it encountered, examining the ideas of improvement and public purpose that drove colonial town planning in Calcutta. I argue that property owners discovered that they could reinterpret Hindu religious texts as a legal tool to block the Trust from seizing their property. In all of its improvements, the Trust steered clear of religious structures to avoid communal outbreaks. When property owners observed this, they transferred all lands, and the structures that stood on them, to their family deities. This made their property *debutter* (for Hindus) and *waqf* (for Muslims), signifying in each case that the right of ownership lay in deities that made the land inalienable. Investing their property with deep religious meanings, property holders constituted new urban spaces and with it, communities founded on religious identities.

Investing symbolic and legal ownership in the deities, property holders also refashioned their own identities primarily as Hindus or Muslims. They explained their neighbourhoods as spaces constituted by shared religious beliefs. The shaping of this religious identity remained independent of parallel processes of nation building, through which nationalists crafted a religious identity to highlight their difference from the British. Separate from the nationalist production of a Hindu identity, Indian property owners deployed religion in their everyday struggles with the state to recast their identities as Hindu, over all other defining qualities.

An Improvement Trust for Calcutta

In October 1905, a group of Bengali men occupied downtown Calcutta. Picketing stores and barricading storefronts, their goal was to shut down business in the city. They torched vehicles and engaged in armed conflict with the police to block the streets. These men were part of the Swadeshi movement, an economic boycott campaign that came to exert a powerful influence in the city. Upholding economic nationalism, Swadeshi protesters appealed to city dwellers to reject goods manufactured in Britain and to buy Indian products. The movement took a violent turn when the British announced their decision to partition Bengal. Arguing that the British were planning to partition the state as a way to pacify the movement, demonstrators took to the streets and set vehicles on fire.

The Swadeshi movement started in 1905 and over the next few years, the protests grew and became routine. Other than being an economic boycott, the movement was unique for its use of public space to draw state attention. The protesters gathered in the streets, barricaded them, destroyed stores, and put the city on high alert as a way to make their voices heard. Their routine demonstrations shook the foundations of British rule. In 1911, in the face of these growing protests, the British decided to transfer their capital from Calcutta to Delhi.

The transfer of the capital, however, did little to stop the growing tide of street protests in Calcutta. Upsetting daily life and barricading streets night after night, the protesters kept drawing public attention. The government of Bengal finally decided to take stricter measures to control unrest. It decided on a new plan for the city that would relocate Indians to distant neighbourhoods and restrict their entry to the city centre.

Government officials soon realized that such a plan would be impossible to implement because no single authority had complete jurisdiction over all areas of the city. The part of Calcutta that was under the jurisdiction of the High Court was different from the section administered by the Calcutta Municipal Corporation, which oversaw municipal administration. While the erstwhile Circular Road marked the limits of the High Court's jurisdiction, municipal Calcutta extended to adjoining villages. Yet another municipal subdivision, called Greater Calcutta, comprised metropolitan Calcutta and some village districts, grouped together for census purposes. These complex subdivisions— all under separate administrative authorities—challenged colonial plans to implement a complete reordering of the city.

Faced with the limits of its jurisdiction over the city, the Bengal government sought advice from Herbert Risley, a British ethnographer. Risley had earlier surveyed ethnic groups in India and written extensively on the significance of caste in moulding Indian society. His assessment of caste informed a new school of thought that explained caste as a racial or biological phenomenon

The Calcutta Improvement Trust

rather than a system based on profession.[3] He argued that anthropomorphic studies of individuals, their facial features, height, weight, and behaviours, determined their caste. Inscribing caste with racial meanings, the British turned India into a ground for experimentation in racial pseudoscience.

The Bengal government believed that Risley's exhaustive knowledge of race and caste would help him invent extrajudicial provisions in their plans for Calcutta. These provisions would help British town planners, as they could reorder the city without having to worry about the jumble of jurisdictions. In 1905, the same year Swadeshi activism began, Risley had warned British and Indian health officials at an advisory meeting that epidemics were a growing threat in Calcutta and that Indians were to blame.[4] Imagining hygiene as a racial phenomenon, he argued that Indians were characteristically unclean but that certain castes were more unsanitary than the others. He described the Marwaris, a dominant business group who had migrated from Rajasthan to Bengal, as the most unclean and explained that plague had first taken shape in their houses and warehouses.

Given the sanitary unawareness of the Marwaris, the location of their houses at the city centre, Risley explained, would lead to a series of epidemics. He advised the state to declare a health emergency at once and to summon a town planning committee to clear the city centre of Indian houses.[5] He recommended that the state invest this town planning committee with absolute powers to acquire land across all municipal jurisdictions, both in Calcutta and in the suburbs. The risk to the city's health justified such an authoritative committee, he insisted.

The state followed Risley's advice and commissioned the Calcutta Improvement Trust in 1911. The Trust's constitution made the state supreme authority in matters of land management and transfer.[6] A committee of eleven members comprised a board of trustees that oversaw the work of the Trust. This board represented the interests of the state, as well as the city's powerful businesses. The state, however, had ultimate authority to review and authorize improvement plans.[7] The state also invested the Trust with the Land Acquisition Act of 1894, which permitted it to acquire any land, without restrictions, under an 'urgency' clause. In addition, the Trust operated its own court of law, squashing resistance by deciding all lawsuits in its own favour.

In the early twentieth century, concerns of hygiene drove the British to appoint similar improvement trusts in all of its colonies. These agencies worked to upgrade housing, clear congestion, demolish informal settlements or 'slums', and carry out sanitation campaigns to restore hygiene.[8] At the very outset, the work of the trusts was similar to the provisions of the British Housing of the Working Classes Act of 1890. The Housing Act authorized local committees to demolish slums for reasons of public health.[9] The scope of the trusts' work, however, was much larger. The trusts were staffed with experts in town planning and armed with scientific knowledge to implement a massive reordering of cities.

The work of the colonial improvement trusts was, in fact, similar to the Glasgow Improvement Trust of 1866, which had demolished some of the most crowded parts of the city.[10] Like the Glasgow Improvement Trust, colonial improvement trusts pulled down numerous properties to sanitize cities. Yet, unlike its predecessor in Glasgow, which had targeted poorer neighbourhoods, colonial improvement trusts demolished native neighbourhoods indiscriminately, both wealthy and poor. The colonial trusts operated on a racialized notion of hygiene, describing non-European neighbourhoods as inherently filthy dens of disease.

Before the Calcutta Improvement Trust started its work, senior engineer E. P. Richards surveyed the city to determine the routes along which it could expand. In 1910, working with a small staff of two Indian surveyors and an Indian clerk, Richards complained about the impossibility of trying to plan a city that housed a quarter of a million people and a geographic area spanning thirty thousand acres.[11] It took him fifteen months, a physical breakdown, and a forced departure from the city before he could actually submit his report.

Richards envisioned Calcutta as a port city. The port had earlier been a thriving centre of commerce but had not determined the city's spatial orientation. For the first time, the Trust made the port the nucleus of urban life in Calcutta, reconfiguring all other spaces around it. This reconfiguration inscribed a *value* on land that was determined by a region's proximity to the port. The trustees argued that the most valuable parts of the city—the spaces near the port—should grow as centres of commerce. Borrowing city plans from Berlin, Paris, London, and even Venice, Richards tried to zone Calcutta according to the use-value of land (residential, office, and so on).

New York City was among the earliest American cities zoned for the dual purposes of police regulation and state surveillance. But in 1912, when zoning was still only an idea in New York, Richards produced a detailed plan to zone Calcutta. Along the west bank of the river Hooghly, where pilgrims and traders assembled, he envisioned a modern industrial district. He appealed to the state to bar Indians access and to instead develop the area as an industrial zone. He planned to open the city centre to banks and government offices. He made the

The Calcutta Improvement Trust 73

south Calcutta suburbs residential zones and designed boulevards served with tram lines to provide easy connections between the city's new zones.

Within a few years of commencing work, the Trust built wide, asphalt boulevards to provide capacious corridors between zones. These boulevards brought with them a new aesthetic of space that emphasized speed and the easy circulation of people and goods as the core principle of city building. J. M. Maden, an engineer working with the Trust, explained that 'speeding up does not mean increasing speed. It means removing obstructions'.[12] The trustees followed Maden's advice in laying out the new boulevards; for instance, in building the Central Avenue, a major boulevard that connected north and south Calcutta, they built sidewalks to stop pedestrians from holding up traffic, ordered electric wires to be laid overhead, and began fining vendors who encroached on the streets. To free the streets of all obstruction, the Trust also demolished all houses, shops, and businesses that fell in the path of the new boulevards.

The Trust employed the languages of public purpose and improvement to justify its demolitions. Public purpose meant that the Trust was working to improve the health of a large number of people—the public—which authorized it to dissolve the rights of individuals or private citizens. Underlining the public over the private, public purpose carved out a distinct mode of governance that made it impossible for individuals to challenge the state and its policies. Although many individuals lost their rights, like the right to hold private property, the Trust argued that this loss was negligible when measured against the collective good that the acquisitions served. The language of improvement, which empowered the state to improve the conditions of the masses, also helped it to closely supervise individuals. For instance, to find out whether a given site posed a threat to the rest of the city, health officers were authorized to thoroughly inspect the most intimate of spaces and residents.

The language of public purpose, however, was not an invention of the Trust. It had steered British public works in India from its earliest days. The preamble of the Bengal Regulation I of 1824 had for the first time declared that property owners were bound to give up their lands to the state for building roads, canals, and other works of public utility.[13] Some of the major public works carried out by the British, like the railways, were possible because public purpose approved unrestricted land acquisitions.[14] In 1863, the state modified the clause of public purpose to authorize private companies to acquire lands. Act XXII of 1863, for instance, empowered the state to acquire land for private companies.[15] This Act proclaimed that it was no longer necessary for the government to initiate land acquisitions: local authorities, societies registered under the 1860 Societies Registration Act, and co-operative societies established under the Co-operative Societies Act of 1912 could also acquire land on behalf of the government.

In 1882, the Indian Trusts Act had defined a 'trust' as an establishment to transfer property to a beneficiary. It explained that a trust was an 'obligation of ownership of property, arising out of a confidence reposed in and accepted by the owner for the benefit of another individual or group'.[16] The Act, however, did not authorize the trustees to acquire religious or charitable endowments. This was the context in which the colonial state enacted the Land Acquisition Act of 1894, which made up for the loopholes in the Trusts Act. The Land Acquisition Act expanded the meaning of public purpose and authorized the state to acquire all lands—including religious and non-religious endowments—during 'urgencies'. This meant that if the government thought that an urgent situation necessitated land acquisitions, it could dissolve all claims of private ownership. The state had simply to issue a notice stating what the exact nature of the emergency was. Based on that notice, it could acquire the land within a fortnight.[17]

Both in Calcutta and in the adjoining villages, the trustees followed similar procedures to acquire land. Once they decided which land to acquire, they served legal notices informing property owners of the *urgency* of the acquisition. After they published these notices, it was lawful for them to survey and dig trenches in the land. The property owners had to vacate the premises within a fortnight of receiving eviction notices. The only difference between the Trust's method of acquiring land in the city and the way it proceeded in the villages was that in the villages, it had to wait for the consent of the state to serve eviction notices.[18] But the state quickly approved these notices.

Investing the Trust with unlimited powers to acquire land, the Act of 1894 also crafted the widest possible meanings of the word 'land'. Besides the ordinary meanings of land, the word 'land' as used in the Act included all benefits that emerged from it, 'profits from things attached to the earth or permanently fastened to anything so attached'.[19] In this sense, the word 'house' used in the Act meant not simply structures but also rents and profits from land. As the trustees explained, 'land' included anything that could be inherited, whether corporeal or non-corporeal, including future rights in land or contracts. Armed with the Land Acquisition Act of 1894, the Trust hoarded land both in Calcutta and its neighbouring villages, consolidating these under a single authority, that of the Calcutta Municipal Corporation. In 1916, for instance, the chairman of the Calcutta Corporation informed the state that

The Calcutta Improvement Trust

'the Trust was effectively bringing the suburbs within its municipal and legal jurisdiction'.[20]

Two main purposes guided the Trust's land acquisitions. First, it aimed to reorder the city to spatialize colonial discourses on race and hygiene. The town planners employed the discourse of hygiene to create a white-dominated city centre by dismantling Indian neighbourhoods and dislocating and resettling non-white populations in the suburbs. Second, in disassembling Indian neighbourhoods, the Trust found the right opportunity to eliminate all threats to the state's intention of taking over and monopolizing the cotton trade. They responded to the growing influence of Marwari traders, who controlled the largest share of the cotton trade, by labelling them inherently unsanitary and arguing that their houses and warehouses were filthy dens of disease that had to be demolished. Acquiring the land, the Trust sold it to private builders who introduced new types of housing—suburbs and 'flats'[21]—that segregated the city along lines of race, class, caste, and religion.

From Barrabazaar to South Suburban Municipality

As early as the seventeenth century, the Marwaris had moved from villages in Rajasthan in western India to take part in the active jute trade in the Bengal delta. Mostly upper caste, they spoke the language Marwari from which the community derived its name. They worked as bankers and moneylenders and also as grain merchants and cloth and salt traders. Their houses and business premises in Calcutta were in Barrabazaar, a locality near the port. Property value in Barrabazaar was high. This resulted in four- and five-storey buildings with very little space between them. The Marwari houses bordered their business premises and warehouses. Some Marwaris also lived in floors above their offices and shops.[22] Living close to their businesses was convenient because their families helped them run these businesses.

The Marwari cotton traders had always been an influential economic group in Calcutta. In 1900, the Marwari Chamber of Commerce, an association formed to advance Marwari economic interests, controlled 80 per cent of Calcutta's cotton trade. The traders also established political associations to petition the state about the persistently increasing import taxes and the lack of fairness in the arbitration of trade disputes. This threatened the British, who took part in the same cotton trade and hoped to gain dominance.

Plague broke out, strangely, at about the same time that the Marwaris were growing as a powerful political force in the city. The British retaliated

76 A Hygienic City-Nation

by warning city dwellers that Marwari neighbourhoods bred plague. They explained the unique intersection of residential and office premises in these neighbourhoods as the reason for congestion and ensuing unsanitary conditions. When Plague officers discovered infected rats in Marwari warehouses, they condemned the traders for transporting the plague from Bombay and ordered them to sever all trade ties with Bombay. Following this, the state decided to demolish Marwari warehouses and reorder Barrabazaar in sanitary ways.

In 1915, the Calcutta Corporation that oversaw municipal administration had appointed Patrick Geddes, a Scottish town planner, to plan Barrabazaar as a modern business district. Geddes was at the time formulating his own principles of town planning, which emphasized the need to preserve old city spaces in new plans.[23] While redesigning Barrabazaar, he first wanted to learn how the Marwaris envisioned their neighbourhoods. He carried out a survey of Barrabazaar, walking every street and by-lane, entering all houses and warehouses, and meeting with the Marwari residents. Based on this survey, he explained that a strong community feeling existed among the Marwaris and a successful new plan for the region should keep community spaces like clubs and temples intact. In addition, he pointed to the unique intersection of work and residence that sustained Marwari trade and argued that it should inform the new plan.

Geddes failed, however, to convince the Corporation that it should preserve community spaces in Barrabazaar. The Corporation rejected his plan, arguing that it did not open the region to enough sunlight and fresh air.[24] The Calcutta Improvement Trust intervened at this point and proposed a sixty-feet-wide asphalt thoroughfare—Central Avenue—to demolish unsanitary Marwari houses and ventilate and bring light to Barrabazaar.[25] The Trust served the Marwaris of the neighbourhood with eviction notices, ordering them to evacuate their houses and businesses within a fortnight.

Faced with this attack on their property, the Marwari traders broke out in revolt. In 1915, they organized a street protest to condemn the Trust for initiating 'improvements' that left them homeless. They argued that the Trust was actually trying to replace their houses, stores, and commercial premises with British businesses.[26] They particularly condemned the Trust for the violence with which it lashed out against their ancestral houses or *bastubhita*s.[27] As the protestors pointed out, ancestral houses were not simply impersonal, generic living quarters but were invested with meaning: they embodied family histories. Several generations of Indians lived in the same house to preserve the space their forefathers had built. For some families, bastubhitas were also

The Calcutta Improvement Trust   77

sources of income; these houses were large, with many rooms that the owners rented out. A cotton trader, Motichand Nakhat, for instance, petitioned the Trust not to demolish his ancestral house specifically because it constituted part of his livelihood.[28] His neighbours, two widows, Nitya Manjuri Dasi and Nistarini Dasi, wrote providing evidence that rents from their ancestral houses were their *only* source of income.[29] Their neighbour, yet another cotton trader, Makhon Lall also petitioned the Trust not to destroy his house as rents that supplemented his income from business met the rising expenses of his family.[30] When the trustees refused to read these petitions and moved forward with their plans, the petitioners were left both homeless and impoverished.

In June 1919, Marwari property owners met once again to demonstrate against the Trust. This time, an iron merchant named Hari Hor Sett led the protests.[31] He described that the Central Avenue scheme purposely displaced Marwari trade networks, especially for the gold, silver, iron, sugar, rice, and spice trades. He explained that the Trust's efforts to improve hygiene were in fact meant to separate Marwari businesses from residential premises with the sole objective of impairing trade. Along with the other merchants, he pointed out that the intersection of home and work sustained Marwari trade; the families of merchants advised them on matters of trade and also supplied free labour when required. For that reason, the Marwaris needed to live near their businesses. Neither the Trust's plans to rebuild Barrabazaar nor its rehousing schemes authorized the intersection of home and work. Like Geddes, Sett explained that the Trust's plans should preserve the tradition of Marwari neighbourhoods where home and work overlapped.

As with the earlier protests, the Trust refused to make any alterations to its existing plans for demolition. Instead, the Trust sent its surveyors to the Marwari neighbourhoods on a routine basis to inspect houses and decide on which houses to demolish first. These intrusive actions of the surveyors resulted in growing agitation among the Marwaris. Their discontent resulted in a third protest that took place on a Sunday morning in January 1927 at a high school in Barrabazaar. Like the earlier demonstrations, protestors met to condemn the Trust's hoarding of land, which, they argued, coloured its 'improvements'.[32] To widen the scope and impact of the protest, the Marwari traders invited Bengali teachers and activists to speak at their meeting. Sir Deviprosad Sarvadhikary, a teacher at the Metropolitan Institute, presided over the meeting. Baidyaratna Kaviraj and Jogindranath Sen, both school teachers, joined him in condemning the Trust's forceful demolitions, evictions, and insufficient compensation.

Professor Subhas Chandra Ray, who delivered a speech at the meeting, remarked that the 'president (Sarvadhikary), like the knights of the middle ages, had come to rescue the affected old citizens and residents from the hands of the Calcutta Improvement Trust tyrants'.[33] To this, Sarvadhikary replied, 'civics will not tolerate the Trust's extreme Haussmannizing of this city'.[34] The Trust's work in Barrabazaar indeed was remarkably similar to the Haussmannization of Paris.[35] In nineteenth-century Paris, the French administrator Georges-Eugène Haussmann designed a network of straight boulevards meant to improve sanitation. In constructing these wide streets, the city destroyed all properties that fell in their way.[36] Haussmann had explained that the boulevards would facilitate a system of subterranean sewers, which would keep the city clean. What the streets did, however, was to clear the city centre of its poorer inhabitants. Like Haussmann, the trustees in Calcutta initiated urban renovations to clear populous neighbourhoods and improve hygiene. Working to advance British trade, the Trust's schemes aimed to remove Indians from the city centre, disperse their trade, and subdue anti-colonial demonstrations.

Evicting Indians from the northern and central parts of Calcutta, the Trust rehoused them in newly built southern suburbs. As Table 2.1 shows, this movement brought about a southward displacement of the Indian population from the north.[37]

Table 2.1 As the Calcutta Improvement Trust improved the northern parts of Calcutta, property owners were evicted and forced to move to the southern parts of the city from improvement schemes 7, 7B, 7C, and 7D in the north to 5 and 4A in the south.

Improvement Scheme Numbers from which homeowners were displaced	Improvement Scheme Number in which they were rehoused
7 (Central Avenue-Machuaabazaar Street to Beadon Street)	5 (Bhowaneepore)
7C (Manicktola Spur)	5 (Bhowaneepore)
7D (Central Avenue-Bowbazaar Street to Prinsep Street)	5 (Bhowaneepore)
7B (Central Avenue-Coolootollah Street to Bowbazaar Street)	4A (Russa Road)

Source: Compiled by the author from Annual Reports of the Calcutta Improvement Trust for the years 1921 to 1930.

In 1897, Ebenezer Howard, a British planner, designed garden cities as independent communities bound by agricultural greenbelts to house individuals away from the urban centre. Howard's work inspired the Trust to build southern suburbs as independent residential zones located away from the city centre. They spanned the area between Ballygunge Railway Station and King

The Calcutta Improvement Trust

George's dock, by the river. New boulevards, served by tramways, connected these suburbs to the city centre.

Analysing the complex interconnections between colonialism and urban planning, Liora Bigon has argued that city plans of Europe took different shapes in the colonies.[38] Bigon shows that the idea of the garden city that materialized in Europe was a much-contested space in the colonies—shaped in translations and contestations that colonialism produced. In Calcutta, the Trust demolished existing settlements to build garden cities. The Trust officials described the region they were developing as the garden suburb—the southern suburban municipality—as 'wetlands with *hogla* (wild trees) bushes'. This, however, was far from true. The Trust had demolished populous neighbourhoods to build the garden suburb. Residents who were evicted, such as Gopal Chandra Sarkar, Khetra Mohan, and Bidya Dhori Devi, wrote petitions detailing the Trust's forceful acquisitions of their huts to open the area as a garden suburb. Khiroda Mohan Devi had fiercely protested when the Trust filled in a pond near her home for building purposes.[39] Residents of nearby Ishwar Chandra Ganguly Lane had challenged the Trust when it tried to acquire their huts.[40] When complaints from property owners started to pour in, the trustees met at a school to hear their grievances. At this meeting, several residents of South Russa Road, Mohin Halder Street, and Monhorpooker Road questioned the legitimacy of improvements that targeted their homes and businesses. The Trust refused to give credence to these grievances and offered nothing other than meagre compensation to the property owners.

In March 1919, the Trust acquired premises that belonged to a certain Haridas Banerjee to construct a public thoroughfare. As compensation, it assigned him land in the southern suburb.[41] Banerjee accepted the geographically distant land but refused to accept the small plot. He explained that local customs required him to split his property equally between his three sons. He appealed to the Trust for a larger plot, similar to what they had acquired. When the Trust informed him that it could not give him more land, he arranged for accommodations elsewhere. Similar to Banerjee, evictees from the Trust's scheme in north Calcutta who were used to living in large houses refused the small plots of land in the southern suburb. The Trust then sold these empty plots to private builders who introduced a system of housing that brought about a vertical expansion of the city and also segregated city space into ethnic enclaves.

The Trust's land acquisitions reveal that British policies on land in urban areas like Calcutta were different from what they were in the Bengal

80 A Hygienic City-Nation

countryside. While the British fixed ownership of land in the villages for perpetuity, they stripped it of private ownership in the city.[42] In the villages, the British introduced the Permanent Settlement in 1793 to create a new class of landowners. In the city, they appointed town improvement committees that worked to make the state the biggest landowner. Improvement served as the rationale for the hoarding of land in which the Trust engaged. Acquiring land for reasons of hygiene, it then sold the land to private builders at very high rates. The private builders were not always big construction companies.[43] Individuals who wanted to build houses or stores also bought land from the Trust.

Land Speculations Craft a New Order of Space

The idea of improvement, and the urgency associated with it, authorized the Trust to acquire as much land as it wanted and in any part of the city. These acquisitions shaped a land bank based on which the Trust engaged in a massive speculation in land. Acquiring plots of land at cheap rates, it implemented a few inexpensive improvements and then sold the plot at a much higher rate. Well-known auctioneers Mackenzie and Lyall traded land on behalf of the Trust. An advertisement in the *Amrita Bazar Patrika* in 1918 showed that, by instruction of the Trust's chairman, Mackenzie and Lyall had sold six plots of land on North Russa Street and seven plots near Shambhu Nath Pandit Street on the south side of Calcutta.[44] Receipts from these auctions reached a record high in 1919, adding forty-two lakhs of rupees to state coffers that had been devastated by World War I.

Benami, illegal transactions, were common at the Trust's auctions. Benami meant that the Trust negotiated land prices with an individual but transferred the land to someone else. This person bought the land at a very high price, leading to a sudden surge in land price. In December 1919, the Trust acquired the ancestral home of a person named S. N. Banerjee.[45] Banerjee claimed preemption, or the right to buy back his own land. A co-sharer of the property named Fanindranath also made similar claims. The Trust decided to hold an auction between the two, and Fanindranath won the land. Meanwhile, an earlier tenant, Upendra, informed the Trust that Fanindranath had already sold the plot to him at a price that was much higher. Fanindranath supported Upendra's claims, asking the Trust to transfer the land directly to him. The Trust agreed, giving the land to Upendra in a benami way.

The Trust also hired agents to sell surplus lands using private treaties. In the summer of 1926, the trustees hired Mr Shrosbree and Babu Benoy

The Calcutta Improvement Trust

Kumar Mukherjee as agents to sell lands using private treaties.[46] The trustees informed the agents that it would give them a commission on the total revenue they generated from the sale of the land. Shrosbree and Mukherjee then sold the land at an inflated rate and received a heavy commission. Likewise, in 1933, the Trust employed Talbot and Company, K. P. Chatterjee, and P. B. Chakravarty to sell surplus lands using private treaties.[47] The Trust promised them a commission on the total sale on land. To offer the agents a free hand in determining land value, the Trust advertised the sale in local newspapers but did not fix a standard price on plots. This resulted in the agents selling land at very high rates, leading to a hike in land prices across Calcutta.

English property laws assisted the Trust in tightening its control on lands and increasing its income from acquisitions. The Trust imported principles of exemption, recoupment, and betterment from the corpus of English property laws to further boost its income from the land market. Exemption meant that property owners could pay a fee to stop the Trust from acquiring their lands. The Trust could then earn a lump sum only by serving property owners with notices. The Trust, however, charged very high exemption fees, making it difficult for middle class owners to pay that amount. The residents of Dhakuria in south Calcutta, for example, complained that the Trust charged exemption fees that were ten times the actual value of their lands. [48] In addition to exemption, the Trust practised the principle of recoupment. Recoupment meant that the Trust could purchase property, both houses and lands, near the site of improvement, for a lower price, to meet the costs of its renovation projects. This made it legal for the Trust to acquire surplus lands for sale.

The Trust's speculations caused land prices in Calcutta to spike. The Calcutta Municipal Corporation appointed a committee in 1920 to inquire into the reasons for high rents. The committee reported that the Trust's improvements were leading to massive increase in rents.[49] The Bengal Legislative Council in 1918 had passed a resolution requiring the Trust to acquire surplus lands proportional to the land required for improvement. According to the committee's report, the Trust almost always evaded this regulation and carried on with its unrestrained acquisitions. As a result, land values flared up and reached an all-time high in January 1920 (Table 2.2).[50] Along central thoroughfares like Theatre Road and Camac Street, rents had increased threefold. With high land values, housing conditions in Calcutta deteriorated. In the winter of 1920, city dwellers checked into hotels, finding them cheaper than apartments.[51] The rent inquiry committee advised the Trust to invest more in housing as a means of bringing down land prices.

Table 2.2 A steep increase in land prices, calculated per *cottah* (32 cottahs make 1 acre), between May–June 1919 and January 1920.

Town–Improvement Scheme Number	Rate Per Cottah of Land (in Indian Rupees) in May and June 1919	Rate per Cottah of Land (in Indian Rupees) in January 1920
IV	3,620	9,050
VII B	2,023	5,800
V	1,683	4,000

Source: Compiled by the author from Annual Reports of the Calcutta Improvement Trust for the years 1919 and 1920.

The Trust did dabble in rehousing evictees and also invested in housing the general public. It passed on the land it acquired to builders who erected 'flats' or apartments to rehouse evictees, but later sold these flats to the general public. The concrete and steel structures of the flats differed from the ancestral houses and huts of the Indians.[52] Typically, in Indian neighbourhoods, ancestral houses bordered green fields and temples offering spacious living conditions. In sharp contrast, flats standardized the amount of space an individual could occupy in the city; this space was much smaller than what the Indians had in their neighbourhoods. Although smaller in size, the builders named the flats mansions, clearly signalling that they were building them for the wealthy.

The first flats clustered around the posh Park Street area in central Calcutta. Here, the Trust had sold several building sites directly to the private builders Mr A. Stephen and J. C. Galstaun who built modern flats to replace the former Indian houses and shops.[53] With tennis courts and swimming pools, the rents of these flats were extraordinarily high. Flats like the Cohen Mansion on Ripon Street and Elliot Mansion on Elliot Road were similar to expensive cottages in England in terms of amenities they offered, but their rents were three times those of the cottages.[54]

From Park Street, the flats spread to the southern suburban municipality—which had initially been built to house evictees of the Central Avenue scheme. The builders, however, transformed this area into a paradise for wealthy Bengalis: flats, villas, and the small palaces of commercial groups populated its spaces.[55] Dhakuria Lake stood at the heart of the southern suburbs, with its rowing clubs, cricket clubs, and gardens crowding the lakesides and displaying the region's affluence. In the 1930s, poet Buddhadeb Basu lived in a flat on Rashbehari Avenue in the south suburban municipality. The Trust had earlier filled up a small stream at the heart of Old Ballygunge neighbourhood to build the Rashbehari Avenue. With its tramlines and tree-lined expanses, the

The Calcutta Improvement Trust

Avenue was quickly becoming the centre of a 'New Ballygunge' neighbourhood. Basu recounted how, from his flat on the Rashbehari Avenue, he could see the rows of modern flats that populated New Ballygunge. The demographic and structural difference from Old Ballygunge, he explained, was striking.[56] The flats here were all upscale, fitted with modern chimneys and electric fans and charging exorbitant rents. A new class of urban professional Bengalis—'flat dwellers'—lived in these neighbourhoods.[57] They worked mostly in the city centre; they commuted on the trams running up and down the boulevards.

The flats also introduced a new aesthetics of space, offering a mixed model of living that combined residential with commercial premises. Although the Trust had earlier condemned similar intersections of work and residence in Barrabazaar, the builders leased floors to residents, retail shops, showrooms, and offices in the same building. At the junction of Chowringhee and Sudder Street in central Calcutta, a private builder, Chowringhee Commercial Properties Limited, built a new complex of flats with ground floors leased to commercial showrooms.[58] The architect, P. N. Logan, designed a four-storey building with two office suites on each floor. A similar mixed-model flat stood in the vicinity of the Empire Theater on Chowringhee Road. This was a six-storey building with offices, flats, showrooms, garages for fifty motorcars, and servant quarters.

The Trust's housing schemes split the city along lines of class and religion. The Trust planned new suburbs in Kalighat and Chetla for Hindu commercial groups. It assigned plots of land south of Alipore and west of Diamond Harbor Road to wealthier traders to build detached houses.[59] To rehouse the working and poorer class evictees, the Trust built tenements on Ward Institution Lane and Karbala Tank area. On Ward Institution Lane, the Trust built three blocks to house twelve hundred working-class men and women. It reserved one of the three blocks for Muslim workers.[60] The Trust also built separate tenements at Bow Street for the Eurasian population.

By the early twentieth century, town planners had globally condemned tenements for creating corrupt living conditions and degrading the moral lives of city dwellers. Responding to the global critique of tenements, in India, urban planner Charles Mulford Robinson called for increased regulations on tenements.[61] He pointed to the Bombay *chawl*s (tenement-like row houses where textile mill workers lived) to argue that they produced abject lifestyles. The Trust in Calcutta ignored Robinson's warnings and claimed that, in many ways, 'public housing in other cities, many years ago, is exactly applicable to Calcutta of-today'.[62]

Farhan Karim has argued that improvement trusts built tenements out of a sense of 'duty' towards the working classes, who featured in the Trust's scheme as apolitical, abstract, and voiceless receivers of charity.[63] In Calcutta, the Trust kept the cost of building tenements low, and the tenements turned out to be unfit for human habitation.[64] In the Ward Institution Lane tenements, in the blocks reserved for the sweepers, residents on the top floor lacked water for weeks at a time. In the block reserved for artisans, water supply was limited to an hour in the morning and an hour in the evening. In all three blocks, the water pressure was too low to flush cisterns. H. B. Moreno, an activist campaigning for better housing for Eurasians, described the Bow Street tenements as 'very damp, smoky, smelly, badly drained; the lower flats are overbuilt, and the bathing accommodation is most unsatisfactory'.[65]

In addition to building tenement-style housing, the Trust commissioned thirty-nine detached houses in the Karbala Tank neighbourhood to rehouse Muslim middle-class evictees. The houses were meant to accommodate the evictees on a temporary basis, with the Trust encouraging residents to build their own houses and move out as soon as possible.[66] Once the evictees moved out, it sold these houses to the general public. Like the tenements on Ward Institution Lane, the Karbala housing scheme was extremely unpopular. The detached houses were in fact semi-detached, forcing residents to share spaces like stairways and courtyards with strangers.

As H. V. Lanchester, a prominent town planner, had earlier warned the Trust, rehousing schemes that did not follow Indian customs were bound to fail. The religious beliefs of the Hindu upper castes prohibited them from sharing residential premises with non-Hindu and lower castes.[67] Semi-detached houses and apartments where residents had to share spaces such as stairs and hallways thus posed a problem for them.[68] They refused to live in these houses, leaving many of the semi-detached houses vacant. Indians preferred to live in the more vibrant parts of the city, so the Trust's plan to rehouse them in quiet garden suburbs, away from the urban core, troubled them. Added to this, the Indians refused to live on the top floors of houses, which they found too quiet and removed from the rest of the city. The Trust finally had to give up on its rehousing schemes and opened these to the general public.

Although the Trust's rehousing scheme was a failure and improvements led to a massive increase in land prices, the engineers paved, drained, and metalled roads; the trustees transferred land to private builders, and flats and tenements kept going up where Indians' ancestral homes had once stood. The reason, of course, was the Trust's land speculation and the booming real estate market.

The Calcutta Improvement Trust 85

An independent tribunal—a law court—assisted the Trust's acquisitions in land and also made land easily transferable from private owners to the private builders. The tribunal carried out 'small dispensations' or legal trials outside the court to free land for the Trust's speculations.

The Improvement Trust Tribunal

While scholars have studied colonial improvement trusts as town planning authorities, they have not written about the trusts' role as a court of law.[69] As the state machinery to acquire land, the Trust was both a town planning committee and a court of law. The state equipped it with an independent tribunal to settle land disputes. The tribunal was composed of a president and two assessors. The state appointed the president and one of the assessors. The Calcutta Municipal Corporation appointed the second assessor. The president, however, wielded supreme authority in all matters of law and procedure; his decision was final.

The tribunal resolved disputes in makeshift courts—held in the offices of the Improvement Trust or in a room in a city-school, on street-sides, at local municipal offices, and in rooms or courtyards of neighbourhood houses—that provided unconventional judicial spaces for deciding land disputes. Although these spaces were different from a law court, the Court of Small Causes (the local designation for small claims court) enforced all order of the tribunal as if it was their decree.

In January 1918, a debate on whether the Improvement Trust tribunal indeed constituted a 'court' reached the High Court. The debate began when an Indian property owner Nandoo Lal Ganguli brought a case against the president of the tribunal for not prosecuting a certain gentleman for perjury.[70] The High Court ordered the president to prosecute that person. The president, however, refused to do so, arguing that the tribunal was only a body of arbitrators; it had no prosecutorial power as it was not a court of law. The word 'court', he explained, included judges, magistrates, and all persons legally authorized to take evidence. That was not the case with the tribunal. The Justices of the High Court challenged him, ruling that the tribunal was indeed a law court not simply a body of arbitrators. Following this, the tribunal functioned like a court under section 195 of the criminal procedure code.

The tribunal's idea of justice in the settlement of disputes was informed by the utilitarian concept of public purpose. It upheld the principle of 'salus populi suprema lex', which meant that the interests of the public were paramount and that private property and local customs were subordinate to its interests.[71] The tribunal's emphasis on public purpose rationalized the Trust's land acquisitions as efforts to improve the 'moral and physical welfare of *its* people'. In other words, the tribunal facilitated the Trust's acquisitions by representing them as necessities and creating a space for extrajudicial dispute arbitration.

In 1917, the tribunal met at a high school to hear objections to its Central Avenue scheme. At the meeting, Marwari traders pointed to the sentimental value attached to the lands the Trust wanted to acquire.[72] The tribunal stalled all proceedings for 2 months to rethink its scheme but later reconvened and decided not to amend existing plans. The tribunal argued that demolitions would result in the Marwaris losing their ancestral houses but that this loss was minor compared to the public good that the demolitions would serve by opening neighbourhoods to sunlight and air.

Similarly, when the Trust decided that the neighbourhood where school teacher Basanta Kumar Basu lived was crowded and unsanitary, it ruled that it should be torn down. Challenging the Trust, Basu argued that only a few people lived in the neighbourhood and that it was not unsanitary at all.[73] The tribunal met at the local municipal office and decided to inspect the neighbourhood before actually demolishing it. No inspection took place for days, and the tribunal finally rejected Basu's appeal, arguing that the Trust needed to acquire the property, not simply to sanitize the adjoining neighbourhood but for the more general public purpose of improving the health of the city.

The tribunal decided against the Trust only once in its history. In 1916, the case of Chandra Kanta Ghosh took Calcutta by storm. Ghosh owned a plot of land where he had cleared trees and built a two-storey house.[74] Carrying out an improvement scheme in the vicinity, the Trust found the property unsanitary and served Ghosh with an evacuation notice. Ghosh filed suit, arguing that the notice was ultra vires, exceeding the court's jurisdiction. When the tribunal took up the case, it surprised the Trust by deciding against it. The trustees took the matter to the High Court, where they lost the case once again. The High Court accepted the tribunal's decision that the Trust's acquisition was entirely for profit—for meeting the costs of other improvements—and therefore authoritarian, forceful, and unsolicited.

Nonetheless, Chandra Kanta Ghosh's case failed to influence subsequent jurisprudence. The same year, the Trust acquired property belonging to a man named Mani Lall Singh. Singh refused to give up his land, explaining that the Trust was not acquiring his land for purposes of improvement but rather to meet the costs of other improvement work. Like Ghosh, the tribunal decided

The Calcutta Improvement Trust

the case in favour of Singh. The trustees then took the dispute to the High Court. This time, the judge decided in the favour of the Trust arguing that the 'vesting of a local authority with powers to acquire land for the purpose of meeting costs of improvement could not be described as arbitrary'.[75]

The verdict in Singh's case called the accuracy of the decision in Ghosh's case into question. In deciding Singh's case, the judge did not follow the precedent set in Ghosh's case. Instead, he followed the municipal laws of England. The authoritative English laws granted the trustees complete freedom to acquire surplus land to pay for its projects. The judges then described that the decision in the Chandra Kanta Ghosh case had been a mistake and that the Trust was free to acquire surplus lands to meet the costs of improvements. Following the court's verdict in the Mani Lall Singh case, the judges relitigated the Chandra Kanta Ghosh decision. This time, the case was settled in favour of the Trust. This decision reversed the ruling that had long impeded the Trust's work in Ghosh's neighbourhood. The Trust could now acquire the premise it wanted to.

As Table 2.3 shows, after Singh's case, the tribunal decided all subsequent lawsuits in favour of the Trust.

Table 2.3 The Calcutta Improvement Trust Tribunal decisions between 1922 and 1926.

Year	Number of Suits Filed Against the Trust	The Tribunal Decisions
1922	Five suits filed in small claims court, seven ejectment suits in small claims court	All decided in favour of the Trust, except one ejectment which remained pending
1924	Twelve suits in Calcutta small claims court	All decided in favour of the Trust
1926	Twenty-four suits in small claims court	All decided in favour of the Trust
1928	Fourteen rent suits	All decided in favour of the Trust

Source: Compiled by the author from Proceedings of the Calcutta Improvement Trust, 1921–1927.

With the tribunal deciding all cases in favour of the Trust, property owners searched for new strategies to resist its appropriation of land. Because the law failed to protect their interests, they turned to customs as a legal basis on which to try to hold on to their property.

Debutter property

In 1914, the Trust decided to widen Russa Road, an arterial thoroughfare in what today constitutes south Calcutta. Shifting the tramway to a separate track, it expanded the northern stretches of the road. Once this was done, the Trust proceeded to widen the southern portions of the road, as well. The difficulty in widening this part lay in the fact that numerous houses of middle-class Indians crowded the sides of the street. Any widening would require the Trust first to tear down these houses. The Trust served the usual eviction notices to the homeowners. Panic ensued; property owners drafted petitions to force the Trust to dismiss its plans.[76] They described their houses as having been passed down through generations, which made these symbols of their family's histories. They also explained that their families were large, growing, and extended and that they simply lacked resources to rebuild houses as big as their ancestral homes. The Trust heard their grievances but moved forward with its plans of demolition. Lack of funds, however, soon forced it to give up its plans. The trustees informed the property owners that it no longer required their properties. The property owners heaved a sigh of relief but soon realized that this would only be a temporary respite.

Four years later, the Trust had accumulated enough resources to take up the south Russa Road improvement scheme once again. It served new notices to property owners informing them that it would now proceed with its earlier plans. The property owners realized from their previous experience that simple petitions would fail to convince the Trust to not demolish their houses. Studying the Trust's other schemes, however, they observed that it always steered clear of religious structures. They used this information to fashion a new language of resistance that recast all of their properties as holdings invested with religious meanings.[77] They revised their earlier petitions to argue that their ancestral houses did not simply preserve the memories of their forefathers but that the family deities *owned* these premises, which made them debutter, inalienable properties.

A complex system of customs governed land in Calcutta when the Trust commenced its work. Customs were different from laws; they were not documented and followed oral traditions. Property owners did not register land transfers. They simply passed land through generations as gifts. Rather than bureaucratic processes like the signing of official titles, the transfer of land involved rituals that celebrated its passage from father to son.

The complete absence of land deeds that prevailed in Indian society made it difficult for the British to comprehend patterns of landownership. They realized that trusts were subject to regulations pertaining to some of the most difficult local customs. Two major laws pertaining to estates in property—the legal (vested in the trustee) and the equitable (vested in the beneficiary or trust)—informed trusts in England. The English lawmakers stipulated that

The Calcutta Improvement Trust

89

the trustees could maintain an estate for the upkeep of a trust and also for profit. In India, customs forbade the trustees from holding an estate for more than what was required to maintain a trust. Besides, properties inscribed with religious meanings overlapped with private alienable lands, making property rights even more complex.

The term debutter designates a property belonging to a deity (*deb*). A property became a debutter when its owners dedicated their lands to the deity. Hindu customs did not require a governing body of trustees to dedicate land to an idol. Rather, a performance of rituals transferred land to the deity. The property owner first made the land grant to the priest. The priest then performed three rituals—*sankalpa, samarpan*, and *pratistha*—to officially make the deity the owner of the land.[78] Sankalpa signalled the landowner's decision to transfer land to the idol; samarpan was the very act of granting ownership of the land to the deity; and pratistha meant moving the idol of the deity to a temple or a sacred room near the plot of land and performing rituals to invest it with life. The rituals performed for these ceremonies included the recitation of *mantra*s or holy hymns, the spluttering of holy water on the idol, and the giving of sacred items (certain plants, food, incense sticks, and so on) either on the ground or in the hands of the deity. Along with the land, the property owners could also gift the deity water tanks and gardens as *utsarga* (tribute).

In 1918, the residents of Russa Road argued that several properties adjoining south Russa Road were debutter, inalienable sites. They further claimed that these debutters had temples that served as 'a sacred place of salvation for the Hindus'. They explained that in the evenings the neighbours met there to offer prayers. The temples also provided space for the celebration of annual festivals. The prayers and festivals brought neighbours together as a 'Hindu community'.[79] The property owners thus petitioned the Trust as a Hindu community. They argued that if the Trust demolished the temples it would not simply leave them homeless, but would also destroy a religious community. For fear of inciting communal riots, the Trust abandoned the Russa Road scheme. The gambit had worked.

The remarkable change in the language used in the petitions drafted by the residents of Russa Road, one written in 1914, the other in 1918, points to the growing importance of religion in exchanges between the Trust and property owners. This paralleled but was different from how anti-colonial nationalists employed religion to showcase their difference from the British and to mobilize the population as a Hindu nation. Starting in the late nineteenth century, the nationalists led a movement founded on the idea of difference that imagined an autonomous spiritual domain for the Indians where nationalism took shape. They carved a Hindu identity in organized forums and through institutional means, such as legislative councils, in debates against colonial laws (an example of this would be the debates centring on the Age of Sexual Consent in 1891), in country-wide protests, and planned anti-colonial demonstrations. The anti-colonial movement, however, did not inform the processes by which property owners invested their land with religious meanings and made their Hindu or Muslim identity paramount over other elements of identity. Property owners inscribed emotive and material meanings to land as part of their everyday strategies to resist the Trust. In the process, their own identities as members of a religious community were reflexively produced.

An army of flats in Park Street and in the southern suburbs of Calcutta was gradually transforming the urban fabric in the 1920s and 1930s. Flats threatened existing neighbourhoods with demolition and the anonymity of flat dwellers contrasted with the family-like bonds of neighbourhood communities. Petitions filed by neighbours in the northern parts of the city, however, show that flats did not make their presence felt in this part of the city: here the anti-Trust movements and protests against land developers were rather strong. In south Calcutta, flats were more common but failed to wipe out existing neighbourhoods: old neighbourhood communities survived alongside new flats. Petitions filed by neighbours in Russa Road and Bhowaneepore bear testimony to this.

Property owners routinely wrote petitions investing their lands with religious meanings as a strategy to resist the Trust. In 1917, the Trust decided to demolish the ancestral house of a school teacher Haripodo Chowdhury because it fell in the path of its improvement scheme in Watgunje Street.[80] Served with an eviction notice, Chowdhury drafted a petition that explained that the Hindu god Panchanan (another name for Shiva) owned the land and his house, and the property was debutter. The petition elaborated that the deity was the holiest in the country and the sacrificial altar in the courtyard was the oldest in the city. On days of worship, devotees from across the country assembled at his home and the roofed-in courtyard provided them shelter at night. Convinced of the importance of the temple for the Hindu community, the Trust abandoned its plans for widening Watgunje Street.

The success of one group of property owners in deploying religion to resist the Trust inspired others to do the same. In December 1919, the residents of Entally petitioned the Trust as a Hindu community to call off the widening of Entally Road.[81] They explained that this would demolish the temple of

The Calcutta Improvement Trust 91

Dharma Thakur, a very old Hindu temple in the neighbourhood. That same year, residents of Khidderpore asked the Trust not to destroy a courtyard where a temple of the deity of Panchanan stood and where neighbourhood Hindus met to celebrate festivals.[82]

The Trust soon realized that Indian property owners had begun considering their properties in religious terms in order to resist expropriation. It responded by trying to separate *public* debutter from *private* debutter. In such efforts, the Trust harked back to 1876, when a court ruling in the case of Doorganath Roy versus Ram Chunder Sen had mandated, 'where the temple is a public temple, the dedication [land right] may be such that the family itself could not put an end to it; but in the case of a family idol, the consensus of the whole family might give the estate another direction [that is, it may be alienable]'.[83] In other words, while public debutters were generally inalienable, the consent of the family could make private debutter alienable. The reason why public debutters were inalienable was that they served the public, especially the poor. With public debutter, the endowment of land was for the upkeep of the temple for public worship and also to support itinerant spiritual teachers, homeless persons, orphans, poor widows, and travellers who sought refuge at the temple. These temples offered food, *bhog* and *prasad*, to all devotees. In contrast, property set aside for the worship of the family deity did not serve the public in any way. Unlike public debutter, which served a community, private debutter properties were for the use of the family, and the Trust could acquire them if the family agreed to transfer the land to the state.

The work of separating public from private debutter turned out to be much more difficult than the Trust expected. A dispute in Ahiritola Street pointed to the impracticality of determining whether a debutter was public or private.[84] Residents of Ahiritola Street had resisted the Trust's expropriations by pointing to a temple that fell in the path of demolition. The trustees challenged the property owners by arguing that the temple was only an insignificant shrine of the goddess Sitala, which made the land an alienable 'private debutter'. The Trust's argument met with fierce resistance. The homeowners explained that it was impossible to separate public debutter from those that were private; the boundaries between the two could not be fixed and generally overlapped in the form of *mixed* debutter. Mixed debutters were the most common landholding tenures in Calcutta. A debutter was mixed when its temple could keep its premises open to the public on certain days of the year and closed on others. When the temple was open to the public, devotees from the entire city gathered there to offer their prayers and take part in rituals.

In addition, a local custom permitted all heirs of debutter property to worship the deity in *pala*s (turns). When it was an heir's *pala*, the heir organized the day's worship, offered gifts to the deity, fed Brahmins, and collected tributes that the other devotees offered to the deity. Some famous families in the city, like the Halders of Kalighat, sold their turn of worship or pala to strangers, making their personal and inalienable rights of worship alienable. Those who bought these rights performed the worship for the day and, in turn, collected the offerings and gifts that the devotees made to the deity. It depended entirely on these buyers of the rights of worship whether they wanted to keep the temple open to the public on their pala day.

The customs governing land challenged the Trust's efforts to categorize debutter into neat binaries of private and public. Customs also challenged the Trust's goal of following British laws as precedents in Indian land dispute cases. The British had earlier tried to replace customs with written deeds and contracts when, in the 1895 Bhagobotty versus Guruprosonno dispute, the district court declared that under Hindu law, an idol could hold property but had to 'express words of gift in the shape of a trust' in order to create the valid endowment.[85] The court made it clear that religious ceremonies like sankalpa and samarpan were inadequate instruments for the transfer of property. Indian property owners had nonetheless carried on with their rituals, clearly indicating that the British had failed to rewrite local customs.

Far from accepting Indian autonomy in matters of religion, the Trust routinely interpreted religious tenets and decided on the weight of customs that informed land-holding systems in Calcutta. In 1916, a major dispute ensued between the Trust and the owners of 25, Gopi Krishto Pal Lane, after the Trust reported deplorable living conditions in the neighbourhood.[86] The Trust planned a new street, meant to bring fresh air into the 'dark and insalubrious neighbourhood'. A section of the road passed through the house of Mathur Mohan Sen. Sen's house had a *thakurbari* (temple) located right in the path of demolition. Almost a hundred years before, a trader named Babu Goyaram Sen, who lived in the lane, had the idol of the deity Radhakanto built in his family dwelling.[87] He engraved his name on the left foot of the deity and engaged in elaborate worship. But within a few years his business failed, and he ordered the family priest to take the idol away, believing that it had brought bad luck. The priest then gifted the idol to the forefathers of Mathur Mohan Sen, who were also traders and lived in the neighbourhood.

When the Trust informed Mathur Mohan Sen that his house and the temple would be demolished, debates took place between the coparceners or equal

The Calcutta Improvement Trust 93

share-holders of the property. They met at the thakurbari to discuss whether they should consent to the Trust's plans. Their meeting clearly revealed that the coparceners were not unanimous in their interpretation of Hindu scriptures and in their resistance to the Trust. Instead, the coparceners were divided into two groups and came up with very different interpretations of Hindu religion to argue for and against the thakurbari's demolition.[88] The differences revealed that the property owners had started to deploy their Hindu identities to both side with the Trust, and also challenge it, making religion central to all dialogues between the state and property owners.

The coparceners who opposed demolition argued that the thakurbari constituted an inalienable public debutter. They pointed out that during their pala they allowed the neighbours to enter the temple and offer prayers. This meant that the temple served the public. The coparceners who challenged him pointed out that the devotees could not enter the thakurbari without their permission. This, they argued, made the thakurbari private.[89]

The neighbours joined in the debate, making the discussion on the thakurbari's private or public character a matter of public debate. In August 1916, coparcener Babu Krishna Chandra Ghosh led the neighbours in arguing that the thakurbari was indeed a private debutter.[90] They wrote to the Trust that the temple was not a temple at all; its premises did not carry *lokkhon*s (indications) of a temple: a trident, a tower, or a flag.[91] Instead, the building was a *fulbaganbati* (garden house). Mathur Mohan Sen had placed the deity in the fulbaganbati to make the place look like a 'chapel in a gentleman's park'.[92] The neighbours further argued that the site was not a debutter because some security guards lived there and used it for purposes other than worshipping the deity. The land was thus used for reasons beyond serving the spiritual needs of the family members.

The neighbours concluded that the temple was neither a public temple nor a debutter estate but had been 'built in a certain style and fashion without bearing characteristic indications and not consecrated in the manner enjoined in *Shastras*'.[93] For instance, the image of the deity was merely *located* at the site and not vivified with mantras as the Shastras required. Mathur Mohan Sen had not performed a second *pran pratistha* (spiritual vivification) because the idol could not be vivified twice. This made the idol moveable, the neighbours explained. In addition, Babu Goyaram Sen, who had performed the pran pratistha of the deity, belonged to the *savarna banik* (merchant) caste. The neighbours argued that individuals who did not belong to that caste could not offer prayers at the temple for fear of excommunication.

The neighbours also warned each other that if the Trust did not destroy the thakurbati, it would destroy the *vedi*s or spiritual seats in the neighbouring Baburam Ghose Lane.[94] A rare and peculiar planetary configuration determined the orientations of these vedis: built of expensive materials mentioned in the Shastras, these had historic significance. Seated on these immovable vedis, the famous Pandit Panchanan had performed his spiritual *sadhana* (meditation) and attained *siddha-hood* (sainthood). Hindus from all over the country gathered here to worship these vedis. The neighbours argued that, as devout Hindus, they did not approve the demolition of these vedis.[95]

Meanwhile, B. N. Mallick, another coparcener, brought together a different group of neighbours, who took the opposite stance, petitioning the Trust that the temple was a public debutter. This group explained that the Hindu and Vaishnava communities had been offering their prayers at the temple for over one hundred and fifty years.[96] Their petition said, '[W]e, the neighbours, have the prescriptive right to perform these ceremonies.'[97] For religious ceremonies like Annacoot (the worship of the Hindu deity Annapurna who is the god of nourishment), Janmastami (Hindu festival celebrating the birth of Lord Krishna), Dolejatra (a Hindu festival of colours, also known as Holi), as well as ceremonies like marriage and *sradh* (funeral), the temple was the only place available in the neighbourhood. Every year in the month of Kartik (the seventh month in the Bengali calendar), the ladies of the neighbourhood congregated at the temple to watch the worship or the *mangal araati* (worship that includes offering lights—lamps or candles—to the deity). The temple offered the devotees shelter and prasad.

The conflict in Gopi Krishto Pal Lane reached its height when the Trust intervened and subpoenaed Hindu *pundit*s (experts) to decide on whether the property was public or private debutter.[98] Unfortunately, the pundits themselves were divided on this question. Experts like Dr Satish Chandra Vidyabhushan, pundit Promotha Nath Tarkabhushan, and pundit Parbati Charan Tarkatirtha supported the group that argued that the idol in the thakurbati was moveable.[99] Chandi Charan, a teacher at the Sanskrit College, took the opposing view, holding that the deity had been installed with the proper recital of mantras and was therefore not movable.[100] Chandi Charan believed that in order to relocate the idol, the coparceners had to perform heavy *prayashchitta* (act of repentance).[101]

These debates over public and private debutter expanded the meaning of property beyond a system of real estate rights, transforming it into a cluster of religious principles that layered land with transcendent meanings. The

The Calcutta Improvement Trust

debates represented a new territory of power that moved away from conflicts over actual property rights to a struggle over who could best decipher the multiple layers of meaning that constituted property. Disputes among property holders, and between them and the Trust, centred on who could interpret the meanings invested in land and decide whether the land could be transferred. The Trust's participation in analysing religious investitures in land departed from its post-1857 strategy of non-interference in matters of religion. Like the coparceners of a property, the Trust also took to religious canons to challenge property owners, and their autonomy in the religious sphere, in order to argue, naturally, that certain lands were indeed alienable. Ascribing their lands with religious meanings, the property owners went beyond demanding private property rights. Instead, in their conflict with the state, they described land as their religious right. In such efforts, they recast their own identities in the language of religion: as Hindus and Muslims.

Waqf and public purpose

Like debutter in Hindu custom, waqf signified inalienable property in Islamic law. It implied an endowment by a Muslim of property—moveable or immovable, tangible or intangible—to Allah. As a legal transaction, *waqifs* (settlers) appointed themselves or another truthful person as *mutawalli* (manager) in an endowment deed (*waqfnamaah*) to oversee the waqf.[102] Following the true spirit of Islam, Muslim property holders dedicated property, land, and its revenue rights to *awqaf* (plural of waqf), for maintaining mosques, *madrasas* (schools), *qabristans* (graveyards), *yatimkhanas* (orphanages), and other charitable institutes. As a surrender of properties to Allah, a waqf deed was perpetual and inalienable.

Like debutter, waqf could be either private or public. The difference was based either on the relationship between the donor and the beneficiaries or on the nature of the donation itself. The waqf that supported the welfare of the destitute was public. The private waqf benefited the family and relatives of the endower. In the case of private waqf, only when the specified beneficiaries expired, the waqf was transferred to benefit the public.

In Shambazaar, the Trust's improvements targeted numerous properties in the vicinity of the Cornwallis Street. The Chairman of the Trust described the houses there as 'bustees of filthy huts'.[103] It decided to demolish these and rebuild the area. The neighbourhood's residents, mostly Muslim, challenged the Trust by arguing that one of the huts they planned to demolish was a mosque and that the land on which it stood was a waqf and therefore inalienable. Abdul Latif, a tailor who lived in the area, led a group in collecting subscriptions to improve sanitation on their own.[104] Abdul Waheb, another neighbourhood denizen, wrote petitions to the Trust warning it to not interfere in religious matters. Waheb was a member of the Bengal Muslim league, a rival of the Indian National Congress. His involvement in the anti-Trust demonstrations attracted Muslim nationalist leaders.[105] Moulavi Fazal Ul Haq of the Muslim League took an active interest in protecting the mosque and organized demonstrations in the neighbourhood.[106]

Although the Muslim community wanted the Trust to dismiss this scheme, the Trust's chairman, C. H. Bompas, wrote to the government of Bengal that the mosque was a *jhupdi* (shack) that served no purpose. He hired Muslim scholars Sultan Ahmed and Hedayat Hussain to support his view. Ahmed and Hussain surveyed the neighbourhood to determine whether the mosque was important to the residents. In these enquiries, they found that the mosque was well-regarded and a popular place for prayers. For twenty years, it had played a meaningful role in bringing neighbours together. Moulavi Rahman Khan, who lived in the neighbourhood, verified this information. The Imam of the mosque argued the same. Ahmed and Hussain then went against the Trust, concluding that the mosque was public and the land a public waqf and inalienable.

The Trust, of course, did not agree with the findings of Ahmed and Hussain. Instead, it engaged in interpreting Islamic laws on its own to argue that the land on which the mosque stood was not a waqf. It pointed out that the site had originally belonged to a certain Shaik Moniruddin Amin, who on his death bed had passed the land to his two sons and daughters.[107] The mosque had gone to one of the sons, Abdur Rouf. Following this, there had been several mortgages and re-conveyances. Several Hindus had held the property. The last mortgage Rouf paid was to Babu Netto Chandra, who was a Hindu. He later sold the property under a mortgage decree to another Hindu, Babu Krishna Behari Mukherjee. All of this meant, the Trust contended, that the land was not a waqf and that the mosque was a private structure.[108]

The Trust's furious exchanges with another Muslim property owner, the Tayeb family, once again showed its efforts to interpret Islamic laws on land. In 1895, Muhammad Tayeb, a property owner on Durga Road, died and left behind his widow, five sons, and three daughters.[109] A few months prior to his death, Tayeb had converted his property—a house, a plot of open land, and a mosque—into a waqf. He clearly stated that his family should use the income

The Calcutta Improvement Trust

from the land for their upkeep and invest the remainder in the mosque to support pilgrims and poorer city dwellers. In 1925, when the Trust planned an improvement scheme near Tayeb's property, his daughter wanted to transfer her share to the Trust in return for substantial compensation. The Trust, however, refused to accept this property, arguing that it was a public waqf.

Similar to Hindu property owners, Muslim property owners also employed religion to inscribe land with sacred meanings and engage in a debate with the state over alienable and inalienable property rights. Religion helped them to intervene in the Trust's acquisitions and reordering of the city. Yet their responses to the Trust's improvements were much nuanced and layered instead of simple resistance. Tayeb's daughter responded that the property violated several clauses of a public waqf including the idea of *musha* that mandated that the waqf should not be used for profit. She showed that her mother had parcelled out parts of the waqf to other women and drew monthly rents from them. For months, the Trust refused to accept her claims and the tribunal decided against her. The trustees insisted that the property was a public waqf and inalienable.

Tayeb's daughter took the matter to the High Court. Reading Islamic laws and examining land deeds, the Trust argued that the waqf followed *marz-ul-maut*. Marz-ul-maut was a complex doctrine that referred to processes that turned properties into waqfs; different schools of Islam interpreted it in different ways. The Trust described marz-ul-maut as the Islamic custom that allowed property owners, on their deathbeds, to convert their property to waqf without following procedural formalities. The Trust explained that Tayeb had used this principle to make his property a waqf. Tayeb's daughter, however, questioned whether Tyab's illness was actually fatal and whether he was on his 'deathbed' when he undertook the marz-ul-maut. In February 1895, paralysis of the lower limbs hit Tayeb leaving him tied to the bed. Paralysis of the lower limbs meant that he remained in bed and had to be helped to a sitting posture, but his brain was functioning.

On the day Tayeb made the waqfnamaah, his sons took him in a palanquin to the *cutcherry* or court of the Office of the Registrar. At the cutcherry, he participated in turning his holdings into a waqf. Tayeb's daughter pointed out that because her father's mental faculties remained unimpaired, he had no right to claim marz-ul-maut. She brought some neighbours who supported her and said they saw nothing in Tayeb suggestive of senile decay, apart from the paralysis of his lower limbs. Tayeb was therefore not on his deathbed when he converted his property into a waqf. Although the Trust cited the marz-ul-maut, Tayeb's daughter's insistence led the Court to rule against it, deciding in her favour. The High Court decreed that the property was not a public waqf and that the Trust could acquire it in lieu of paying compensation to Tayeb's daughter.

The Trust's interventions ascribed private property with sacred meanings. Property no longer meant land or structures as such. It enmeshed these physical forms in religious implications that turned conflicts centred on land into intense struggles over the meaning of religious texts and customs. Disputes over property made religion the loci of conflicts between the British and Indians. With Indian property owners defining their properties as rooted in customs that rendered them inalienable, the British realized it was impossible to disengage from religion while governing Indians. Indeed, as founders of a new market in land, they had to engage in religious texts and arbitrate on customs even more. As conflicts over property ownership increased in the 1920s, sparked by the sharp rise in land prices, property emerged as a contested terrain on which Indians and British fought some of the most arduous struggles over the interpretation of religious principles and customs that governed landed property. These struggles, as we have seen, informed the urban spaces of neighbourhoods as well as urban identities of city dwellers.

Conclusion

The Trust's constructions—boulevards, parks, squares, flats—which ostensibly aimed to improve Calcutta's hygiene also facilitated circulatory processes that authorized colonial power in new spaces in the city. The boulevards evicted Indians from the city centre, striking at the heart of their protests, weakening them and forcing them to move to distant suburbs. Colonizing the organic growth of the city and stifling anti-government protests, the Trust built suburbs, flats, and tenements to stratify the city along racial, economic, religious, and caste lines with the goal of rendering impossible the unity that the anti-colonial protests otherwise needed. Adding to this, the Trust's zoning reinforced a dichotomy in the experiences of the rich and the poor, the Hindus and Muslims, and the Indians and Europeans.

The Trust's urban reconstruction projects also made private property the recurring locus of conflict between city dwellers and the Improvement Trust. At the focal point of these debates were religious metaphors that became transposed in urban space. This, in turn, added to private property a public value weaving together neighbourhoods or *para*s as Hindu communities. The

The Calcutta Improvement Trust 99

new identity of the neighbourhood as a Hindu or Muslim space was thus an outcome of the complex contestations over property and of the struggle to control the built environment. At the heart of these struggles were sets of social relations constituted through meanings invested in space. These new social relations led to the carving out of new identities, including the sharpening sense of self-identity in the backdrop of widening social and economic polarities in the city. As the next chapter will show, within the space of the para, the production of Hindu self-identities also entailed changing relationships between the body and the built environment.

Notes

1. Victoria Kelley, *Soap and Water: Cleanliness, Dirt and the Working Classes in Victorian and Edwardian Britain* (London; New York: I. B. Tauris, 2010), 7.

2. David Arnold pointed to the hegemonic attributes of colonial medicine that was of value to both the British and Indian elites. See David Arnold, *Colonizing the Body: State Medicine and Epidemic Disease in Nineteenth-Century India* (Berkeley: University of California Press, 1993), 241. Mark Harrison described public health as a colonizing discourse, but also emphasized that indigenous medicine appropriated Western medicine. He described voluntary associations, popular among Indian elites, that provided instruction in Western hygiene. See Mark Harrison, *Public Health in British India: Anglo-Indian Preventive Medicine, 1859–1914* (Cambridge: Cambridge University Press, 1994), 88.

3. Herbert Hope Risley, *The Tribes and Castes of Bengal: Ethnographic Glossary* (Calcutta: Bengal Secretariat Press, 1892).

4. Abinaschandra Ghosh, *The Laws of Improvement and Acquisition in Calcutta: With Complete Commentaries and Forms* (Calcutta: Eastern Law House, 1919), iii.

5. Ibid., iv.

6. Howard Spodek explained that British improvement trusts had absolute authority in 'planning' Indian cities. See Howard Spodek, 'City Planning in India under British Rule', *Economic and Political Weekly* 48, no. 4 (2013): 53–61.

7. Calcutta Improvement Trust, *The Calcutta Improvement Act, 1911 & Allied Matters* (Calcutta: Calcutta Improvement Trust, 1912).

8. Improvement trusts carried out similar atrocities in Britain's other colonies too. See Brenda S. A. Yeoh, *Contesting Space in Colonial Singapore: Power Relations and the Urban Built Environment* (Singapore: Singapore University Press, 2003), and William Cunningham Bissell, *Urban Design, Chaos, and Colonial Power in Zanzibar* (Bloomington: Indiana University Press, 2011). In India, brutal demolitions and rebuilding activities of improvement trusts in colonial cities

like Bombay and Delhi have been discussed by Prashant Kidambi, *The Making of an Indian Metropolis: Colonial Governance and Public Culture in Bombay, 1890–1920* (Burlington, VT: Ashgate Publishing Company, 2007); Sandip Hazareesingh, *Colonial City and the Challenge of Modernity: Urban Hegemonies and Civic Contestations in Bombay 1900–1925* (Bombay: Orient Longman, 2006); and Jyoti Hosagrahar, *Indigenous Modernities: Negotiating Architecture, Urbanism, and Colonialism in Delhi* (Milton Park, Abingdon, Oxon; New York, NY: Routledge, 2005), among others.

9. M. J. Daunton, *Wealth and Welfare: An Economic and Social History of Britain, 1851–1951* (Oxford; New York: Oxford University Press, 2007), 361.

10. The Glasgow Improvement Trust acquired nearly ninety acres of land in the most crowded parts of the city. Acquisitions were slow; there were instances when the private builders who bought these lands opposed the Trust and refused to agree to land settlements, further slowing down the process. See Thomas Martin Devine, *Glasgow* (Manchester: Manchester University Press, 1995).

11. E. P. Richards, *Report by Request of the Trust on the Condition, Improvement and Town Planning of the City of Calcutta and Contiguous Areas: The Richards Report* (Ware, Hertfordshire, England: Jennings & Bewley, 1914), 11.

12. James Maden and Albert de Bois Shrosbree, 'City and Suburban Main Road Projects, Joint Report, 1st July 1913' (Calcutta: Calcutta Improvement Trust, 1913) [TBLA].

13. Bengal Regulation I of 1824 in D. Sutherland, *The Regulations of the Bengal Code, in Force in September 1862 with a List of Titles and Index* (Calcutta: Bengal Printing Co., 1862). The preamble to the regulation stated that it was necessary for individuals to surrender their property for the purpose of general convenience of communities.

14. Act XLII of 1850 in Richard Clarke, Bengal (India), and East India Company, *Digest, or Consolidated Arrangement, of the Regulations and Acts of the Bengal Government, from 1793 to 1854* (London: Printed by J. & H. Cox, 1855).

15. Act XXII of 1863 in *High Court Reports; Being a Re-Print of All the Decisions of the Privy Council on Appeals from India and of the Various High Courts and Other Superior Courts in India Reported Both in the Official and Non-Official Reports from 1862 to 1875* (Madras and Trichinopoly: T. A. Venkasawmy Row and T. S. Krishnasawmy Row, 1915).

16. William Fischer Agnew and M Krishnamachariar, *The Law of Trusts in British India* (Calcutta: Thacker, Spink & Co., 1920).

17. Om Prakash Agarwal, *Compulsory Acquisition of Land in India and Pakistan, Being an Exhaustive, Critical and Analytical Commentary on the Acquisition Land Act I of 1894 and Other Allied Acts* (Allahabad: University Book Agency, 1950), section 17.

The Calcutta Improvement Trust   101

18. 'Letter of H. F. Samman, Secretary to the Chairman of the Trust', Bengal Municipal Proceedings and Consultations of the Government of India and of its Presidencies and Provinces, July 1913 [TBLA].

19. Ghosh, *The Laws of Improvement and Acquisition in Calcutta*.

20. 'Proceedings of the Chairman of the Calcutta Corporation', in *Annual Report of the Calcutta Municipal Corporation, 1916* [TBLA].

21. In Calcutta, apartment buildings are called flats, different from the Western usage where flats mean a self-contained housing unit that occupies only part of a building.

22. 'Report of the Barrabazaar Improvement Sub Committee, Appendix D', in *Annual Report of the Calcutta Improvement Trust, 1926* [TBLA].

23. Patrick Geddes, *Barrabazaar Improvement: A Report to the Corporation of Calcutta* (Calcutta: Calcutta Corporation Press, 1919), 27.

24. Government of Bengal, Municipal Department, 'Proposal for developing a modern business area west of Darmahatta Street', Proceedings of the Bengal Government, Municipal Branch, 1922 [TBLA].

25. 'Report on Barrabazaar Improvement Subcommittee. Resolution No 1', in *Annual Report on the Operations of the Calcutta Improvement Trust, 1926* [TBLA].

26. 'The Marwari Protest', *The Times of India*, 14 May 1915.

27. Ibid.

28. 'Precis of Objection, Proceedings of a Committee to hear objections to the Scheme VII, held at the Trust's Offices, July 21, 1915', Proceedings of the Calcutta Improvement Trust, September 1916 [TBLA].

29. Ibid.

30. Ibid.

31. 'Letter from The President of the Iron Merchant Association of Barrabazaar to the Chairman of the Trust', in *Report on the Barrabazaar Improvement Schemes as Adopted by the Improvement Trust Special Committee* (Calcutta: Calcutta Corporation Press, 1919) [TBLA].

32. Government of Bengal. Municipal Department, 'Protest Meeting on the revised scheme of XXVI of the Calcutta Improvement Trust', Proceedings of the Bengal Municipal Department, 1927 [TBLA].

33. 'Protest Meeting on the revised scheme of XXVI of Calcutta Improvement Trust', Proceedings of the Calcutta Improvement Trust, 1928 [TBLA].

34. Ibid.

35. Partho Datta explained the overlaps in Richards' plan for Calcutta and Haussmann's ideas of improvement; see Partho Datta, *Planning the City: Urbanization and Reform in Calcutta; c. 1800–c. 1940* (New Delhi: Tulika Books, 2012), 212.

36. David Harvey, *Paris, Capital of Modernity* (New York: Routledge, 2006), 141.
37. Keya Dasgupta wrote that in the early twentieth century, the Sikh community of Calcutta moved from the central parts of the city to the sparsely populated localities of Bhowaneepore in the south. In Bhowaneepore, the Improvement Trust had laid tramlines transforming the region into a residential neighbourhood with connections to the city centre. See Keya Dasgupta, 'Mapping the Places of Minorities: Calcutta through the Last Century', in *Calcutta Mosaic: Essays and Interviews on the Minority Communities of Calcutta*, ed. Himadri Banerjee, Nilanjana Gupta, and Sipra Mukherjee, 23–70 (New Delhi: Anthem Press, 2012), 49.
38. Liora Bigon, *Garden Cities and Colonial Planning* (Manchester: Manchester University Press, 2017).
39. 'Petition of the Residents of the Hazra Road, February 13, 1919', in *Annual Report on the Operations of the Calcutta Improvement Trust, 1920* [TBLA].
40. 'Petition of the Residents of the Russa Road to the Trust Office at Clive Street, December 19, 1920', in *Annual Report on the Operations of the Calcutta Improvement Trust, 1921* [TBLA].
41. 'Resolution No. 13, Meeting of the Tribunal on March 12', in *Annual Report of the Calcutta Improvement Trust, 1920* [TBLA].
42. Patrick McAuslan, *Land Law Reform in East Africa: Traditional or Transformative?* (New York: Routledge, 2015), 161.
43. Ibid.
44. *Amrita Bazar Patrika*, 2 September 1918.
45. Proceedings of the Calcutta Improvement Trust, June 1920 [TBLA].
46. Proceedings of the Calcutta Improvement Trust, May 1927 [TBLA].
47. 'Disposal of Land', in *Annual Report on the Operations of the Calcutta Improvement Trust, 1933* [TBLA].
48. 'Objections under Section 43, Letter from inhabitants of western portion of Dhakuria to the Chairman of The Board of Trustees', Proceedings of the Calcutta Improvement Trust, August 1916.
49. Bengal (India), Calcutta Rent Enquiry Committee, *Report of the Committee Appointed to Enquire into Land Values and Rents in Calcutta* (Calcutta: Bengal Secretariat Press, 1920) [TBLA].
50. Manindranath Kanjilal, *The Calcutta Rent Act, Bengal Act III Of 1920, Annotated, etc.* (Calcutta: Bengal Secretariat Press, 1920).
51. *The Statesman*, 12 October 1921.
52. Nikhil Rao provides a fascinating account of apartment living as part of suburbanization in colonial Bombay, where apartments catered to upper-caste migrants from the southern parts of India. See Nikhil Rao, *House, but No Garden. Apartment Living in Bombay's Suburbs, 1898–1964* (Minneapolis: University of Minnesota Press, 2013), 97.

The Calcutta Improvement Trust

53. Proceedings of the Meeting of the Calcutta Improvement Trust, 8 July 1918 [TBLA].
54. Calcutta Domiciled Committee Enquiry Committee, *Report of the Calcutta Domiciled Committee 1918–1919* (Calcutta: The Bengal Secretariat Press, 1920) [TBLA].
55. 'Appendix E, Papers Related to the disposal and sale of Land, Meeting No. 97', Proceedings of the Calcutta Improvement Trust, 1934 [TBLA].
56. Buddhadeb Basu, *Amar Joubon* (Calcutta: M.C. Sarkar and Sons, 1977).
57. Ibid., 34.
58. 'Park Street Transformed', *The Statesman*, 29 June 1922.
59. 'Meeting No. 107, August 3, 1928', in *Annual Report on the Operations of the Calcutta Improvement Trust, 1929*.
60. *Annual Report on the Operations of the Calcutta Improvement Trust, 1935*.
61. Charles Mulford Robinson, *The Improvement of Towns and Cities; or, The Practical Basis of Civic Aesthetics* (New York: G.P. Putnam's Sons, 1901).
62. *Annual Report on the Operations of the Calcutta Improvement Trust, 1917*.
63. Farhan Karim, *Of Greater Dignity than Riches: Austerity and Housing Design in India* (Pittsburgh: University of Pittsburgh Press, 2019), 45.
64. Ibid.
65. H. W. B Moreno, *Anglo-Indians and the Housing Problem* (Calcutta: Central Press, 1917).
66. *Annual Report on the Operations of the Calcutta Improvement Trust, 1925*.
67. H. V. Lanchester, 'Calcutta Improvement Trust: Precis of Mr. E.P. Richards Report on the City of Calcutta Part II', *The Town Planning Review* 5, no. 3 (October 1914): 214–24.
68. 'Rehousing of the Poorer Classes', Proceedings of the Calcutta Improvement Trust, April 1926.
69. Datta, *Planning the City*; Kidambi, *The Making of an Indian Metropolis*; Eric Lewis Beverley, *Hyderabad, British India, and the World* (Cambridge: Cambridge University Press, 2015); Karim, *Of Greater Dignity than Riches*; Bissell, *Urban Design, Chaos, and Colonial Power in Zanzibar*.
70. *The Statesman*, 30 January 1918.
71. M. N. Gupta, *Land Acquisition Acts and Principles of Valuation* (Calcutta: S. C. Sarkar & Sons Ltd., 1939).
72. 'Proceedings of a Meeting of the Committee Appointed to Hear Objections to Scheme No VII, Held at the Office of the Marwari Association, Machuaabazaar Street, March 15, 1917', Proceedings of the Calcutta Improvement Trust, 1918.
73. 'Objections under Section 43, Letter from Inhabitants of Western Portion of Dhakuria to the Chairman of the Board of Trustees', in *Annual Report on the Operations of the Calcutta Improvement Trust, 1925*.

74. 'Chandra Kanta Ghosh versus the Calcutta Improvement Trust, August 22, 1916', Proceedings of the Calcutta Improvement Trust, August 1917.
75. 'Mani Lall Sing versus the Trustees for the Calcutta Improvement Trust, 14 August, 1917', Proceedings of the Calcutta Improvement Trust, May 1918.
76. 'Petition from the Inhabitants of Russa Road against Street Widening, 1914', in *Annual Report on the Operations of the Calcutta Improvement Trust, 1915*.
77. 'Petition from the Hindu Inhabitants of Russa Road to the Calcutta Improvement Trust, 1918', in *Annual Report on the Operations of the Calcutta Improvement Trust, 1919*.
78. Jogendra Chunder Ghose, *The Law of Impartible Property: Rajas, Chieftainships, Zemindaries, Taluks, Tekaiti-Gadis, Military and Other Service Tenures, Polliems, Ghatwalis, Digwaris, Vatans, Inams, Tarwads &c.* (Calcutta: R. Cambray & Co., 1916).
79. 'Petition from the Hindu inhabitants of Russa Road to the Calcutta Improvement Trust, 1918', in *Annual Report on the Operations of the Calcutta Improvement Trust, 1919*.
80. 'Letter from Haripodo Chowdhury to the Chairman of the Trust, October 8, 1917', Proceedings of the Calcutta Improvement Trust, February 1918.
81. 'Objections to the Proposed Public Street No III of the Gobra Main Road by Residents of Hatibagan, December 1919', Proceedings of the Committee to Hear Objections to the Scheme, 18 July 1920.
82. 'Petition of the Khidderpore Residents to the Improvement Scheme XVI', Proceedings of the Calcutta Improvement Trust, February 1920.
83. 'Doorganath Roy versus Ram Chunder Sen, 1876 (Before the Privy Council, November 30, 1876)', in *Annual Report on the Operations of the Calcutta Improvement Trust, 1899*.
84. 'Letter from Bompas to the Secretary of the Government of Bengal', Proceedings of the Calcutta Municipal Corporation, May 1919.
85. Arthur Phillips and Ernest John Trevelyan, *The Law Relating to Hindu Wills, Second Edition, Revised by Sir E.J. Trevelyan* (London; Calcutta: W. Thacker & Co.; Thacker, Spink & Co., 1914), 233.
86. Proceedings of the Calcutta Improvement Trust, March 1917.
87. 'True Copy of Srijuta Mohendra Nath Sen, of 85 Years of Age, May 9, 1916', Proceedings of the Calcutta Improvement Trust, July 1917.
88. 'Letter from Bully Chunder Sen to the Chairman of the Municipal Corporation, May 1, 1916', Proceedings of the Calcutta Improvement Trust, August 1917.
89. 'Letter of Krishna Chandra Ghosh to the Chairman of the Trust, June 24, 1916', Proceedings of the Calcutta Improvement Trust, February 1917.
90. Ibid.
91. 'Humble Petition of the Mathur Sen Garden Lane Inhabitants, August 31, 1916', Proceedings of the Calcutta Improvement Trust, December 1917.

The Calcutta Improvement Trust

92. Ibid.
93. Ibid.
94. 'Humble Petition of the Inhabitants of Baburam Ghosh Lane to the Chairman of the Trust, June 15, 1916', Proceedings of the Calcutta Improvement Trust, November–December 1917.
95. Proceedings of the Calcutta Improvement Trust, June 1917.
96. 'Letter of B. N. Mallick and other hundred, June 1916', Proceedings of the Calcutta Improvement Trust, May 1917.
97. Ibid.
98. 'The Humble Petition of the undersigned Inhabitants of Mathur Sen Garden Lane, Goppee Kristo Pal Lane to the Chairman of the Trust', Proceedings of the Calcutta Improvement Trust, June 1918.
99. 'Opinion of the Hindu Pandits Relating to Scheme VII', Proceedings of the Calcutta Improvement Trust, August 1918.
100. Ibid.
101. 'Opinion of the Hindu Pandits Relating to Scheme VII', Proceedings of the Calcutta Improvement Trust, December 1920.
102. K. D. Gangrade, *Social Legislation in India* (Delhi: Concept Publishing, 1978), 195.
103. 'Letter of Mr. Bompas to the Secretary, Government of Bengal, May 19, 1916. Papers Relating to the Mosque at No. 1 Akshay Kumar Bose Lane', *Annual Report on the Operations of the Calcutta Improvement Trust, 1916.*
104. 'Appendix 1, Papers relating to the Mosque of No. 1 Akshay Kumar Bose Lane to the Secretary to the Government of Bengal, General Department, Municipal Branch', in *Annual Report on the Operations of the Calcutta Improvement Trust, 1916.*
105. Ibid.
106. 'Letter from Moulavi Fazlul Ul Haq to the Trust, August 10, 1915', in *Annual Report on the Operations of the Calcutta Improvement Trust, 1916.*
107. 'Report of Estate Manager Mallinath Roy, March 24, 1916', in *Annual Report on the Operations of the Calcutta Improvement Trust, 1917.*
108. *Annual Report on the Operations of the Calcutta Improvement Trust, 1925.*
109. 'Karimannessa Bibi versus Hamedulla Alias Raja and Ors', Proceedings of the Calcutta Improvement Trust, May 1925.

3 A City-Nation

Paras, Hygiene, and *Swaraj*

> Yet the *para* was not precisely a space, but a structure loosely superimposed
> upon the urban landscape, a way of understanding the complex identities
> generated by the city.[1]

In Calcutta, the month of Ashwin—October—is marked by the annual
autumnal ritual of Durga Puja. The Puja memorializes the mythical event
of Hindu goddess Durga's victory over buffalo-demon Mahishashura.
Kalikapurana, a Hindu epic, describes Durga as the embodiment of Shakti,
the force that governs all of human existence. The collective energies of the
Hindu gods Shiva, Vishnu, and Brahma went into creating her. Armed with
divine powers, she killed the buffalo-demon Ashura, whom no other god or
human could defeat. Week-long celebrations of the Puja in Calcutta relive the
moment when Durga slayed Mahishashura. Variously described as a street-
art festival, a festival to preserve village folk-art traditions in the city, and a
heavily commercialized rendering of a religious event, the Puja is primarily
expressed in street carnivals.[2] Neighbourhood clubs erect *pandal*s (decorated
canopies) on the sides of streets and in the city's parks. They festoon these
pandals with lights and play loud music. Inside the pandal, they place an idol
of Durga and engage in elaborate rituals. City dwellers crowd the streets all
day and all night. They tour the pandals and offer their prayers to the deity.

Durga Puja did not always include magnificent pandals and public
celebrations, however. In the late nineteenth century, it was a household
festival. Hindu merchants worshipped the deity in the private recesses of their
house.[3] Their houses were enormous, containing an inner central courtyard.
Surrounding the courtyard were *dalaan*s (a verandah or open hall for receiving
visitors); they placed the idol on these platforms and engaged in day-long rituals.
It was only in the twentieth century that the Puja evolved into a public festivity.
Neighbourhood clubs replaced merchants, organizing *sarbojonin* (public) Durga
Pujas in the public spaces of Calcutta.

A City-Nation

In this chapter, I argue that the transitions in Durga Puja celebrations, from a private worship to a public festival, undergirded a much bigger shift in the socio-spatial configuration of Calcutta. This shift took shape at the local, everyday spaces of neighbourhoods or *para*s that emerged as spatial units of a Hindu, and Bengali nation.[4]

In Persian, the word 'para' means 'part of [a village]'. Translated literally, the word 'para' means 'neighbourhood'. But paras are more than geographic spaces. Neither the state nor town planners design the para; a simple dismissal of the state's claim to define subjects and spaces characterize the para. People who live in the para set its physical limit and shape its spaces. More than planned spaces, paras are spatial communities built on kinship-like ties.[5] In the para, neighbours live like extended families and address each other in familial terms like *dada* (brother), *didi* (sister), *mashi* (aunt), and *kaka* (uncle). A shared cultural life reinforces the quasi-kinship bonds of the para and also moulds its spaces. Neighbours living along the same street, who pay *chanda* (subscriptions) to the same annual festivals, belong to the same para.

In Chapter 2, I argued that Indian property owners described their paras as Hindu or Muslim spaces to resist the Calcutta Improvement Trust's expropriation. I also argued that their efforts were everyday strategies, different from the organized anti-colonial nationalist movements that imagined India as Hindu. In December 1922, a group had branched out of the Indian National Congress, a premier nationalist association that steered agitations against the British. This group that separated from the Congress demanded a more intense programme of agitation and believed elections could lead to *swaraj* or self-government. They formed the Swaraj Party in 1923. That year, they also had a sweeping victory at the Calcutta municipal elections. In this chapter, I argue that when the Swarajists (members of the Swaraj Party) took up municipal administration, they appropriated the everyday spaces of paras and reconfigured these as microcosms of a nation. They conflated urbanism with nationalism to shape a 'city nation'—a city that was equipped to bring together a Hindu and Bengali nation.

The Swarajists collaborated with *bhadralok*s—propertied, upper-caste, English-educated Bengali men—to shape the city nation. The Calcutta Improvement Trust had earlier targeted the ancestral houses where bhadraloks lived and threatened them with eviction. The bhadraloks responded by marshalling their para as a Hindu community and arguing that an eviction could incite riots. After 1923, they worked enthusiastically with Swarajists to reinforce the Hindu identity of their paras. With Swarajist assistance, they launched a pedagogic training programme that found expression in health campaigns, fitness programmes, festivals, sports, and cultural events in their para. In these campaigns, urbanity manifested as interventions in conduct: a civilizing process reinforced the training programme, trying to inculcate neighbours in what bhadraloks thought was conduct fit for the city and the nation in formation. The bhadraloks offered these as the normative practices of urban modernity.

Bhadraloks led surveys that involved new institutional forms of control and systematic collection of information of para dwellers. The regulation of the body, its gradual incorporation within a network of rules and behavioural codes not only was an outcome of an increasingly urbanized modernity but also reflected a strategic intervention on the part of the bhadraloks in shaping a nation.

While defining their paras as Hindu, bhadraloks arranged for festivals, theatres, music, book clubs, and so on that evoked the spirits of a new Bengali nationalism. Swarajist separatism from Gandhian nationalism had mandated a distinct regional identity for Bengal. When Gandhi called for a boycott of British products in 1920, he encouraged Indians to manufacture goods locally. In the wake of Swadeshi, an economic boycott movement in 1905, Bengalis had opened factories. Most of these factories failed, however.[6] The Bengali Swarajist leaders were therefore unsure whether an economic boycott was the road to freedom. They also questioned whether the silent methods of Gandhi— the peaceful demonstrations and civil disobedience—were powerful enough to pressure the British into leaving India. They explained that Bengal needed a different self-expression and proceeded to shape a distinct regional identity that could bring together a Bengali nation and also set it free.[7]

Bengali newspapers and books in the late nineteenth century had shaped an intellectual ferment that opened dialogues on Bengali-ness. Bankim Chandra Chattopadhyay, a celebrated writer, reflected on the meanings of a Bengali identity in his mid-nineteenth-century writings. He explained that language (he used the Bengali language to describe both geography and community) and caste (he described Brahmins as descendants of Aryans) were the two main pillars of the Bengali identity.[8] Meanwhile, in the *mofussils* (satellite towns), political discourse in Bengali awakened Bengali nationalism.[9] I argue that the pedagogic training programme that bhadraloks led culminated in the public celebrations of Durga Puja and carved a material and discursive environment that contributed to the nationalist need of constructing cities in such a way that their inhabitants behaved like members of a nation, in this case, a Hindu-Bengali nation.

A City-Nation

Kinship, City Space, and the Everyday

In both Western and non-Western cities, public areas shape more than city space; they also shape relations among city dwellers. In shared common spaces, like streets, cafes, and parks, city dwellers meet to discuss matters of national importance. These meetings craft interpersonal ties beyond family and kinship. In the city, an individual is a product of interactions and responses to public spaces and not of their private, family lives.[10] Contact and socialization among city dwellers on sidewalks, for example, foster the development of civic virtues or citizenship.[11] In public spaces, city dwellers can meet as individuals. Unfettered by familial ties, they behave in public as rights-bearing citizens. Their meetings and discussions, formal and informal, are participatory processes that feed public opinion and keep democracy alive. A public sphere needs public space; the spatial order of the city is therefore critical to the functioning of democracy.

As philosopher and sociologist Jurgen Habermas has pointed out, in the wake of print capitalism, the bourgeoisie in Europe met as individuals in the public spaces of cafes and salons to debate pressing matters. This shaped a civil society that kept the government in check.[12] But space for individuals to interact is not inherently redemptive. Habermas' critics have shown that public space can work to further exploitation. Social inequalities like class and race often restrict an individual's access to public spaces, making only the voices of influential groups heard. Habermas does not mention, for instance, the struggle that women had to undergo to make their voices heard in the public sphere.[13]

In countries like India, with a long colonial past, public spaces are heavily policed and are usually instrumentalized in order to discipline citizens. The British in India passed laws that censored public gatherings and anti-colonial speech. Given these discriminatory laws, public debates in India were far from organic. Discussions in the public sphere focused primarily on meaningful ways to fight the British. Nationalism worked as a disciplining force that inflected all debates in the public sphere, side-lining voices of the lower castes, non-Hindus, and women who protested against discrimination among Indians themselves.

The anonymity that aided the rise of the individual in Europe was also quite impossible in India, where a person was seen in the context of their family, caste, religion, and so on. In this context, the space of the neighbourhood in South Asian cities offers the most visible challenge to the public/private divide that is key to the shaping of a public sphere. The public sphere comes to life when individuals interact with each other as rights-bearing citizens rather than as members of families. The public sphere builds on the divide between the public and the private. In South Asian cities, these divides are much blurred. The neighbourhood, which is a public space, is instead shaped by private, kinship-like ties between neighbours; the public space of the neighbourhood becomes an extension of the private space of the family. For example, the *moholla* in Bombay is a tight-knit neighbourhood community that is governed by a family-based governing council of the elderly (a *jamaat*).[14] This unique form of control that the elderly exerts over the moholla, treating it as a family, eliminates the line between public and private.

As Geert De Neve and Henrike Donner have described, neighbourhoods in Indian cities are sites of a plethora of actions—here social and gender relations get constituted, political organizations and labour movements take shape, kinship ties, ritual performances of religion, and enactments of political and national sentiments occur.[15] Above all, they explain, this is where individual and social identities are produced in festivals, economic cooperation, and political mobilization. Arjun Appadurai, on the other hand, pointed out that the neighbourhood is different from 'locality'.[16] The nation-state can appropriate the locality as a site of commemoration and events. Such appropriation is not possible in neighbourhoods because these are social formations where lived experiences of residents mould space. Shaped by the lifeworld of residents, each neighbourhood is different from the other; Appadurai argued that neighbourhoods, marked by difference and autonomy, challenged the efforts of the nation-state to standardize space and through it regulate the public.

Scholarship on neighbourhoods in South Asian cities celebrates their everydayness. At the focus of scholarly works are the kinship-like ties between neighbours that make neighbourhoods resemble extended families. In most Indian neighbourhoods, religion cemented ties between neighbours. In cities in Rajasthan, for instance, temples and shrines marked the boundaries of mohollas that were organized along religious lines and named after the caste of their residents.[17] Resisting colonial town planning, religion shaped public spaces of the moholla. The residents of the moholla came together as a family to run the temples. But at the same time, religion also formed the axis along which moholla residents interacted with state authorities, including the police. For example, in mohollas in colonial Bombay, residents had to engage with the police when the latter started issuing licenses for Muharram processions.[18]

Religion, however, was not the only thread that held together neighbourhoods as kinship-like communities in colonial Indian cities. Neighbourhoods were, after all, lived spaces, where no one logic could determine the order of space. Neighbourhoods in workers' villages in the district of Girangaon near the

A City-Nation

Bombay cotton mills, for instance, were quite secular. Workers in this district had moved from their villages to live in one-room apartments in tenements or *chawls*. Leisure activities and entertainments such as magic show in these neighbourhoods made them feel at home in an unknown city.[19] The continuance of rural entertainments created the comfort of a community that brought neighbours together. In a similar way, festivals, theatres, and football tournaments between paras produced a sense of belonging in the otherwise irregular and seemingly arbitrary configurations of these spaces.[20]

My analysis of the para, however, questions its everydayness. I argue that although paras defied state-control, these were far from organic city spaces: who were the 'people' who shaped paras? Did diverse groups of Indian city dwellers, divided along caste and religion live in the same para? I depart from existing scholarship that underscores the everydayness of neighbourhoods to argue that hierarchies of caste and religion, together with anti-colonial nationalism, stifled the organic growth of paras.[21] I draw on Ranajit Guha's argument that the everyday in South Asian cities is in fact a much-regulated and disciplined everyday.[22] Guha offered the example of the 'office-para' to explain how colonial time-discipline invaded and reshaped everyday spaces in colonial Calcutta—festivals, he argued, marked a temporary suspension of this discipline. Adding to Guha's work, I argue that paras provided a productive space for nationalists to launch a ground-level movement against the British; they exploited the kinship-like ties between neighbours to craft a Hindu-Bengali nation. In the nineteenth century, paras were organized along lines of caste and religion, but they were not exclusionary. The exclusionary practices of the para stemmed from it being an ideational space innately linked to the urban, upper-caste, Hindu-Bengali identity in the twentieth century. A heavy politicization of the paras took shape in the wake of Swarajist municipal rule in the city. The Swarajists targeted the para, co-opting these spaces as the spatial unit of a Hindu-Bengali nation.

Samaj, Para, and Kinship

In sixteenth-century Bengal, a Brahmin scholar named Panchanan Ganguly received a *jagir*, a land grant, from the Mughal emperor Akbar. He decided to build a new *samaj*.[23] In those days, samajes, Hindu spatial communities, were common in Bengal. They took shape as an upper-caste response to the long period of Muslim rule in the region. As early as the thirteenth century, the Delhi Sultanate—Muslim rulers who came to India from Central Asia—

ruled over the northern parts of the subcontinent. After a brief interval when less-powerful overlords, both Muslims and Hindus, ruled the region, the Mughals—another Muslim dynasty from Central Asia—gained control over Bengal. Starting in the sixteenth century, the Mughals ruled over northern India for three hundred years. This Muslim dominance caused Hindus to worry about their religion and property. They feared that as Muslims became more powerful, they would force Hindus to convert to Islam and seize their property, as well. Faced with these fears, the upper castes formed samajes or sovereign communities to live together, practise their religion, and protect their properties.[24]

Samajes had a distinct spatial arrangement based on the caste of the settlers. A samaj usually took shape when a member of the upper caste received a jagir from the Muslim ruler. First, they built their houses and administrative offices at the centre of the property. They then distributed the remaining plots to arriving settlers according to their castes. Caste moulded the space of the samaj, shaping what became paras or neighbourhoods where families of the same caste lived together—the upper castes lived at the centre of the samaj, the other castes lived in paras surrounding them.[25]

When Panchanan Ganguly received his jagir, for instance, his first move was to invite Yajurveda Brahmins (Bhattacharyas) to live at the centre of his plot. He built schools where the Bhattacharyas instructed Hindu boys in reading scriptures. The neighbourhood where the Bhattacharyas lived was named after them as Bhat-para. When young Hindu boys (*kumars*) started attending the schools, the vicinity of the school came to be known as Kumar-para. Ganguly distributed land to the different service classes to enable them to live nearby and make the paras self-sufficient: fishermen (*jeley*) lived in Jeley-para and the milk sellers (*goyals*) lived in the Goyal-para.[26] Other worker paras, the Muchi-para (shoemaker neighbourhood), the Dhali-para (guard neighbourhood), the Das-para (domestic help neighbourhood), the Kumor-para (sculptor neighbourhood), and the Duley-para (palanquin-bearer neighbourhood) formed tightly held skeins surrounding the Bhat-para.

Samajes resembled small, self-contained villages where upper caste houses and *cutcherries* (offices to collect revenues) formed the nucleus of a network of caste-based paras. In 1608, when Panchanan Ganguly's grandson Lakshmikanta received a jagir of eight villages from the Mughal emperor Jahangir, he also decided to build a samaj on this land.[27] He lived in the village of Halisahar but built his cutcherry in one of the eight villages he received as jagir. The area near the cutcherry came to be known as Sabarna-para after

A City-Nation 113

his Sabarna-Brahmin caste. He distributed the land near the cutcherry to his sons-in-law, who were all *kulin* (a sub-caste of Brahmins). This shaped the Kulin-para. As his grandfather had, he allotted land to the service classes near the Kulin-para, shaping Muchi-para, Kumor-para, and the Duley-para, thus bringing together Hindus as self-sufficient spatial communities within the broad framework of Muslim rule.[28]

Writing about samajes, historian S. N. Mukherjee explained that these rural social formations did not continue in the colonial city. According to Mukherjee, samajes were usually under the control of a single leader and largely dependent on the discretion of that leader.[29] The new colonial laws, and the lack of caste laws, made such individual, discretion-based rule impossible in the city. Mukherjee described that *dal*s, groups of influential Hindu men led by merchants, replaced samajes in Calcutta; dals preserved the caste practices of their members. Multiple dals often competed with each other to gain influence in the city.

I argue that a closer look at everyday urban life in the paras can tell us a different story of the samaj. Colonial laws failed to transform the samaj; British law courts could not dismiss the merchant's kingly status or the role of religion in governing space. For that reason, paras organized along kinship-like ties continued to resist colonial town planning, just as they had previously resisted potential interference by Muslim rulers.

Yet paras were not everyday spaces in the sense Michel De Certeau uses the term. According to De Certeau, everyday acts like walking, talking, reading, and so on empower individuals to reclaim autonomy from established rules.[30] Paras certainly demonstrate a form of everydayness in planning that have roots in the daily acts of individuals; they resist the more formal plans of the state. Given the colonial history of Bengal, paras, nevertheless, served to extend the influence of certain social groups over the others. I argue that starting in the late sixteenth century, when the earliest paras took shape, these assisted upper-caste Hindus to exert their influence over Bengal. By the late nineteenth century, anti-colonial nationalists employed Hindu religion to mark their difference from the British—they spatialized their discourses by appropriating paras as spatial units of the Hindu nation.

Hindu Merchants, Their *Danas*, and Early Paras

When the merchants of the East India Company first reached Bengal in the seventeenth century, they described the banks of the river Hooghly as 'marshy, forested terrains, infested with wild animals'.[31] This description, however, was far from true. French, Dutch, and Portuguese merchants had earlier established trade networks in Bengal; overseas and inland trade had moulded the river banks, shaping new settlements and markets. The earliest settlers on the riverbanks were the agrarian and fishing communities.[32] Their boats travelled up the tidal creeks and the many tributaries of the river up to its estuary. The lively port of Satgaon stood here, connecting the region with the networks of global trade.

Portuguese traders in the early seventeenth century reached the riverbank and took part in an active trade in muslin, sugar, and rice with the Indians. Their trade 'filled the bazaars with the hum of men and the rivers with their boats'.[33] This trade did not continue for long. Silt accumulated at the mouth of the Hooghly and the harbours declined. With the river changing its course, the Indian merchants moved downstream. They established a new *haat*—a seasonal market—that became famous as the Sutanuti haat (market for cotton bale). As the haat expanded, the Indian merchants established new samajes near it. When the British merchants arrived, they settled immediately below the Sutanuti haat. In 1757, they defeated the Bengal Nawab at the Battle of Plassey, officially inaugurating British colonialism in India.

The British reordered the spaces along the river bank, transforming villages into a colonial city that facilitated both trade and government. Standing on the banks of the river Hooghly, Fort William housed the British military, while also segregating the region into racial enclaves with separate black and white towns. The Indians lived to the north of the fort in the black town, the British to the south in the white town. Wide streets and spacious bungalows in the white town displayed a British spatial knowledge that was markedly different from Indian knowledge of space. The Indians built houses with little space between them in order to minimize the afternoon sun. They built streets with corners where neighbours could congregate for idle conversations. As discussed in Chapter 1, the British described the closely built houses and crowded streets as pre-modern spaces and took up the work of building colonial cities as part of their goal of modernizing Indians.

British colonial cities were tools of exploitation that reinforced ideas of racial superiority while clearing the way for Anglo-Indian trade. The British built these cities by decimating and displacing the local population and reordering existing spaces to fit a model of what Anthony D. King has called 'culture-contact situations' that justified their presence in the colonies.[34] Culture-contact projected the British technological society as modern and superior to the Indian traditional, craft-based society. The colonial city

A City-Nation

demonstrated this difference spatially, with the white town representing the space of technology and the black town embodying the pre-modern, craft-based, agrarian community that the British understood as needing to change. But at the same time, the culture-contact situation could not be strictly enforced because markets and trade required passages between white and black towns. These passages shaped urban modernity in the colonial city into a series of negotiations between individuals, communities, the state, and the ideational and physical space in which norms of private and public were reworked and modern subjects produced.[35] The para was not a formal, administrative category. Nor did colonial town planning impact it in a direct way. Yet its spaces were informed by a series of negotiations that took shape in the minds of Bengalis and centred around questions of Indian and British visions of space.

The Indian vision of space blurred the line between public and private space in the paras. A painting of a Hindu temple and neighbouring huts by the British officer Charles D'Oyly (Figure 3.1) shows the unique arrangement of huts and streets that rejected the borders between the public space of the street and the domestic, private space of the family. The household life of the hut dwellers can be seen spilling into the streets, filling its spaces with people and animals.

Figure 3.1 Hindoo *mutt* (temple) in the Chitpore Bazaar. Sir Charles D'Oyly's twenty-eight 'Views of Calcutta and its Environs' [Object no. R2566-24].

Source: Victoria Memorial Hall Archives, Kolkata. By kind permission of the Trustees of Victoria Memorial Hall, Kolkata.

Hindu traders who took part in cotton trade with the British shaped the first paras of Calcutta. They moved from their villages in the region to settle near new markets that came up by the river Hooghly. While settling near the Hooghly, memories of their villages were still fresh in their minds. They established new samajes on the banks of the river to preserve the social space of their villages in the new geography. The spatial configuration of the samajes imparted a sense of familiarity and helped to build communities in an otherwise unfamiliar land. The paras that the merchants shaped resembled rural spaces; these were a mix of brick buildings and huts separated by temples, water tanks, blooming hedges, cattle sheds, coconut trees, and green fields. Trees shaded the paras. Neighbours sat in the shade of the trees, engrossed in hour-long, casual conversations (*addas*) that shaped their kinship-like ties.

Both upper- and lower-caste merchants took part in trade, but only the upper castes such as the Setts and the Basacks engaged in long-distance trade.[36] They dominated the Sutanuti haat and shaped some of the earliest samajes near it. Their first act was to clear land and erect a temple to the Hindu god Kali.[37] They then invited the *sebayat*s, Brahmin worshippers of Kali, to live near the temple. The houses of the sebayats formed the nucleus of a new samaj. The merchants distributed the rest of the land to settlers according to their castes. The caste-based distribution of land configured paras that resembled neighbourhoods in the villages of Bengal.

This unique caste-based spatial orientation of the para was also central to mixed practices of production and consumption that sustained the colonial city. Upper-caste merchants established *karkhana*s or workshops near the haats to supply the British with cotton yarn. The Setts, for instance, helped two thousand weavers settle near the Sutanuti haat, offered them *dadan* (advances), and established a karkhana for the yarn.[38] On the one hand, karkhanas divided artisans according to specialized skills that turned them into wage labourers.[39] On the other hand, the service classes who lived close by served the samaj and the merchants' gardens supplied the haats, shaping a subsistence mode of production and consumption in the samaj. The haats met under trees in open fields near the merchant's house or administrative offices. Fishermen and vegetable sellers sat with their wares spread in front of them.[40] The mixed economy challenged the transformative potential of Anglo-Indian trade by assisting both traditional (subsistence) and British mercantile interests to coevolve.

Although a mixed economy secured the merchants' hold over the samaj, they explained their power as divinely ordained, their status quasi-kingly. According

A City-Nation

to Kiranchandra Datta, author of the most detailed history of Baghbazaar, a bustling part of Calcutta, the region was 'as Hindu as possible'.[41] In 1830, a wealthy merchant, Shankar Ghosh, who lived in the area erected a temple to the goddess Kali near his house. In the eastern wing of the temple, he engraved a tablet that read *Shankarer hridoy majhe, Kali biraje*, or Kali dwells in the heart of Shankara,[42] alluding both to his own name as well as to Lord Shiva, also known as Shankara, to whom Kali was betrothed. The temple of Gokul Mitra was nearby. Like Shankar Ghosh, he was a rich merchant who had built an architecturally magnificent temple. On full moon nights, he invited Brahmins to lead prayers at this temple.

As Hindu leaders, the merchants engaged in city-building as a form of *dana* or gift to the Hindu community. In Sanskrit, dana means gift, but implies much more than a simple gift: dana is a religious duty. Hindu scriptures like the *Rig Veda* describe dana as an act of gift-giving to a community without expectation of reciprocity. For an ordinary person, the practice of dana promises a better afterlife. For kings, it reinforces their royal stature. Danas attest to kingly status by demonstrating both generosity and devoutness. Legends about successful Hindu kings, such as Samudragupta and Chandragupta II, describe their generous danas at length.

The danas of Hindu merchants marked the city with religious architecture that stood freely alongside the secular. They built roads, dispensaries, and schools as their dana to the Hindu community.[43] Merchants like Nayan Chand Mullick and Baidya Nath Raj Bahadur earned the title *daanbir*, heroic gift-givers, when they built roads and dispensaries for the Hindu community.[44] Krishnaram Basu, a moneylender to the East India company, earned a similar title for building shelters for Hindu pilgrims. His sons carried on the family's tradition of dana, setting up dispensaries and schools in the samaj. The merchants also invested in sacred spaces, such as *ghat*s (bathing platforms). Ghats served as a site for religious festivals, where pilgrims assembled to take holy dips in the river. Hindus performed their last rites at the ghats. The ghats the merchants built were spacious, complete with changing rooms and shelters for pilgrims. Some merchants chose to spend the later days of their life at the ghats in the hope of a better afterlife.[45] When gold merchant Nilmani Mullick realized that his death was imminent, he requested his family to take him to a ghat, where he sat reciting Hindu scriptures and later distributed silver coins to the poor.

Similar to Calcutta, philanthropy drove the urbanization of colonial Bombay. Preeti Chopra in her detailed study of Bombay has explored urbanization as a joint enterprise or a partnership between the state, merchants, philanthropists, engineers, and craftsmen.[46] Chopra explains that the native elites—the wealthy merchant group of the Parsis—offered financial help to the British and also assisted them in implementing urban development projects. While working with the British, Indian craftsmen appropriated urban structures by inscribing their religious or cultural motifs on building designs. But as Chopra argues, Indian elites were partners of the British and they built the city jointly. Chopra's study focuses on the Parsi community that configured the city differently from how the Hindu-Bengali merchants of Calcutta acted. The Parsi merchants worked with the British to implement a colonial plan for Bombay. In sharp contrast, the Hindu-Bengali merchants engaged in city building to reinforce their kingly status and saw infrastructure as their gift to the Hindu community.

In 1904, a certain Siddha Mohan Mitra authored a historical work on philanthropy that explained how Hinduism required a king to care for the poorer masses. They had to maintain *annachattras* (or *chattras*), public kitchens that distributed rice to the poor.[47] According to Mitra, there were no Western-style workhouses for charity in India.[48] It was part of the king's religious duty or *dana* to provide the poor with food and clothes. The merchants maintained chattras for distributing rice and clothes. Their generous dana in running these chattras elevated them to the rank of kings and commanded the respect of the people.

A variant of the chattra was the *atithisala* (boarding house), which the merchants built with the temples they erected. Atithisalas housed pilgrims and poor Hindus. The *sadabrata* was a similar place, a special type of atithisala in which merchants assigned the poor to cooking stalls and provided them fresh ingredients and utensils to prepare food.[49] Makeshift chattras on the days of festivals were common. On days reserved for the public recitals of Hindu texts like *Astadash Maha Puran*, for example, the merchants ran chattras that distributed food, clothes, shawls, pearls, necklaces, and silver dishes to Brahmins and Hindu indigents.[50]

The merchants employed Hindu religion to design public spaces in the para and also shape a caste-based government in the samaj. This comes alive in the memoir of wealthy trader Moti Lal Seal, who wrote that the prejudices of the British courts and their indifference to caste had forced him to maintain his own court and private army.[51] Like Seal, merchants across Calcutta maintained independent courts of law and private armies. These *jatimala* cutcherries (courts) resolved disputes by taking into consideration the religion, caste, and social standing of the petitioners.[52] They were held in the outer wing of the merchant's house along with the other offices, the *azbegi daftar* (petition

A City-Nation

collecting office), the *munshi daftar* (office of the secretary), and the *mal adalat* (financial office).[53] The merchants also maintained private armies comprising *lathials* (club men), who wielded the *lathi* (club) to settle property disputes and discipline rent defaulters, and through it brought to force a new mechanism of resolving conflicts, independent of the state and its law courts.

Acts of philanthropy and religious devotion culminated in the grand celebrations of the Durga Puja at the merchant's home. On the days of the Puja, the merchants arranged for lavish rituals that placed their wealth on display. As Rachel McDermott explains, the expensive celebrations of Durga Puja were tied to the merchants' thirst for status, and in that sense the displays can be connected to Bourdieu's social capital or capital that ensures social prestige.[54] Writing in 1845, the Reverend Alexander Duff described Durga Puja festivities at the home of a Bengali merchant: 'on one side [of a quadrangle] was a spacious hall, opening along the ground floor, by many folding doors to piazzas and verandahs on either side. These are crowded by the more common sort of visitors'.[55] Coloured silk and paper, gold and silver tissue covered the walls of the house, and chandeliers radiated a flood of light that dazzled vision. Musicians and dancers, dressed in their finest regalia, roamed the piazzas performing for the spectators, who were also entertained with fresh fruits and sweetmeats.

One of the earliest Durga Pujas in Calcutta took place in the house of Nabakrishna Deb, who worked as a *munshi* (clerk) for the British East India Company. The Puja at his house was marked by an atmosphere of exchange. The British attended and took part in revelries. Musical performances, rituals, gift giving, and a grand feast complemented the strict worship of the idol; Deb offered several hundred pounds of rice as gifts to the deity and invited musicians and dancers to perform in spectacular rooms built for the occasion.[56] These grand displays of wealth tightened his control over the neighbourhood. On the days of the Puja, local invitees gathered at his house to take part in the rituals as a family. They sat together listening to music and watching dance performances. Deb's conspicuous expenditure engendered feelings of awe and respect in their minds. At the same time, day-long camaraderie strengthened kinship-like ties between neighbours.

The spectacle of Durga Puja at Deb's mansion set a precedent for similar Pujas in Calcutta. Accounts that survive of these Pujas point to massive wealth that the merchants displayed on the days of the Puja. One account explains that the gold merchant Dutts scrubbed their palace floors with rose water on the days of worship.[57] Yet another describe that they dressed in muslin and smoked hookahs studded with diamonds, emeralds, and pearls. At night, they sacrificed hundreds of buffaloes, goats, pumpkin, sugarcane, betel nut, and fish and offered these to the deity. Although the exact amount that the merchants expended for the Puja cannot be verified, repeated assertions of wealth demonstrate that the displays of affluence were an essential part of the Puja.

Spectacular celebrations of Durga Puja at the merchants' residences, scholars have argued, displayed the growing Anglo-Indian collaboration symptomatic of colonialism. The Indian merchant is at the heart of scholarship describing colonialism as a collaboration between Indian and European mercantile interests.[58] As agents of indigenous capital, their financial ties with the British steered the subcontinent's transition to early capitalism. Economic processes that empowered the Indian merchant also helped the British East India Company graft itself onto Indian society. Meanwhile, British–Indian financial ties have led scholars to revisit relations between the Indian merchants and rulers. C. A. Bayly, for instance, has argued that the British exploited the relations of the weak merchant-princes to appropriate political power.[59] In a more recent study, Lakshmi Subramanian has described how rival power blocs built up in western India, with the Mughals, the Marathas, and the British each trying to secure better trading rights for their brokers.[60] In this struggle, the collaboration between the Indian and British merchants helped the Company to secure an edge over rival claimants.

The grand celebrations of Durga Puja at the merchant residence, however, point to a splintering of the merchant's economic and political ambitions. The strict observance of Hindu rituals at the Puja is evidence that it was not necessarily Anglo-Indian economic partnership that paved the way for British political hegemony. Rather, ritual performances pointed to the deep Hindu foundations of Indian society recasting Indian merchants as leaders of Hindu communities that the British could never govern. The merchants used the returns of their trade with the British to meet the expenses of the Puja. To describe the Puja solely as Indians 'hobnobbing with the British'[61] is to tell only part of the story. The problem with such an argument lies in the fact that these overlook the role that the Puja itself played in displaying the idea of Indian difference and how it reinforced the merchants' perceived role as Hindu kings.

Durga Puja at *zamindar* Govindram Mitter's house, for instance, followed strict Shastric rituals. He attached gold leaves to the body of the idol, placed it on a silver throne called a *merr*, and offered *nyvedya* (offerings to the God) in large brazen vessels, the largest of which contained fifty *maunds* (four thousand pounds) of rice.[62] On the ninth day of Puja, which coincided with a full moon, he distributed clothes, silver coins, and food to a thousand Brahmins. These

A City-Nation

121

rituals did not simply display his wealth but portrayed Mitter as a pious leader of a Hindu community. Shastric rituals at the Puja conveyed to the British the Hindu identities of merchants and the deep religious roots of their society.

Occasionally, decors at the Puja did display British cultural motifs that celebrated the Queen of England. Models of equestrian Scot Highlanders, fairies, birds, flowers, and lotuses made of pith at times formed the backdrop of the idol.[63] Paintings of gown-clad fairies playing the trumpet and bearing flags and insignias of the British Empire adorned the podium on which the idol was placed. Replicas of the Queen's unicorn and the royal crest were also put on display; these adaptations, however, had very little to suggest that the merchants desired anything more than to include British political symbols at the Puja for purposes of trade. The decors bear no evidence that the merchants were paving the road for British colonial rule.

Although performed as a Hindu festival, the merchants encouraged creative cultural exchanges on the days of the Puja. They invited *baijies*—female Muslim musicians—to perform at the Puja. Nurbaks, Ilhajan Banu, and Zinat came from Lucknow to perform at the merchants' mansions.[64] For these performances, the merchants erected special dance halls and decorated podiums with gold and silver. In 1832, a landlord from a village near Calcutta was caught up in work in the city and arranged for the Puja there. On the final day of the Puja, he organized a dance performance of the baijies on a boat on the river Ganges. He wrote back home that such performances were common in the city and that the Puja was considered incomplete without these.[65]

A painting by Russian artist Alexis Soltykoff (Figure 3.2), shows a panoply of performers at the merchant's house on the days of Durga Puja.

Muslim women dancers, indicated by their dress, can be seen standing at the centre with male musicians. Brahmins sit on the floor. Standing by them are performers dressed in costumes for plays. The idol of Durga is in the backdrop. The room has impressive chandeliers and expensive drapery. We can see the British attending the Puja with their families. Everyone stands in close proximity—the British, the Indian merchants, Muslim women, and the Brahmins—in what appears to be an inclusive celebration of the Puja.

Almost a hundred years later, Durga Puja celebrations changed in significant ways. The merchants still arranged for the Puja, but the most popular Pujas in the city had become sarbojonin or public worship celebrations that neighbourhood clubs organized in their paras. The Puja stopped being a creative exchange between diverse communities. The clubs censored performances by Muslim women, describing them as obscene. They also stopped inviting the British to their Puja.[66] In its place, the clubs encouraged demonstrations of muscular strength and other cultural performances that celebrated a bourgeoning Hindu-Bengali nation. In addition, the Puja no longer displayed wealth. Instead, it was celebrated in democratic ways where the para paid chanda to meet expenses.

Figure 3.2 Europeans visiting a princely home in Calcutta to witness Durga Puja. A painting by Alexis Soltykoff (1859).

Source: Catalogue of the exhibit 'Puja and Piety: Hindu, Jain, and Buddhist Art from the Indian Subcontinent' by Susan S. Tai in collaboration with Pratapaditya Pal, Santa Barbara Museum of Art, 17 April–31 July 2016.

The transitions in the celebrations of Durga Puja, I argue, was an outcome of growing cultural nationalism in late nineteenth-century Calcutta. These sentiments were spearheaded by a new group of urban Bengali men, the bhadraloks born out of British economic and cultural imperialism. By the late nineteenth century, colonial import duties and tax policies threatened Indian merchants with impoverishment. Trade was no longer the route to upward mobility in Calcutta; instead, an English education and government job helped individuals to lead respectable lives.[67] The British introduced English education in India in 1835. The Bengali men who received this education secured salaried jobs in government offices. They constituted a new group of urban, professional men: the bhadraloks, who staffed British offices. English education helped them to find jobs in British offices; discrimination at the workplace, however, soon produced discontent. While working for the government, bhadraloks emphasized their difference from the British and crafted a language of anti-

A City-Nation

colonial nationalism that was deeply spiritual. They employed the language of religion, Hinduism, to explain how they were different on a spiritual (inner) level.[68] In their discourse on difference, religion fuelled cultural nationalism and recast their identities primarily as Hindu and Bengali.

Armed with the new education, bhadraloks challenged the wealth-based authority of the merchants and the caste-based character of their para, calling for democratizing space. They soon replaced the merchants as leaders of their para. They worked with the Swarajists to engage in an urban management of space that became the basis of their new power in the city.

Exploring Swarajist municipal administration of Calcutta, the next sections question the everydayness of the para. I argue that in the colonial city, paras evaded British control, but this did not mean that they were beyond external control. The everyday in the colonial city, as Ranajit Guha observed, was truncated: while a part of it retained autonomy from colonial control, colonial discipline permeated and transformed the other half.[69] I argue that Swarajists preserved the freedom the para enjoyed from British control, but transformed its spaces into a microcosm of the city-nation.

Swaraj in Calcutta's Paras

> Human families grow in cities like plants in the tubs more or less isolated from the vital currents of the life of their neighbours.... (Bipin Chandra Pal)[70]

Bipin Chandra Pal, who taught at the University of Calcutta and later became an outspoken Swarajist, explained that city life was marked by social isolation. The spatial constitution of the city, unlike the village, he argued, did not help individuals to develop a consciousness of identification with the space they inhabited. In cities, families lived separate from their neighbours, indifferent to their joys and sorrows. The Swarajists in their municipal government drove to create attachments between city dwellers and city space.

Motilal Nehru and C. R. Das, members of the Indian National Congress, had established the Swaraj Party in 1923. A subsidiary of the Congress, the Swaraj Party believed in self-government. Though they accepted the entire programme of the Congress, the Swarajists added to it clauses regarding political freedom and increased representation of Indians at the legislative level. The founding of the Swaraj Party dovetailed with a mass nationalist movement led by the Congress, and which Mahatma Gandhi returned from South Africa to lead. He created the Non-Cooperation and Civil Disobedience movements, which called on Indians to abstain from all partnerships with the British.

As historian Sabyasachi Bhattacharya has described, Gandhi's movements were never entirely embraced in Bengal. Instead, Bengalis came up with several alternatives, from revolutionary nationalism to Left radicalism.[71] The Swarajists were part of this alternative milieu. While Gandhi proposed Non-Cooperation, the Swarajists pushed for the increased participation of Indians in municipal administration and legislative councils. They argued that instead of Non-Cooperation, active participation of Indians in colonial political and legislative structures could steer the country towards freedom.

While encouraging all city dwellers to participate in legislative and political assemblies, the Swarajists described the nation and nationalism in an overtly Hindu language. They borrowed from Hindu philosophy the concepts of *tamasik, rajasik,* and *sattwik,* the three attributes of human nature, to describe three different forms of nationalism.[72] Tamasik meant a destructive mode of existence; rajasik, an instinctive mode; and sattwik, the rational.

According to an employee of the Calcutta Municipal Corporation, B. C. Ghosh, these three modes of existence drove Indians to nationalist activism. Speaking for the Swarajists, he wrote in the *Calcutta Municipal Gazette,* a Swarajist organ, that tamasik activism resulted in the disruption of meetings, howling down of speakers, and the obstruction of the opposition. Rajasik activism, on the other hand, worked through petitions and policies that subordinated the interests of people to groups. Sattwik activism, which the Swarajists preferred, sought common purposes like religion for the just distribution of resources for the whole community or nation. The Swarajists openly endorsed sattwik nationalism, seeing in Hindu religion a common purpose that could bring together Indians. The nation, they imagined, was thus wholly Hindu.

In 1923, the Swarajists won the municipal elections in Calcutta. They formed a majority in the Calcutta Municipal Corporation, which oversaw city administration. The British had established this elected body in 1876 to supervise municipal administration in the city. In its earliest days, the Corporation was far from participatory. The British dominated its executive councils. With the Swarajist victory at the elections, British domination came to an end. The Swarajists inaugurated an era of municipal socialism articulated in a paternal language. They drew on the politics of Social Democrats in Red Vienna to describe the Calcutta Corporation as *pouropita,* the 'city father', responsible for educating and caring for the masses.[73] The Corporation officers pledged to offer free education, medical facilities, fitness programmes, and food and shelter for all city dwellers, particularly the poor.

A City-Nation

As pouropita, the Swarajists decided to build infrastructure to facilitate the civic uplift of the masses. They explained that civic uplift was possible only when city dwellers shared a civic consciousness.[74] They argued that individualistic lifestyles in the city prevented Calcuttans from developing a shared civic consciousness.[75] As described earlier, Bipin Chandra Pal had pointed to the social isolation of city dwellers and explained that only collective life of the villages could sustain a shared consciousness.[76] He wrote that city life contrasted with the strong emotional ties between people in the villages, where neighbours shared happiness and sorrow as a family. Social life in the villages took shape spontaneously through long associations, often continuing from the life of previous generations. In the city, individuals did not know each other and a shared consciousness was not natural—it had to be cultivated.

As pouropita, the Swarajists envisioned street-level institutes to include all city dwellers not simply as subjects to be educated in civic consciousness, but also as the medium in which to produce this consciousness. In such efforts, they practised what Radhakamal Mukerjee, a philosopher and historian, had earlier termed as 'civicization'.[77] In his much-celebrated thesis, *Principles of Comparative Economics*, Mukerjee had described an ideal city as a cluster of villages with goals different from that of the agrarian society. In a perfect city, he wrote, administration and procedure of rural self-government continued but with activities satisfying larger civic life and consciousness: a process he called civicization. He pointed to the paras, suggesting that these spaces could preserve certain structures of rural self-government in the city.

The Swarajists adopted from Mukerjee the idea of civicization, seeing paras as clusters of villages in the city. They worked with bhadraloks to exploit the kinship-like ties of the para to manufacture a national consciousness. Bhadraloks partnered with the Swarajists to lead public health campaigns that surpassed individual interests and instructed para dwellers to think about public good—as a nation—thereby transforming the para into a spatial unit of the nation. They conceived these health campaigns at their para clubs, a room in the neighbourhood, where they met in voluntary associations in the evenings.

Para clubs

Voluntary associations of bhadraloks from mid-nineteenth century onwards had crafted a deeply patriarchal public sphere in Calcutta. Christine Furedy has called these associations 'political clubs'.[78] Usually secular in nature, the clubs—literary societies, chambers of commerce, professional and trade associations—influenced municipal administration, particularly after the 1870s when municipal systems with elected representatives allowed participation of elite Indians and solicited the opinion of their clubs in crafting legislations. Furedy pointed out that the political clubs connected associational life with institutional development and through it connected ideology with action. The clubs that the bhadraloks established in their paras drew on the general atmosphere of associational life that configured urban politics in late nineteenth-century Calcutta.

At the heart of each para stood a club—the centre of the para's social and cultural life. A room in the para that a resident generously offered for free housed the club. Here, bhadraloks met after work to engage in lively discussions on literature and politics over tea. They also planned for cultural events: religious festivals, musical events, painting classes, and sports tournaments that brought neighbours together as a community. A library at the club doubled up as the office for the para's literary and cultural associations. Para theatre groups rehearsed at the club in the evenings. [79] Each para had its own football team that practised in open fields that bordered the club premises.[80]

The clubs shaped a public sphere that exteriorised sociability based on kinship, something usually associated with private, domestic spaces. This public sphere, however, was wholly exclusionary: women were not allowed to socialize at the clubs. [81] Bhadraloks condemned women loitering in public spaces as obscene and discouraged their presence at the clubs. The Four Arts club in south Calcutta had attempted a mixed coterie of friends, but the experiment was short-lived; the only exception was the Baikali club, where female members used to meet once a week in a clubroom for a couple of hours.[82]

Existing scholarship on civic associations in late nineteenth- and twentieth-century Calcutta has described at length the importance of English education in shaping the figure of the bhadraloks and their associations.[83] But absolutely no research exists on bhadralok work at the para clubs. This is surprising because bhadralok activism in Calcutta can hardly be understood without examining their work at the clubs—their addas, their involvement in cultural programmes, football matches, and Durga Puja festivals made clubs into the wellspring of Bengali culture. At the same time, bhadraloks took pride in their clean bodies and spotless houses to emerge as supervisors of hygiene at the clubs, a position that elevated them to the ranks of city leaders.

Bhadralok supervision of their paras introduced new ideas of hygiene that they themselves developed. They drew on Hindu scriptures to shape hygiene as

A City-Nation

a form of bodily comportment and a technology of self that shaped a profoundly spatial urban subjectivity. This new language of hygiene led bhadraloks to craft physical routines that included new standards of fitness, diet, nutrition, and conduct. They instructed their neighbours to follow this routine as informed members of a Hindu city and nation.

Hygiene served as the tool that drove the transformation from merchant-led paras to the government of the bhadraloks. While both merchants and bhadraloks tried to preserve a Hindu community, their methods and scope were widely different from each other. For instance, merchants believed that infrastructure was a gift, an act of philanthropy that reinforced their roles as Hindu kings. In contrast, bhadralok focus was more on shaping social perceptions of how spaces and bodies should appear. They borrowed from the Western notions of hygiene that was rooted in racist dichotomies of 'dirty natives' and 'clean colonizers' and conflated it with Hindu imperatives of a nationalist state to shape principles of modern Hindu hygiene. This new language of hygiene targeted both bodies and spaces, tightening bhadralok hold over their paras.

Hygiene also served as the meeting ground between bhadralok sanitarians and the Swarajists. The Swarajists employed hygiene to create a new language of public health that effectively transcended the interests of individuals and groups and became a civic concern shared by all.[84] They encouraged bhadraloks to take charge of their paras and instruct their neighbours in this new language of hygiene. Clubs worked as street-level institutes that led sanitation campaigns in the paras facilitating Swarajist political-scientific control of space and intertwining questions of spatiality with the surveillance of populations. In other words, the clubs initiated health programmes to train city dwellers in conduct fit for the city and Hindu nation. They engaged the neighbours in raising civic awareness by recruiting the para youth and sending out enthusiastic volunteers to advise people on the importance of clean spaces and bodies.

Para health associations

On a Sunday morning in March 1926, a para in north Calcutta woke up to the songs of the local theatre group. The group performed a *prabhat feri* (morning procession), singing songs as they walked the streets of the para.[85] They had written these songs for the first anniversary of the para's health association. The neighbours joined the group's procession, walking the streets in the scorching sun. As they played the *khol* (percussion) and *kartal* (cymbals) to raise sanitary awareness in the para, the procession looked more and more like a religious parade.[86]

Within a year of their victory in the municipal elections, the Swarajists divided the city into 'blocks' and assigned one health association for each block. The blocks covered one or more paras. The health associations worked closely with para clubs, carrying out routine health check-ups and administering vaccines. Each health association had a medical officer, appointed by the Swarajists, and locally enrolled health workers who were *sevak*s (volunteers).

Bhadraloks assisted the local health associations by offering rooms in their houses and additional space to set up clinics. They also worked directly with the association as sevaks.[87] As sevaks, they surveyed the para, inspected its houses, and reported the health conditions of its residents to the medical officer. As representatives of the health association, bhadraloks explained the benefits of good health, helping indigent patients to adopt sanitary measures, and carried ailing patients to hospitals.[88]

For the British, hygiene was an individual practice tied to rational thought. Bhadralok urbanists borrowed the concept of hygiene from the British but departed from the belief that hygiene was an individual practice. In its place, they explained hygiene as a community virtue: a national duty that qualified individuals as members of a collective, that is, a nation. Their campaigns appealed to para dwellers to maintain clean spaces—not simply to improve their personal health but also as a way to express their religion and caste identities as members of an emerging nation.

One of the earliest projects the bhadraloks carried out as health association sevaks was to resolve the long-unsettled dustbin dispute. In the 1880s, the Corporation had assigned three dustbins for each municipal subdivision of the city and placed these bins at the doorsteps of Indian houses.[89] This inconvenienced the Bengalis, particularly the upper castes. They were repelled by the communal use of the bins that individuals belonging to different caste and religion used to dump refuse. The refuse piled up during the day and municipal carts took it away the next morning. Given the communal use of the bins, the upper castes had to wash themselves every time they walked past these bins. They had earlier written to the Corporation to remove the bins from their doorsteps. The Corporation had refused to reply. As sevaks, the bhadraloks stressed the importance of caste in ordering space in Bengali neighbourhoods. Describing the bins as a threat to their caste practices, they

A City-Nation 129

recruited the para's youth to move the bins. They described moving the bins as a 'national duty' linked to the rights of all citizens to exercise their caste choices. Repositioning the bins from the doorsteps, they placed it on the street-sides.

As sevaks, the bhadraloks constituted health promotion societies that advanced ideas of Hindu hygiene in the paras. In April 1926, a neighbourhood health promotion society, Svasthya Vikash Samiti in Manicktola, worked with the health association to deliver lectures on hygiene. A schoolteacher who lived in the para recited passages from Hindu scriptures to inaugurate the event. [90] The sevaks delivered lectures that drew on Hindu scriptures to set new standards of hygiene. In the evening, the society led a procession that sang songs to celebrate hygiene as a Hindu value. The sevaks spent hours expostulating, arguing, and persuading the residents to follow Hindu diets and partake in a Hindu fitness programme.

The Swarajist Corporation assisted bhadraloks with the health promotion events they organized in their para. In February 1930, vaccination superintendents of the Corporation delivered lectures on smallpox at the health exhibition that the sevaks arranged on Sukeas Street.[91] At the health exhibition in Entally, Corporation health officers delivered lectures on nutrition that schooled the para's residents in diets prescribed by the Shastras.[92] But were all residents of paras where the health associations advanced ideas of Hindu hygiene Hindus? Street directories of Calcutta reveal a different reality. A street directory published in 1915 shows that most paras were ethnically diverse. The religion and caste composition of residents of Manicktola, where Svasthya Vikash Samiti was headquartered, and Entally, where health officers instructed residents in the Shastras, were rather mixed.

Boxes 3.1, 3.2, and 3.3 show that in Manicktola and Entally, Hindu, Muslim, and Christian houses bordered each other. In Shombhubabur Lane, a bustling part of Entally (Box 3.2), Christian neighbours DeCosta, Currie, and Victor lived by the house of Warisali Ahmed Hossain, a Muslim. A mosque bordered the house of Hossain beside which lived two Hindu neighbours. In Chattubabu Lane and Simla Road, shops and mosques stood near Hindu and Muslim houses. In addition, 'bustees', or huts leased at cheaper rents, adjoined middle class houses making the paras mixed class. Although paras were ethnically diverse, Hindu bhadraloks working as sevaks for health associations believed their neighbourhoods were Hindu. They trained their neighbours in practices of Hindu hygiene, forcing Hindus and non-Hindus to follow its standards.

Box 3.1 A neighbourhood in Simla Road, Manicktola.

Manicktola (Simla Road)

Motilal Seal, Purnachandra Bagh, Prasanna Kumar Santra lived at house number 135; Adwitoocharan Das and Nandalal Das lived at house numbers 136 and 137, a Muslim washerman lived at house number 138, a mosque stood at 139, **bustees** covered plots 140-146, Baikunthanath Ghosh lived at house number 147.

Source: Compiled by the author from Jayanta Bagchi, *Kolikata Street Directory, 1915*, ed. Samik Bandyopadhyay and Debasis Bose (Calcutta: P. M. Bagchi and Company Private Limited, 2017).

Box 3.2 A neighbourhood in Shombhubabur Lane, Entally.

Entally (Shombhubabur Lane)

F. W. and A. W. DeCosta lived at house number 21, M. Currie and E. A. Victor lived at house number 22, Munshi Warisali Ahmed Hossain lived at house number 23, Munshi Ahmed Hossain lived at house number 23/1, a Mosque stood beside this house, Ramrakhal and Shahsibhushan Ghosh lived at house number 24.

Source: Compiled by the author from Jayanta Bagchi, *Kolikata Street Directory, 1915*, ed. Samik Bandyopadhyay and Debasis Bose (Calcutta: P. M. Bagchi and Company Private Limited, 2017).

Box 3.3 A neighbourhood in Chattubabu Lane, Entally.

Entally (Chattubabu lane)

Shops and **bustees** stood on plot number 53, a Bihari mess stood on plot 54, Abhiram Datta lived at house number 55, Harimohan Mitra lived at house number 56, Abinash Chandra Nag lived at house number 57, Ananda Chandra Kundu lived at house number 58, **Bustees** occupied plots 59 and 60, Ramlal Das lived at house number 61, H. G. Woodward lived at house number 62, a School stood at plot 63, Majed Ali lived at house number 63/1.

Source: Compiled by the author from Jayanta Bagchi, *Kolikata Street Directory, 1915*, ed. Samik Bandyopadhyay and Debasis Bose (Calcutta: P. M. Bagchi and Company Private Limited, 2017).

The health sevaks' argument that hygiene was a duty of all Hindus, however, did not go uncontested. In some paras, residents challenged the sevaks. In 1926, when sevaks in south Calcutta launched an anti-cholera campaign, encouraging their neighbours to undergo inoculation as their national duty as sensible Hindus, the residents resisted. While the eastern half of the para agreed to vaccination, the western half did not. Unable to convince them, the health association sent inoculators to their houses. Scared of the inoculators, a crowd became violent, burning cars and attacking medical officers. Nonetheless, the sevaks carried on with their health campaign. They made further arguments that not only the neighbourhood was unclean but the cholera epidemic had

A City-Nation

shown that Indians had strikingly low levels of fitness. This observation led to a gradual modal shift that moved the locus of bhadralok intervention from the spaces of the para to bodies within the para.

An anti-spitting campaign followed the anti-cholera push; it was one of the earliest Swarajist urban improvement initiatives that manifested as interventions in conduct. An anti-spitting pamphlet published by the Swarajists in 1930 described 'cleanliness means control' (Figure 3.3). Spitting was a common practice among Bengalis. Although they understood cleanliness as keeping their houses clean, they did not extend the same interest to the space outside. Being under municipal jurisdiction, they believed that the space outside and its cleanliness depended on municipal authorities.[93] The pamphlet had little on the need to maintain clean public spaces for reasons of good hygiene. Instead, it advanced ideas of self-control. It described how Bengalis could cultivate habits of self-control by regulating their practices of spitting, sneezing, and coughing in public spaces. The emphasis on self-control in the pamphlet was part of the broader plea that the bhadraloks made to neighbourhood residents asking them to behave as informed members of an emergent Hindu-Bengali nation.

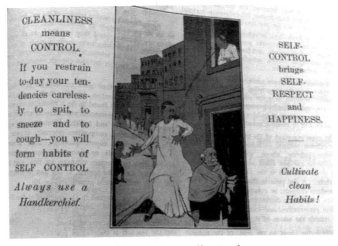

Figure 3.3 Swarajist pamphlet on cleanliness as self-control.
Source: Calcutta Municipal Gazette, 1931. Courtesy of Kolkata Town Hall Archives.

The anti-spitting campaign made urbanism as much a *bodily* intervention as it was *spatial*. Urbanism—commonly understood as the theory and practice of the built urban environment—now became a series of spatial shifts effected through interventions in conduct. Advising their neighbours to display self-control and not spit on the streets, the bhadraloks transformed Bengali bodies into a politicized terrain around which the nation derived a sense of symbolic unity. The discipline acted on and reflected by the Bengalis in displaying self-control and cleanliness carried with them symbolic gestures that were part of the Hindu discipline that bhadraloks envisioned for the city. This discipline was similar to a new brand of nationalism that emphasized physical culture and took shape in sports and wrestling matches throughout northern India. In this new physical culture, the body as a physical reality interacted with the body as a symbol.[94] Bhadraloks led fitness exercises in neighbourhood parks that functioned as what Norbert Elias has described as 'civilizing processes' that marked a reduction in the use of overt physical force and, instead, increased the intensity of self-control: a process that transformed regulation from something that was controlled by others to something individuals controlled themselves.[95]

The final decades of the nineteenth century witnessed a growth in fitness programmes across India. Indians focused on body-building exercises and fitness routines to challenge colonial accusations of Indian effeminacy.[96] *Akharas* (gymnasiums) in northern India trained Indian men in both bodily and moral fitness, developing a certain brand of somatic or bodily nationalism.[97] These centres multiplied with anti-colonial nationalists conceiving ideas of a Hindu nation built by strong Hindu bodies.[98] The wave of physical training exercises also reached Bengal, a region that had long been at the centre of colonial arguments about Indian male effeminacy.[99] Apart from a few works, historians have not explored the history of physical culture and its impact on the crafting of a regional Bengali identity.[100] The following section will trace fitness exercises and scout training programmes that bhadraloks led in their paras to instruct neighbours in bodily standards fit for a Hindu-Bengali nation.

Playground movement: Balak Sangha and Tarun Sangha

Borrowing from the American playground movement, the Swarajists commissioned a special playground committee to advise them on how parks could improve the physical health of the nation. A playground movement had emerged in the United States in 1890 when civic groups opened play lots as breathing grounds in dense housing areas. They urged municipal governments to build playgrounds where children and youth could play in controlled conditions.[101] They explained that supervised play could improve children's mental and physical well-being. By the early twentieth century, these

A City-Nation

groups expanded the movement to include adults. Municipality-controlled parks and playgrounds started to include play leaders and special facilities like gymnasiums and fieldhouses to train adults in physical fitness.

In a similar way, the Swarajist committee on playgrounds suggested creating a position for a games director who could build informal play spaces in the parks and fill these with recreational equipment like swings, see-saw, and merry-go-rounds. The Calcutta Municipal Corporation invested large sums of money to purchase the equipment. A newly hired games director further advised the Corporation on playgrounds that inculcated moral discipline.[102] He explained that young boys spent time after school loitering aimlessly in their para. Not having much to do, they took to petty crime. He believed that parks could solve this problem by attracting the youth and keeping them busy with sports.

In July 1925, a certain S. K. Kar who worked for the Calcutta Corporation was on a leave of absence from his work. He spent most of his time at a small park near his home. In the evenings, he noticed that the para's older boys had a hold over its spaces.[103] They scared away the younger boys and used the park for games like cricket and football. The younger boys spent most of their time at home. Kar grew concerned about their health and happiness. To attract the boys back to the park, he arranged for sports tournaments on Sunday afternoons. When the number of young boys attending the tournaments increased from four to twenty, Kar decided to expand his small enterprise into a full-fledged institute for physical development. He consulted the other bhadraloks of the para and together they wrote to the Swarajist Corporation, asking for help in transforming the playground into a training ground for young boys of his para.

The Corporation—itself engaged in opening playgrounds—agreed to Kar's proposal of transforming the neighbourhood park into a training ground. With financial support from the Swarajists, Kar established Balak Sangha (Children's Club), a free club to train the para's boys in fitness routines. In Sanskrit, *sangha* means a community where members engage in fitness exercises (yoga) together. Similarly, the Balak Sangha instructed local youths in group fitness exercises with the goal of reinforcing their sense of community.

Every morning, the Sangha trained the youth in drills that taught them rapid body movements.[104] Fitness exercises instructed the boys in methodical habits, good manners, punctuality, cleanliness, truthfulness, regularity, and obedience. Free hand drills, pyramid drills, and relay races improved their hand–eye coordination and instructed them to quickly follow orders as a group (Figure 3.4). Additionally, the Sangha trained them in *lathi khela* (game of staves), a sport usually associated with Hindus.[105]

Figure 3.4 The Balak Sangha boys practising drills in a park in Calcutta.

Source: *Calcutta Municipal Gazette,* September 1927. Courtesy of General Research Division, NYPL, New York.

As a community, the Sangha represented a microcosm of the Hindu nation. It was internally divided into the ranks of *sathi, shir, sirdar, nayak,* and *pratinidhi*—ranks of Hindu chiefs. From among the boys, the Sangha selected a leader to discipline the other boys. The leader recorded the conduct of the group and later submitted the report to the secretary of the Sangha. Following the leader, the boys collected chanda from the para to arrange Hindu festivals, such as the Saraswati Puja. Their drills and festivals in the parks displayed a Hindu nation in the making.

In 1931, the editor of the health journal *Physical Fitness* reviewed the fitness programme at the Balak Sangha. He criticized the Sangha for not addressing Indian physical standards in its fitness programmes.[106] He explained that the structure of the Indian body was different from the British, and this difference had to inform the training programme. He advised the Sangha to carry out anthropomorphic surveys at the club and use the information to tailor its fitness routines. Following the advice of the editor, Balak Sangha carried out surveys not only of the boys at the camp but also of the entire para, recording the height, weight, and chest measurements of all para residents.

This anthropomorphic survey helped the Sangha to revise its fitness programme to match the needs not simply of Indian bodies but of Hindu bodies. The Sangha introduced a new system of scout training based on the

A City-Nation

Baden Powel system of command, but revised it to include Hindu commands.[107] The British admiral Baden Powell had created a scouting programme in 1907 to train the British navy. The Sangha drew on this training, but also considered the requirements of the Hindu community and made necessary adaptations.[108] In these adaptations, vernacular alphabets, songs, and games signalled a new system of command. Every morning, the boys woke up to prayers and devotional music. They practised yoga, asana, marital arts, and wrestling designed to train Hindu bodies; they also engaged in lathi khela.[109]

The Sangha promoted vegetarianism, advising the boys on a system of Hindu nutrition that emphasized the need to eat more fruits and reduce the intake of meat. Embedded in the language of an effective diet for the Bengali build the Sangha's push to vegetarianism was in fact aligned with the broader purpose of disciplining bodies and transforming individual food choices to match the needs of an emerging nation that was a creation of upper-caste Hindus. The consumption of meat, usually associated with the lower castes and non-Hindus, increasingly became a marker to separate the upper from the lower castes. In nutrition trainings that aided fitness programmes, the Sangha explained that the diet of Hindus was rich in vitamins. They advised the campers to follow this diet and not consume English food, as it was not nutritious enough.

In June 1930, the Tarun Sangha (Youth Club), a para club similar to the Balak Sangha, organized a scout camp for Corporation employees in a neighbourhood park.[110] Every morning the campers received instruction in fitness and self-control. Tarun Sangha, however, had a history of revolutionary nationalism; the secretary of the club, Benoyendranath Roy, was the assistant secretary of the South Calcutta branch of the Indian National Congress. The British had previously arrested him for assaulting a white police constable.[111] In 1931, they tried him again for conspiracy against the state. Between the two arrests, he established the Tarun Sangha and organized a scout training camp.

A camper wrote in his diary that the day at the camp started with prayers. At six in the morning, campers assembled near the national flag. They stood in *prastut* (attention) as the nayak (leader of the club) hoisted the flag. The Sangha then prayed together; they composed special songs that celebrated strong bodies and a healthy nation. With the flag flying high, the Sangha taught the campers team games. Games like 'follow the leader' and 'the snake and the monkeys', combined with those like 'tug of war' that instructed the campers to promptly follow orders.[112] At the centre of the fitness routine was lathi khela that the Sangha described as Indian tradition, conflating India's past with the Hindu past (Figure 3.5).

Tarun Sangha also instructed the campers in *mukul niti* (Hindu cadet law). This involved instruction in tying knots such as the sheet bend, the reef, the bowline, and the clove hitch on flags knots. In Hinduism, knots carry symbolic meanings. While some knots represent *granthi*s (extrasensory realizations), others represent sacred hymns. Instructors at the camp trained the campers—as Hindus—in the perfect way to tie these knots.

Figure 3.5 The Tarun Sangha boys practising *lathi khela* in a park in Calcutta.

Source: Calcutta Municipal Gazette, September 1931. Courtesy of General Research Division, NYPL, New York.

A City-Nation

Sanghas were classic examples of the efforts of bhadralok sanitarians to discipline the conduct of individuals through changes in urban space. As the boys engaged in fitness exercises, they drove away the poor, the vendors, and people they considered 'unfit' for the park. They discouraged mixed groups of men and women from sitting in the park, explaining such groups as obscene. They kept the park meticulously clean, trimmed the bushes, and cleaned the grounds. The sanitized spaces of the park displayed both moral and spatial cleanliness.

As the para's male population engaged in fitness routines in public spaces, women stayed indoors. An ideal woman of the para would not go out on the streets without a purpose. Author Mahendranath Dutta wrote that in the summer afternoons, neighbourhood women gathered in the dalaan of one of the para's houses after lunch.[113] All houses of the para were interconnected and women did not have to go out to the streets to reach the dalaan. In their afternoon meetings, women exchanged recipes, guidance for childcare, and health tips. They also discussed family matters: stories of their children and in-laws. Everyone knew everything about their neighbours' personal lives—the para resembled an extended village.

In her study of a central Calcutta neighbourhood, Henrike Donner, an anthropologist, has shown how everyday practices gendered local identities.[114] Women, specially newly married women, spent their time in the kitchen completing household chores. Although an extended family, the para offered little scope for her to interact with neighbours and socialize. Public spaces for the use of women barely existed, for it was *lajja* or shame about women's body and sexuality that shaped her ties with the wider community of the neighbourhood. The neighbourhood, writes Donner, was a site of self-discipline, the structure and architecture of which functioned as a panopticon.

Bhadraloks did not allow women to spend time at para clubs, nor did they allow women to partake in fitness camps. Only a few clubs, Balak Sangha among them, offered basic physical training to women. These instructions, however, were delivered in separate and covered enclaves in neighbourhood parks. Every year, the Swarajists sponsored a maternity and women's health week. The clubs offered lectures and set up exhibits on women's health. They instructed women to become better mothers—a role, more than an individual choice, was what the nation required women to play.

Although the clubs offered fitness training, they were different from what akharas or gymnasiums taught their members in north Indian cities—at the para clubs, artistic experimentation was as important as fitness routines.

Bhadraloks encouraged cultural programmes that fuelled a distinct regional identity and brought together a Bengali nation. Writing about culture and identity in Bengal, David Kopf had described agricultural practices, caste, and religious customs shaping local cultures, without merging to create a regional identity.[115] Swarupa Gupta, however, departed from this view. Gupta explained that a regional identity existed in Bengal since precolonial times. Identity, she argued, is not always territorial; it can be cultural.[116] The rulers of Bengal patronized a culture that was regional and drew on religion and the lived experiences of the people. The Bengali identity that this culture shaped was *samaj-ik* or informed by the know-hows of living in a samaj.

Similarly, the idea of a Bengali nation that the bhadraloks shaped at their clubs was also samaj-ik, tailored to invigorate a Hindu and Bengali nation. In music, caricature, comic sketches, and storytelling events at the clubs, neighbours came together to celebrate Bengal's Hindu past. The clubs had libraries filled with books on ancient India meant to familiarize locals with the country's Hindu heritage and take pride in Bengal's role in shaping that heritage. Added to this, the clubs arranged for essay, drawing, and sports competitions that celebrated fitness, compliance, and sympathy for others as Bengali values.

Each para had a theatre group that rehearsed Bengali plays at the clubs and in courtyards and terraces of neighbourhood houses. The well-known Baghbazaar Amateur Theatre group, for instance, took shape in Mukherji para. The group first rehearsed plays in a spare room in the house of a bhadralok who lived in the para. They staged a play on the legend of the Bengali poet and astrologer Khana, *Lilabati*, in the courtyard of a house in the para.[117] They later rehearsed the much controversial play *Nildarpan*, on a major revolt in a colonial Indigo plantation, in the terrace of a bhadralok's house that served as a popular meeting spot in the para.

In addition, the clubs housed libraries to facilitate readings and discussions on Bengali literature. Oral traditions of storytelling were more popular in India than written documents housed in a library. In ancient and medieval times, wealthy kings like the Mughals and the Marathas, however, did have libraries attached to their palaces and religious centres like mosque and temples. The secular tradition of mandatory libraries attached to educational institutions was more of a colonial innovation. Bhadraloks, in their efforts to make their paras more democratic, borrowed from the British secular tradition of libraries as spaces for both reading and public gathering. Other than a reading room, para libraries offered space for small gatherings, like book clubs.

A City-Nation   139

The Swarajists worked with the clubs to bring existing libraries, usually housed at the residences of wealthy merchants to public rooms in the para. The Mudialy Library, for instance, was established in 1876 and was located for more than a century at the home of the merchant Moti Lal Ghose. In September 1929, the Corporation gave the local club money to move the library to a new building.[118] A bhadralok who lived in the para offered land on which the club built a free reading room for the public.

The clubs explained that the success of a library was not only in acquiring books; it had to make sure that the locals visited the reading room. In other words, the work of the library was not simply collecting books but also generating public interest in reading them. To that end, the clubs organized essay competitions in the para to promote reading habits.[119] The Swarajists also awarded medals to those who visited libraries on a regular basis.

The Swarajists influenced the libraries' acquisitions. They offered loans to the para clubs to buy books, while also dictating which books they should buy. The Corporation ordered the clubs to spend 10 per cent of their budget on books on health, hygiene, and physical culture and not less than 15 per cent on religion, morality, history, and travel. In such directives, it forced libraries to buy books with strong nationalist content. The Corporation also exerted direct influence on the libraries by manipulating the constitutions of their advisory boards. When Suhrit Library appealed to the Corporation for a loan to buy books, the Corporation granted the money on the condition that the library had to abolish the existing advisory board, and that the election of the new executive committee must include the local municipal Councillor.[120]

The Swarajists encouraged the flowering of Bengali nationalism at the clubs. On the tenth anniversary of Kantapooker Sporting Club and Library, the Corporation sent its minister of self-government, who sat and listened to a *tabla* (Indian drums) performance by a two-year-old boy, followed by Bengali songs that the women from the neighbourhood performed.[121] Other residents of the para recited Bengali poems, demonstrated muscle-building exercises and even performed comic songs. In a similar way, when Saraswati Samiti celebrated its seventeenth anniversary, the mayor of Calcutta, Subhas Chandra Bose attended the occasion and delivered a speech.[122] Bose was a radical nationalist who broke from the Indian National Congress in 1939 after he thought Gandhian non-violence ineffective in liberating India from British rule. He believed in more aggressive and military strategies in winning freedom. When he arrived at the Saraswati Samiti, the air filled with the shouts of 'Bande Mataram' (hail the motherland); club volunteers gave him

140   A Hygienic City-Nation

a military salute, and the event ended with groups of young boys performing lathi khela and drills.

The importance of the para in shaping a nationalist consciousness comes alive in police officer Durgacharan Bhattacharyya's memoir. Durgacharan grew up in the 1920s in a para in south Calcutta.[123] He lived in a small rented house and attended the nearby South Suburban School. There was a park beside his house where the provincial Congress convened every week. Durgacharan and his four brothers attended these meetings. His brothers started spinning the *charkha* (spinning wheel) in a room in the para when Gandhi launched the Civil Disobedience Movement in 1930, and asked all Indians to boycott British goods. On one occasion, his brothers came home bare bodied after they had set their shirts, manufactured in Britain, on fire at the park. Durgacharan frequented his para club, which he described as a haunt of nationalist men who wanted to fight the British. The club had a library that offered many historical and topical books and authentic records of early British atrocities. Durgacharan explains that he was drawn to nationalist activism after reading these books. He brought together a volunteer group and picketed two liquor stores in the neighbourhood.

The new nationalist culture that found expression at the para health associations, clubs, and libraries eventually transformed the ritual practices of Durga Puja. The clubs replaced merchant houses as the nucleus of the para and transformed the rituals of the Puja to make it into a shared festival of the Hindu-Bengali nation. Every autumn, the clubs organized sarbojonin Pujas that reflected a broad spectrum of social values within the para: the waning merchant authority, the emergence of the bhadraloks as para leaders, the concerns about Hindu hygiene, and the coming together of a Hindu-Bengali city-nation.

Sarbojonin Durga Puja in the Para

Under the supervision of para clubs, the rituals of Durga Puja shifted from a supernatural or socio-cultural event to a public celebration of a Hindu-Bengali nation. The roots of sarbojonin Puja were in the *baroyaari* (organized by twelve friends) Pujas. In 1919, when a merchant denied twelve friends entry to his Durga Puja, they got together to arrange for their own Puja. This started the Nebubagan Baroyaari Puja that the *baroyaar*s or twelve friends organized. At first, they had difficulty finding a proper space to erect a pandal for the deity. Later, bhadraloks of the para met to pay a chanda, expanding the community

A City-Nation

(baroyaari) Puja to a more public (sarbojonin) Puja. Thus began the Baghbazaar Sarbojonin Durgotsav, a Durga Puja that remains popular even today.

The sarbojonin Puja combined nationalist politics and Hindu religion with resounding success; the goddess Durga represented the nation and her worship followed the rituals of *matri aradhana*—the worship of the nation as a mother.[124] This vision of a feminine nation ascribed domestic roles to women. Bhadraloks condemned the performances of baijies, ending the tradition of dance performances by Muslim women at the Puja. In their place, they encouraged demonstrations of muscular strength, music, plays, and dances that celebrated a Hindu nation.

Simla Byayam Samiti, a club in north Calcutta, was the first to celebrate sarbojonin Durga Puja as matri aradhana. Nationalist Atindranath Bosu had initially established the club to train young boys in muscle-building exercises, wrestling, and lathi khela. On the days of the Puja, the Samiti wanted to bring together Hindus across class divides. Hindus who had different caste and class backgrounds were all invited and received training in wrestling and lathi khela. Sports became the common language that brought together young men from diverse backgrounds. Bosu described the Puja as more Shakti Puja than Durga Puja, meaning that he worshipped Durga for her physical strength and not only for her divine existence.[125] On April 20, 1929, the Swarajists wrote supporting the club:

> We would like to take the opportunity in offering our sincerest congratulation to the authorities of the Simla Byayam Samiti on the splendid work they are doing for the improvement of the physique of the boys and young men of North Calcutta and gymnasiums like the Simla Byayam Samiti will help us see our young men stand with their heads erect and walk with their chest forward.[126]

Bosu draped the idol of Durga in *khaddar*, the nationalist fabric, and worshipped Durga as Bharatmata (the personification of the nation as a Hindu goddess). Inside the pandal, surrounding the idol, he placed miniature clay idols of famous freedom fighters. Posters displayed a wide variety of messages that demanded absolute freedom from British rule. The club also arranged for plays, but because of police pressure did not stage political dramas. Additionally, the club provided relief to flood victims and performed social services.[127]

Nevertheless, the Samiti preserved some practices of earlier Durga Pujas held at the house of the merchants. Similar to the merchants, it organized annachattras to distribute rice to the indigents. These were crowded with people on the days of Durga Puja. One year, the Swarajist mayor of Calcutta,

142   A Hygienic City-Nation

Subhas Chandra Bose, visited an annachattra and sat on the floor with the others to eat rice.[128]

Durga Pujas at the clubs served to recast local practices as part of a larger national imaginary. The rituals and ceremonies drew from and evoked a vast repertoire of religious text to craft affectively and visually compelling enactments of ideology so that the practices of the Puja fell under the discursive, visual, and performative sway of a national ideology. The celebration of the Puja as a national festival enhanced the local autonomy of the Swarajists and testified to their envisioning of the para as the unit of the nation. Different from the merchant's celebration of the Puja that marked creative exchanges between Indians and the British, anti-colonial nationalism informed the celebrations at the clubs. Between 1932 and 1934, the Asura at the Durga Puja of the Simla Byayam Samiti started resembling the British, and Durga's slaying of Asura became symbolic of the Indian freedom movement.

With the Puja displaying the ongoing struggle between Bengalis and the British, demonstrations of muscular strength became an indispensable part of the festivities. Celebrating Durga Puja in 1930, the Baghbazaar Sarbojonin Club organized a Virastami festival.[129] The Virastami took place on the eighth day (*astami*) of the Puja. The rituals were the same as the other days, but Hindu women, except for those whose husbands or fathers were alive, observed a fast on this day. During the day, there were athletic displays, hence the name Virastami (Vir means brave/fit/courageous). The Hindus worshipped Durga's weapons with flowers and perfume and offered their prayers to her comrades, the eight Shaktis or powers, also known as the Astanayikas (the eight consorts).

The Baghbazaar Sarbojonin Club first co-opted the ritual of Virastami as a demonstration of nationalist sentiments on the days of the Puja. The para's youth sang patriotic Bengali songs to inaugurate the ceremony. Subhas Chandra Bose, the mayor of the city who espoused the use of force and armed struggle against the British, attended the Virastami festival at Baghbazaar. He delivered a speech on the importance of sports in building strong bodies required to fight the British. Clubs from adjoining paras, Saila Siksha Mandir and Kheyali Sangha performed sword fights and dagger displays for him. A tournament of weight lifting, jujutsu, boxing, wrestling, and high jump followed. Virastami ended with Rakshabandhan, the tying of wristbands to symbolize a Bengali brotherhood.

In yet another Puja, the Kasi Dutta Street Sarbojonin Puja, the unveiling of Durga and her children was done by a famous physician, Dr U. N. Brahmachari. Brahmachari had discovered a new treatment for kala-zaar in 1922. He

A City-Nation

advised Bengalis to exercise to maintain fit bodies. At the Puja, a body-building club called the Young Men's Physical Association performed physical feats.[130] *Byayam guru* (fitness coach) Basanta Kumar Banerjee supervised the programme and instructed young men in the performance of aerial trapeze.[131] He also instructed several other para clubs in north Calcutta like Beniatola Adarsha Byayam Samiti, the Naba Milan Club, and the Mitra Pukur Athletic Union in fitness programmes.

Displays of fitness at the Durga Puja celebrations marked the final phase in the para's transition to a microcosm of a Hindu-Bengali nation. A Hindu festival, the Puja pointed to the religious underpinnings of the bhadralok's vision of the nation. Their attempts to appropriate urban space, create habitats, and negotiate their own existence while working with the Swarajists made them powerful in the city. The bhadraloks incorporated Durga Puja into the broader discourse of national cultural identity. The performative and ideological disciplining of Durga Puja was not simply a top–down process but rather one that occurred in the everyday spaces of the para. The clubs organized the Puja in ways that recast local practices as part of a greater national imaginary that was itself constantly under construction. The celebration of the Puja as a national festival enhanced the local autonomy of the bhadraloks and testified to the alacrity with which they envisioned the para as the unit of a Hindu-Bengali nation.

Conclusion

This chapter has analysed Hindu nationalism built through urban experiences of city dwellers in the everyday spaces of paras. I have argued that the shaping of a Hindu nation was not solely a by-product of top–down political interventions but also an outcome of a new imagined identity channelled through urban practices. I suggest that the physical mass of urban spaces did not construct this identity; it emerged from the narratives embedded in them. Examining these narratives, I have pointed out everyday practices in the para that engendered this new identity by conflating Hindu nationalism with urbanism. Nationhood was institutionalized through urban experiences in the para—the streets, parks, clubs, schools, health associations, and house meetings—where the bhadraloks prompted the agenda and character of Hindu nationalism. The para therefore points to the formation of autonomous spatial communities with self-rule that took shape well before India achieved formal independence.

144 A Hygienic City-Nation

Envisioning paras as microcosms of the nation, the bhadraloks shaped a pedagogic project to school people for collective action and transform society. Through this transformation, they hoped to liberate the country from a foreign occupier. They believed that the people and the seemingly disempowered could defy colonial authority through self-organization and self-improvement. Urbanization was then as much a bodily process as it was a structural intervention. The changing spaces of the para reveal nationalist urban improvement initiatives, as they were deployed to shape discrete spaces as well as bodies. The bhadraloks instructed city dwellers in conduct fit for the city and the nation, making urbanization similar to a civilizing process. This made the bodies of city dwellers the focal point for a plethora of different concerns ranging from the need to produce citizens with strong nationalist sentiments to anxieties over the control of deviant behaviour.

As I will argue in the next chapter, bhadraloks took their civilizing mission beyond their paras to working class neighbourhoods or bustees that bordered their paras. Bustees featured in their campaigns as the foremost critique of colonialism: its unplanned spaces displayed the failure of the state to plan urban space. Bhadraloks, however, followed the colonial portrayal of bustees as filthy hubs of disease but also produced bustees as spaces that contrasted the spatial order and hygiene of their paras, setting these as normative in the city.

Notes

1. Supriya Chaudhuri, 'Remembering the Para: Towards a Spatial History of Our Times', in *Strangely Beloved: Writings on Calcutta* (New Delhi: Rupa Publications, 2014), 118–25.
2. Tapati Guha Thakurta describes Durga Puja as a street-art festival. See Tapati Guha Thakurta, *In the Name of the Goddess: The Durga Pujas of Contemporary Kolkata* (Delhi: Primus Books, 2015). In another essay, Guha Thakurta shows how globalization and a changing economy transformed the artistic traditions of the Puja. See Tapati Guha Thakurta, 'Demands and Dilemmas of Durga Puja "Art": Notes on a Contemporary Festival Aesthetics', in *Bloomsbury Research Book of Indian Aesthetics and Philosophy of Art*, ed. Arindam Chakrabarti (London: Bloomsbury Academic, 2016), 317–53; Jawhar Sircar described the Puja as a traditional folk-art festival in 'Durga Pujas as Expressions of "Urban Folk Culture"', *The Times of India*, 23 October 2011; Anjan Ghosh explained that the Puja was a commercialized religious event. Anjan Ghosh, 'Spaces of Recognition: Puja and Power in Contemporary Calcutta', *Journal of Southern African Studies* 26, no. 2 (2000): 289–99.

A City-Nation 145

3. A detailed account of Durga Puja celebrations in elite Indian houses can be found in the chapter 'Puja Origins and Elite Politics' in Rachel Fell McDermott, *Revelry, Rivalry, and Longing for the Goddesses of Bengal: The Fortunes of Hindu Festivals* (New York: Columbia University Press, 2011), 76–102.

4. I would like to note here that in regular usage, a 'para' can mean any Bengali neighbourhood where residents have diverse religion, caste, and class affiliations. This chapter, however, focuses on paras where significant numbers of Hindu, middle-class residents lived. Calcutta, of course, had Muslim paras, which also transformed with anti-colonial nationalist movements—those neighbourhoods do not fall within the purview of this chapter, as my goal is to understand how Hindu-Bengali nationalists conflated urbanism and nationalism. For a detailed study of Muslim paras, see Anasua Chatterjee, *Margins of Citizenship: Muslim Experiences in Urban India* (London: Taylor & Francis, 2017). Chatterjee traces segregation, based on religion, to bhadralok communal politics in twentieth century Bengal.

5. One direction in existing scholarship focuses on the abstract physical boundaries of paras that carved autonomous spaces within the well-regulated and planned space of the colonial city. Scholars have described certain physical markers—a water tank, a temple, an open field—that set the boundaries of the para. Paras were, after all, spaces shaped by the daily lives of people and not by state plans. See Swati Chattopadhyay, *Representing Calcutta: Modernity, Nationalism, and the Colonial Uncanny* (London; New York: Routledge, 2005), 90; Partha Chatterjee, *The Black Hole of Empire: History of a Global Practice of Power* (Princeton: Princeton University Press, 2012), 132. Yet another direction in scholarship centres on how familiarity and *atmiyata* (close relations) between neighbours shaped these spaces. See S. Chattopadhyay, *Representing Calcutta*; Sircar, 'Durga Puja as Expressions of "Urban Folk Culture"'; Kaustubh Mani Sengupta, 'Community and Neighbourhood in a Colonial City: Calcutta's Para', *South Asia Research* 38, no. 1 (1 February 2018): 40–56.

6. Blair B. King, 'Entreprenurship and Regional Identity in Bengal', in *Bengal Regional Identity* (East Lansing, Michigan: Asian Studies Center, 1969), 75–86.

7. Ibid.

8. Rachel R. Van Meter, 'Bankimcandra's View on the Role of Bengal in Indian Civilization', in *Bengal Regional Identity* (East Lansing, Michigan: Michigan State University, 1969), 61–74.

9. Sabyasachi Bhattacharya, *The Defining Moments in Bengal, 1920–1947* (New Delhi: Oxford University Press, 2014).

10. Richard Sennett, *The Fall of Public Man* (New York; London: W. W. Norton & Company, 1992).

146   A Hygienic City-Nation

11. Jane Jacobs, *The Death and Life of Great American Cities* (New York: Vintage, 1992), 83.

12. Jürgen Habermas, *The Structural Transformation of the Public Sphere: An Inquiry into a Category of Bourgeois Society* (Cambridge, Massachusetts: Polity Press, 2011).

13. Joan B. Landes, *Feminism, the Public and the Private* (Oxford: Oxford University Press, 1998), 434.

14. Jim Masselos points to caste like groups that constituted Muslim neighbourhoods or mohollas; an elderly council of Muslim men, the jamaat, governed these mohollas. See Jim Masselos, *The City in Action: Bombay Struggles for Power* (New Delhi; New York: Oxford University Press, 2007), 19. Also, Prashant Kidambi, *The Making of an Indian Metropolis: Colonial Governance and Public Culture in Bombay, 1890–1920* (Burlington, VT: Ashgate Publishing Company, 2007), 122.

15. Geert de Neve and Henrike Donner, *The Meaning of the Local* (London: Routledge, 2010), 11.

16. Arjun Appadurai, *Modernity At Large: Cultural Dimensions of Globalization* (Minneapolis: University of Minnesota Press, 1996), 183.

17. Mio Minoru, 'Community of Retrospect: Spirit Cults and Locality in an Old City of Rajasthan', in *Cities in South Asia*, ed. Minoru Mio and Crispin Bates, 210–27 (New York: Routledge, 2015).

18. Prashant Kidambi, *The Making of an Indian Metropolis*, 138.

19. Rajnarayan Chandavarkar, *The Origins of Industrial Capitalism in India: Business Strategies and the Working Classes in Bombay, 1900–1940* (Cambridge: Cambridge University Press, 2003), 172.

20. Madhuja Mukherjee has described the connections between club football, history, and identity in Bengal. See Madhuja Mukherjee, 'Football in Asia: History, Culture and Business', in *Football in Asia: History, Culture and Business*, ed. Younghan Cho, 74–92 (New York: Routledge, 2016), 74–92.

21. In scholarship on neighbourhoods, everydayness is a recurrent theme. See Masselos, *The City in Action*; Kidambi, *The Making of an Indian Metropolis*; K. M. Sengupta, 'Community and Neighbourhood in a Colonial City'. Sengupta, however, has pointed to the exclusionary and gendered nature of paras.

22. Guha Ranajit, 'A Colonial City and Its Time(s)', *The Indian Economic and Social History Review* 45, no. 3 (September 2008): 329–51.

23. Bhabānī Rāya Caudhurī, *Baṅgīya Sābarṇa Kathā, Kālīkshetra Kalikātā: Ekati Itibṛtta* (Kalakātā: Mānnā Pābalikeśana, 2006), 12.

24. Swarupa Gupta offers an excellent account of the samaj by tracing the idea of a nation to the pre-colonial social collectivity of the samaj. This connection between samaj and the nation challenges the overarching scholarly inclination to describe the Indian nation as a derivative discourse of European modernity.

A City-Nation

See Swarupa Gupta, *Notions of Nationhood in Bengal: Perspectives on Samaj, c. 1867–1905* (Leiden: Brill, 2009), 160.

25. John Archer argued that the complexity of Indian spatial knowledge reflected in the nomenclature of paras. While streets in the European parts of Calcutta were named after British merchants and officials, paras were named after the caste and villages of the settlers. See John Archer, 'Paras, Palaces, Pathogens: Frameworks for the Growth of Calcutta, 1800–1850', *CISO City and Society* 12, no. 1 (2000): 19–54.

26. Rāya Caudhurī, *Bangiya Sābarna Kathā*, 16.

27. Ibid., 21.

28. Ibid., 22.

29. S. N. Mukherjee, *Calcutta: Myths and History* (Calcutta: Subarnarekha, 1977).

30. Michel de Certeau, *The Practice of Everyday Life* (Berkeley, California: University of California Press, 2008).

31. Randolph Marriott, William Bolts, Claud Russell, Philip Pollock, Peter Michell, Thomas De Grey, and Baron Walsingham, *Appendix of Bengal Papers, 1688–1770.* (London: 1771).

32. A. K. Ray, *A Short History of Calcutta, Town and Suburbs* (Calcutta: Riddhi India, 1982).

33. Charles Robert Wilson, *The Early Annals of the English in Bengal: Being the Bengal Public Consultations for the First Half of the Eighteenth Century, Summarised, Extracted, and Ed., with Introductions and Illustrative Addenda* (London: W. Thacker, 1895–1911).

34. Anthony D. King, *Colonial Urban Development: Culture, Social Power and Environment* (London: Routledge, 2010), 18.

35. S. Chattopadhyay, *Representing Calcutta*, 85.

36. Lakshmi Subramanian, 'Banias and the British: The Role of Indigenous Credit in the Process of Imperial Expansion in Western India in the Second Half of the Eighteenth Century', *Modern Asian Studies* 21, no. 3 (1987): 473–510.

37. Nagendranath Sett, *Kalikatastha Tantu Banik Jatir Itihas* (Calcutta: A. K. Basaka, 1950), 36.

38. Ibid., 38.

39. Irfan Habib, *Essays in Indian History: Towards a Marxist Perception* (New Delhi: Tulika, 2015).

40. Mahendranath Dutta, *Kalikatar Puratan Kahini O Pratha* (Calcutta: Mahendra Publishing Committee, 1973), 59.

41. Kiranacandra Datta, *Bāgabājāra: Atipurātana Nahe, Madhya O Bartamāna Yugera Citra* (Kalakātā: Bāṃlāra Mukha Prakāśana; Mukhya prāptisthāna De'ja, 2009).

42. Ibid.

43. Haradhan Dutt, *Dutt Family of Wellington Square* (Calcutta: Haradhan Dutt, 1995).

44. Dinabandhu Chatterjee, *A Short Sketch of Rajah Rajendro Mullick Bahadur and His Family* (Calcutta: G. C. Day, 1917), 65.
45. Ibid.
46. Preeti Chopra, *A Joint Enterprise: Indian Elites and the Making of British Bombay* (Minneapolis: University of Minnesota Press, 2011).
47. Siddha Mohana Mitra, *Indian Problems* (London: J. Murray, 1908), 17.
48. Ibid., 16.
49. Lokanātha Ghosha, *The Modern History of the Indian Chiefs, Rajas, Zamindars, &C* (Calcutta: J. N. Ghose, 1881).
50. D. Chatterjee, *A Short Sketch*, 23.
51. Dutt, *Dutt Family*, 15.
52. The British recognized the caste courts as formal spaces for legal deliberations. See Mukherjee, *Calcutta: Myths and History*.
53. D. Chatterjee, *A Short Sketch*, 11.
54. McDermott, *Revelry, Rivalry, and Longing*, 24.
55. Alexander Duff, *A Description of the Durga and Kali Festivals, Celebrated in Calcutta, at an Expense of Three Millions of Dollars* (Troy, NY: C. Wright, 1846), 9.
56. Bipinbihari Mitra, *Kalikatastha Sobhabajara-Nibasi Maharaja Nabakrsna Deba Bahadurerea Jibana-Carita* (Calcutta: Stanhope Press, 1879).
57. Dutt, *Dutt Family*, 35.
58. John Gallagher and Ronald Robinson, 'The Imperialism of Free Trade', *The Economic History Review* 6, no. 1 (1953): 1–15.
59. C. A. Bayly, *Rulers, Townsmen, and Bazaars: North Indian Society in the Age of British Expansion, 1770–1870* (Cambridge; New York: Cambridge University Press, 1983).
60. Lakshmi Subramanian, *Three Merchants of Bombay: Trawadi Arjunji Nathji, Jamsetjee Jeejeebhoy, and Premchand Roychand: Doing Business in Times of Change* (New Delhi: Allen Lane, 2012).
61. Tapan Raychaudhuri, 'Mother of the Universe, Motherland', *The Rite Stuff* 1, no. 4 of *The Little Magazine*.
62. A Member of the Family, *An Account of the Late Govindram Mitter and of His Descendants in Calcutta and Benares* (Calcutta: National Press,1869).
63. Kaliprasanna Sinha and Swarup Roy, *The Observant Owl: Hootum's Vignettes of Nineteenth-Century Calcutta: Kaliprasanna Sinha's Hootum Pyanchar Naksha* (Ranikhet; New Delhi: Rupa & Co., 2008).
64. *The Calcutta Journal, or, Political, Commercial, and Literary Gazette*, 2 September 1819.
65. *Samachar Darpan*, 5 October 1832.
66. Rachel McDermott argues that by the 1830s, Christian missionaries had explained the Puja as blind idolatry that did not allow Indians to become

A City-Nation 149

fully civilized. They exercised enough power to dissuade Company merchants from attending the Durga Puja celebrations at Indian houses. See McDermott, *Revelry, Rivalry, and Longing*, 53.

67. Sumit Sarkar and Tithi Bhattacharya have examined the role of English education and salaried employment in shaping the bhadralok group. See Sumit Sarkar, *Writing Social History* (New Delhi: Oxford University Press, 2009), and Tithi Bhattacharya, *Sentinels of Culture: Class, Education, and the Colonial Intellectual in Bengal, 1848–85* (New Delhi, India: Oxford University Press, 2005).

68. Partha Chatterjee, *The Nation and Its Fragments: Colonial and Postcolonial Histories* (Princeton: Princeton University Press, 1993), 120.

69. Ranajit Guha, 'A Colonial City and Its Time(s)', *The Indian Economic and Social History Review* 45, no. 3 (September 2008): 329–51.

70. Bipin Chandra Pal, 'City and City Government', *The Calcutta Municipal Gazette*, 23 November 1929.

71. Sabyasachi Bhattacharya, *The Defining Moments in Bengal: 1920–1947* (New Delhi: Oxford University Press, 2014).

72. B. C. Ghosh, 'Civitas Dei', *The Calcutta Municipal Gazette*, 16 November 1925.

73. Hemendranath Dasgupta, *Desbandhu Chittaranjan Das* (Delhi: Publications Division Ministry of Information & Broadcasting, 2017).

74. Naresh Chandra Sengupta, 'The Bengal Municipal Bill', *The Calcutta Municipal Gazette*, 16 September 1932.

75. Bipin Chandra Pal, 'Civil Service', *The Calcutta Municipal Gazette*, 28 May 1932.

76. Bipin Chandra Pal, 'City and City Government', *The Calcutta Municipal Gazette,* 23 November 1929.

77. Radhakamal Mukerjee, *Principles of Comparative Economics* (London: P.S. King & Son, 1921–1922), 54.

78. Christine Furedy, '"New Men" Political Clubs in Calcutta in the 1870's and 1880's: A Colonial Mix of Self-Interest and Ideology', *Indian Journal of Politics* 13, nos 1 and 2 (August 1979).

79. Joya Chatterji described bhadralok associations—clubs or *samitis*—mostly *palli samiti*s or village associations adding the much-needed earthiness and manliness to their identity. See Joya Chatterji, *Bengal Divided: Hindu Communalism and Partition, 1932–1947* (Cambridge: Cambridge University Press, 2002), 163.

80. The Societies Registration Act of 1860 required all voluntary associations to register with the state as scientific, literary, and charitable (including religious) institutes. The Act authorized clubs to hold property and transfer it tax-free. The numbers of para clubs multiplied after this Act. See Nathuni Lal and

Rajesh Gupta, *Lal's Commentary on the Societies Registration Act, 1860 (Act No. 21 of 1860): States Amendments, State Rules, Model Forms along with Allied Laws*, 2016.

81. Nirmal Kumar Bose, *Calcutta, 1964: A Social Survey* (Bombay: Lalvani Publishing House, 1968). Offering a detailed survey of associations in Calcutta, Bose explained that although there were enough meeting places for individual communities in the city, places that facilitated inter-community meetings, for instance, between Bengalis and non-Bengalis, were absent.

82. *The Calcutta Municipal Gazette*, April 1927.

83. Details of social and political associations of bhadraloks can be found in J. H. Broomfield, *Elite Conflict in a Plural Society: Twentieth-Century Bengal* (Berkeley and Los Angeles: University of California Press, 1968), 57; Rajat Kanta Ray, *Urban Roots of Indian Nationalism* (New Delhi: Vikas Publishing House Pvt Ltd, 1980); Chatterji, *Bengal Divided*, 14.

84. Anand Rao Joshi, 'Educated Indians and the Public Health', *The Calcutta Municipal Gazette*, August 1927.

85. Sundari Mohan Das, 'Sanitary Awakening', *The Calcutta Municipal Gazette*, March 1926.

86. Processions that combined devotionalism with nationalism were common in other cities of colonial India too. In Surat similar processions stormed the streets. See Douglas E. Haynes, *Rhetoric and Ritual in Colonial India: The Shaping of a Public Culture in Surat City, 1852–1928* (Delhi; New York: Oxford University Press, 1992), 277. In Bombay, such processions were also common. See Jim Masselos, *The City in Action: Bombay Struggles for Power* (New Delhi; New York: Oxford University Press, 2007).

87. *The Calcutta Municipal Gazette*, March 1926.

88. 'Ward XI', *The Calcutta Municipal Gazette*, March 1926.

89. *The Calcutta Municipal Gazette*, 22 March 1926.

90. Ibid., September 1930.

91. Ibid., 17 January 1931.

92. Ibid., 11 March 1926.

93. See Dipesh Chakrabarty, 'Of Garbage, Modernity and the Citizen's Gaze', *Economic and Political Weekly* 27, no. 10/11 (1992): 541–7.

94. Joseph S. Alter, *The Wrestler's Body: Identity and Ideology in North India* (Berkeley: University of California Press, 1992), 87.

95. Norbert Elias, *The Civilizing Process: Sociogenetic and Psychogenetic Investigations* (Oxford; Malden, Mass: Blackwell Publishing, 2000).

96. Mrinalini Sinha, *Colonial Masculinity: The 'Manly Englishman' and the Effeminate Bengali in the Late Nineteenth Century* (New Delhi, India: Kali for Women, 1997); Heather Streets, *Martial Races: The Military, Race and Masculinity in British Imperial Culture, 1857–1914* (Manchester: Manchester University Press, 2011).

A City-Nation

97. Alter, *The Wrestler's Body*, 50.

98. Central to philosophies of Hindu nationalism were the workings of the body. Hindu nationalists encouraged a Hindu fitness regime. They trained young boys in these fitness programmes to create loyal cadres. See Banu Subramaniam, *Holy Science: The Biopolitics of Hindu Nationalism* (Seattle: University of Washington Press, 2019), 11.

99. Nupur Chaudhuri, 'Clash of Cultures: Gender and Colonialism in South and Southeast Asia', in *A Companion to Gender History*, ed. Teresa A. Meade, 430–3 (Blackwell Publishing Ltd: Oxford, UK 2008).

100. Joya Chatterji's work on communalism in Bengal points to a growing physical culture. See Chatterji, *Bengal Divided*, 163.

101. Joe L. Frost, *A History of Children's Play and Play Environments: Toward a Contemporary Child-Saving Movement* (New York: Routledge, 2012), 64.

102. P. K. Gupta, 'Health of Calcutta Youth', *The Calcutta Municipal Gazette*, August 1930.

103. S. K. Kar, 'Playground Activities for Children', *The Calcutta Municipal Gazette*, May 1931.

104. 'Balak Sangha: An Open-Air Institution for children', *The Calcutta Municipal Gazette*, 24 September 1927.

105. The training coincided with the Bratachari movement led by Gurusaday Dutta in 1934. Dutta, a writer and folklorist tried to construct a masculine vision for 'effeminate' Bengalis through indigenous folk dance forms. He designed the Bratachari movement to instruct Bengalis in all-round development of their bodies and mind. Unlike the Hindu fitness programmes that the bhadraloks led in their para, the ideology around which the Bratachari movement was built did not draw on Bengali or Hindu sources. It borrowed from the English agenda of the revival of folk traditions and the German idea of *Volksgeist* instead. See Sayantani Adhikary, 'The Bratachari Movement and the Invention of a "Folk Tradition"', *South Asia: Journal of South Asian Studies* 38, no. 4 (2 October 2015): 656–70.

106. S. Mozumdar, 'The Municipal Control of Physical Education-I', *The Calcutta Municipal Gazette*, March 1931.

107. Scholarship on global scout-training is dense. As early as the twentieth-century, scouting in Britain was part of a citizen training programme. See Sarah Mills, '"An Instruction in Good Citizenship": Scouting and the Historical Geographies of Citizenship Education', *Transactions of the Institute of British Geographers* 38, no. 1 (1 January 2013): 120–34. As a global movement, scout-training took on new meanings in Britain's colonies. Timothy Parsons explains that the British encouraged scouting in the colonies to create loyal subjects of the Empire. In Africa, scouting, however, transformed into an anti-colonial resistance movement. See Timothy Parsons, *Race, Resistance,*

and the Boy Scout Movement in British Colonial Africa (Athens, OH: Ohio University Press, 2004), 147.

108. In a remarkable study of suburbs in colonial Cairo, Joseph Ben Prestel explains that as the space of the suburb took shape, fitness regimes became popular. British technical innovations shaped suburbs that encouraged a healthy lifestyle, which, in turn, made fitness routines mandatory. Exercises shaped strong individuals while also instilling in them an emotion—a sense of belonging to a healthy community. See Joseph Ben Prestel, *Emotional Cities: Debates on Urban Change in Berlin and Cairo, 1860–1910* (Oxford: Oxford University Press, 2017). In India, the sense of belonging that physical routines produced, however, was contingent on modes of exclusion. Stephen Legg's work on the Hindu nationalist Rashtriya Swayamsevak Sangh (RSS) in the mohollas of Delhi shows how drills and exercises tried to instil an idea of a Hindu India, while also propagating communalism. See Stephen Legg, 'A Pre-Partitioned City? Anti-Colonial and Communal Mohallas in Inter-War Delhi', *South Asia: Journal of South Asian Studies* 42, no. 1 (2 January 2019): 170–87. Communal riots had in fact ripped apart the urban fabric of Calcutta by 1946. Bengalis fell back on their para for help and support in the communal climate. Their paras provided support, but the solidarity was only short-lived. As Hindus helped Muslims and vice versa, there was a lot of personal risk involved: paras soon turned into centres of communal rioting. See Nariaki Nakazato, 'The Role of Colonial Administration, "Riot Systems" and Local Networks during the Calcutta Disturbances of August 1946', in *Calcutta: The Stormy Decades*, ed. Tanika Sarkar and Sekhar Bandyopadhyay, 267–319 (New York: Routledge, 2018), 267, and Janam Mukherjee, *Hungry Bengal War, Famine and the End of Empire* (New York, NY: Oxford University Press, 2016), 216.

109. Mozumdar, 'The Municipal Control of Physical Education-I'.

110. K. P. Chattopadhyay, 'Scouting in Corporation Schools', *The Calcutta Municipal Gazette*, 10 September 1927.

111. *The Times of India*, 5 August 1929.

112. K. P. Chattopadhyay, 'Scouting in Corporation Schools'.

113. Dutta, *Kalikatar Puratan Kahini O Pratha*, 12.

114. Henrike Donner, 'The Politics of Gender, Class, and Community in a Central Calcutta Neighborhood', in *The Meaning of the Local: Politics of Place in Urban India*, ed. Geert de Neve and Henrike Donner, 141–58 (London; New York: Routledge, 2006).

115. David Kopf, 'Editor's Preface', in *Bengal Regional Identity*, ed. David Kopf, with contributions by Edward C. Dimock, Jr, 1–2 (East Lansing, Michigan: Michigan State University, 1969), 1–14.

116. S. Gupta, *Notions of Nationhood in Bengal*.

A City-Nation

117. Kiraṇacandra Datta, *Bāgabājāra: atipurātana nahe, madhya o bartamāna yugera citra* (Kalakātā: Bāṃlāra Mukha Prakāśana: Mukhya prāptisthāna, De'ja, 2009).

118. *The Calcutta Municipal Gazette*, April 1931.

119. 'Mudialy Library', *The Calcutta Municipal Gazette*, April 1932.

120. *The Calcutta Municipal Gazette*, July 1930.

121. Ibid., December 1930.

122. Ibid., November 1930.

123. D.G. Bhattacharyya, *Random Reminiscences of a Police Officer under Two Flags* (New Delhi: Gyan Publishing House, 2003).

124. A festival similar to the sarbojonin Durga Puja was the *sarvajanik* (public) Ganpati festival of Mumbai. Tilak, a Hindu nationalist, threatened by the British patronage of the Muslim community in 1893 decided to celebrate the household rituals of Ganpati festival as a public parade on the streets. See Kidambi, *The Making of an Indian Metropolis*, 179.

125. Sanat Ganguly and Ashok Das, *Simla Byayam Samiti O Sarbojonin Durgotsover Sonkhipto Itibritto*, 1926–2000 (Calcutta: Published by Simla Byayam Samiti, 2000).

126. *The Calcutta Municipal Gazette*, April 1929.

127. Interview with Sandip Chakravarty, General Secretary of the Badamtola Ashar Sangha Club, 21 May 2012.

128. Interview with Sridhar Kundu, Associate of the Simla Byayam Samiti, 30 May 2012.

129. *The Calcutta Municipal Gazette*, October 1930, 32.

130. *Amrita Bazar Patrika*, 5 September 1941.

131. Ibid.

4 A New Black Town
Recolonizing Calcutta's *Bustees*

Swarajist efforts to transform paras into units of a Hindu-Bengali city-nation coincided with a steady influx of villagers to Calcutta. Groups of villagers first started to move to the city when famines forced them to flee their villages in the late nineteenth century.[1] Between 1850 and 1899, twenty-four major famines had destroyed crops and wrecked villages in India. With the constant scarcity of food and loss of crops, the villagers fled to the cities to find new employment.[2] The Swadeshi economic boycott in 1904 speeded up their movement. Swadeshi activists had called for a boycott on all products manufactured in Britain. They appealed to Indians to set up factories, arguing that only a strong economy could support their fight against colonialism. Inspired by Swadeshi ideals of economic self-sufficiency, nationalists like Dr Rashbehari Ghose and Dr Nilratan Sircar opened soap and match factories in Calcutta.[3] Migrant villagers found employment at these factories. They became workers and earned wages that sustained their lives in the city. The Swadeshi factories attracted villagers not simply from Bengal but from the entire country. In the soap factory, for instance, the workers were from Punjab; in the match factories, they came from Bihar.

The arrival of large numbers of villagers resulted in a housing crisis in Calcutta. Neither the state nor factory owners had the wherewithal to house destitute villagers. When the villagers did not receive any support from the state, they started erecting makeshift settlements where they found empty plots of land. These settlements, known as *bustees*, materialized along busy thoroughfares, railway tracks, and municipal waste dumps, and extended as far as the outer rims of middle-class Hindu paras. The inhabitants of the bustee spoke little or no Bengali. Their diverse language, religion, and caste practices informed their neighbourhoods, distinguishing them markedly from the adjoining Hindu-Bengali paras.

In this chapter, I argue that bhadraloks reacted to the sense of threat they felt from the arrival of waves of non-Bengali, non-Hindu, and lower-caste bustee

A New Black Town
155

dwellers by looking inward. Emulating the British, they described bustees as inscrutable and engaged in a discursive production of bustees as spaces of filth and disease. They worked with the Swarajists to inaugurate a process of spatial *shuddhi*: sanitation campaigns that forced a Hindu spatial order on the working poor and non-Hindus and established the normativity of these customs in ordering city space. Spatial shuddhi worked through bargains: bhadraloks promised improvements in lieu of bustee dwellers giving up practices that contrasted with principles of Hindu hygiene.

The rituals of spatial shuddhi therefore did not endorse the cultivation of secular, modern citizens. Rather, they worked to produce the labouring subject or the Hindu body, disciplined in spirit and physique, which contributed to the nation. In such efforts, bhadralok discourse on bustees involved a mimesis: they produced bustees iteratively, in the course of repetitions that drew on, rehearsed, and remade the colonial imaginary of the black town. Bhadraloks viewed the bustee in much the same way as the white ruling class of the city viewed the black town. Such mimetic projection shaped a new language of urban inclusion-by-exclusion.

The construction of the bustee as a space of 'otherness', in which rational planning could not prevail, fit well within the development discourse of scientific rationality and urban planning. As discussed in Chapter 1, colonial health officers employed the figure of the black town as a discursive tool to translate all Indian neighbourhoods into bustees or zones of poor sanitation. In colonial productions of Indian space, the bustee was the spatial unit of the black town. In the early twentieth century, bhadraloks repurposed the construct of the black town to describe non-Bengali, lower caste, and non-Hindu working-class neighbourhoods as bustees and invested these spaces with new meanings. First, as a geographic unit marked as filth-ridden, bustees served as the other of the hygienic space of the para. Second, by being discursively produced as inscrutable, bustees also served as a counterpoint to the classic construction of the para as a modern space amenable to planning. This antithetical counterpoint played a crucial role in producing and regulating the bustee.

By the 1940s, global shifts in power resulting from the World War II led bhadraloks to question the Swarajist idea of the nation. With yet another devastating famine in 1943, an impending Japanese attack on Calcutta, and the British ban on the Communist Party of India lifted in 1942, bhadraloks argued that the nation had to be more than a Hindu community brought together in its difference from the British. Instead, they defined the Indian nation as a community equipped to fight global fascism. In 1942, when the Indian National

Congress launched a nationwide Quit India movement, demanding that the British leave India at once, bhadraloks led a germinal but powerful movement against fascism in Calcutta. Like the Swarajists, their movement centred on the para and spread to the adjoining bustees. This movement produced a new bhadralok discourse in which, rather than representing unintended urban sprawl, bustees embodied new hierarchies in space and embedded new forms of social control in the city.

Ideas of abjection, citizenship, and public space worked together in bhadralok discourse to form socio-spatial norms of appropriate bodies and actions in urban space. Pitted against the working poor, the upper-caste Hindu bhadralok featured in both Swarajist and Communist discourses as an idealized inhabitant of the city, the 'citizen'. The Communists condemned the Swarajists as bourgeois yet shared with them a focus on hygiene that allowed them to argue that the inhabitants of bustees lacked civic mindedness and required guidance. As I will argue, Communist interventions in the bustees departed from Swarajist goals of shaping a Hindu city-nation but conflated nationalism with antifascism to remould bustees into landscapes that tried to reinforce their hold over the city.

Landscapes of Control

As John H. Broomfield has argued, Swarajist victory at the municipal elections of 1923 provided them with the power that was denied earlier in the Legislative Councils.[4] The Swarajists supervised the Calcutta Municipal Corporation, which oversaw city administration. They now had access to funds and complete autonomy in governing the city. They renamed streets after the nation's heroes and held civic receptions for Congress dignitaries. They made Corporation workers wear *khadi*, the national fabric, and encouraged city dwellers to buy Swadeshi products. Yet, as Durba Ghosh has pointed out, the tide of nationalism in Calcutta in the 1920s had broken with the rest of India—it no longer encompassed Gandhian values but shifted more towards socialism, communism, and militant nationalism.[5]

The Swarajists as city administrators inaugurated a period of municipal socialism. The first Swarajist mayor of Calcutta, C. R. Das, endorsed *daridranarayan*, which meant that the *daridra* (the poor) were *narayan* (god) and that the municipal corporation should take good care of them.[6] Another Swarajist councilor, B. C. Ghosh, described the Swarajist goal as converting Calcutta into a *civitas dei*, or city of god, in which all citizens, rich and poor, had equal rights.[7] Civitas dei, a belief borrowed from Christian philosophy, together with more global principles of socialist administration, practised in cities like Vienna, informed Swarajist reforms. The Swarajists promised free primary education, healthcare, and improved infrastructure for Calcutta's working classes.

Although the Swarajists embraced municipal socialism, repeated worker strikes kept them on constant alert. The Corporation's sanitation workers were the first to strike in July 1928.[8] They demanded higher wages, better housing, and adequate water and electricity supplies in their bustees. The workers first stopped work in north Calcutta. Filth accumulated along the sides of streets and with relentless downpours quickly decomposed, giving off an unbearable stink. The strike soon spread to the whole city. City dwellers warned each other that an epidemic was on the way.

A few weeks later, street and sewer flushers, manhole boys, and brush men joined the sanitation workers in their strike.[9] They met secretly to discuss ways to convince the Corporation to improve their bustees. The Swarajists heard their pleas but simply refused to carry out any improvement work. One group of workers, disappointed by the Swarajist response, resumed work. This resulted in street fights between them and the protestors. The Corporation seized on these fights to deploy the police and force all protestors to go back to work.[10] A bigger reserve of police replaced smaller battalions as the strike carried on. The police arrested seventy workers; several others suffered fatal injuries. The strike went on for weeks with no apparent hope of a solution.

The Swarajist response to the workers' strike revealed that, in practice, their policies departed from the principles of daridranarayan. Instead, they followed the British pattern of bustee management: they accepted bustees as a possible way to house workers, tolerated its makeshift spaces, pointed to the lack of hygiene, and called for improvements—but refused to carry them out. Additionally, they borrowed from the British the belief that bustees were inherently dirty. They led sanitation drives that besides drawing attention to unsanitary spaces, also drove to create a Swarajist foothold in the bustees.

British medical officers who surveyed Calcutta in the early nineteenth century had described bustees as plots of land covered with tiled huts that were unsanitary and in need of reform. Indians mostly lived in tiled huts as these were cooler in the summer. This meant that British health reports considered nearly all Indian neighbourhoods bustees. In 1896, health officer D. D. Cunningham reiterated the main elements of the dominant discourse on the bustee:

> One of the huge evils of Calcutta is the bustee or the land covered with closely built tiled huts. The most elementary principles of sanitation are grossly violated here. These bustee lands are the plague spots of the town, and every form of zymotic disease seems to endemically flourish in their congenial filth and squalor. The existence of these bustees has been condemned many times. They are an acknowledged source of serious danger to public health. Their reconstruction on hygienic principles and even their extinction has from time to time been strenuously advocated by health officers.[11]

Cunningham explained that the reason the bustees suffered from such poor sanitation was that its inhabitants 'violated' the rules of scientific planning. Such accusations of 'violation' removed the brunt of poor sanitation from the state and its failure to build civic infrastructure, placing it on the inhabitants of bustees instead. The state was no longer responsible for not investing in infrastructure—sewers, garbage disposal, and water pumps—in the bustees. 'Violation' meant that it was the bustee dwellers' own resistance to scientific infrastructure that made their houses filthy. Colonial health reports documented instances where bustee dwellers violated hygienic principles, reducing them to criminals and calling for increased surveillance.

Echoing Cunningham, another health officer W. J. Simpson wrote that bustee inhabitants posed 'major threats' to public health. Describing them as a 'sickly population averse to scientific practices', he explained that their ignorance and dirtiness resulted in a general deterioration of public health in the city.[12] Simpson suggested tougher laws to control both bustees and their inhabitants.

The Calcutta Municipal Act of 1876 and its amended versions had already set the stage for the increased jurisdictional authority of health officers to carry out improvements in bustees. The Act gave commissioners unquestionable power to fix territorial limits, allowing them to redraw the boundaries of a bustee and extend their control to newer areas as they saw fit.[13] The Calcutta Municipal Amendment Act of 1899 added to this by targeting existing proprietorial patterns in the bustees. The Act described bustee(s) as 'plot(s) of land or adjacent plots of land not less than ten *cottahs* (thirty two cottahs make one acre) where the building arrangement is such that the tenant of the land is the owner of the hut'.[14] In the previous land tenure system, bustee landlords used to lease their land to a middleman who built huts, leased these, carried out improvements, fixed rents, and collected them. Tenants paid a lump sum to the landlord every month as rent for the land. The Act of 1899 did not acknowledge the middleman; it replaced the middleman with a 'contractor'.

A New Black Town

159

The Corporation appointed the contractor, who collected rents in return for a monthly salary.[15] Unlike the middleman, the contractor did not have the power to build huts or carry out improvements—the Act made the bustee landlord responsible for all improvements.

The Municipal Act of 1923 further tightened state control over bustees. In addition to the contractor, the Act mandated two medical officers to routinely inspect huts and suggest improvements.[16] The officers had the power to break open doors if hut owners refused to let them in. A bustee committee comprising a ward councillor and Corporation officials later met to deliberate on their findings. The committee served legal notices to bustee landlords ordering them to carry out improvements that the health officers argued were necessary. Landlords had to implement these improvements at their own expense. This created confusion because, earlier, the bustee middlemen carried out all improvements. Landlords simply refused to implement any of the changes. But when landlords refused, the municipal commissioners seized their bustees and transferred them to the state.

In 1924, as municipal authorities, the Swarajists followed a two-pronged policy in the bustees. On the one hand, like the British, they held bustee landlords responsible for all improvements. On the other hand, they used infrastructure to shape a pool of loyalist landlords. In bustees where the landlords were not Swaraj Party loyalists, the Swarajists ordered them to carry out improvements at their own expenses. This embroiled the Swarajists in numerous lawsuits. For instance, when they served Barada Prosad Roy Chowdhury, who was not a Swarajist loyalist, with a notice to carry out improvements, he refused.[17] He then informed the Corporation that he intended to remove all huts and demolish the bustee. It was well within a landowner's rights to decide at any point to demolish bustees. Yet, the Corporation did not approve. The Swarajists fined him and threatened him with imprisonment. It was at this point that Choudhury decided to file a lawsuit against the Corporation.

Although the Swarajists would fight legal battles with ordinary bustee landlords, they maintained a non-interventionist policy in bustees that belonged to wealthy merchants and bankers who funded their party. J. M. Sengupta, leader of the Bengal Swarajists, had once explained that without support from landlords, the party could not continue at the legislative councils.[18] He ordered municipal commissioners to avoid using force in bustees that belonged to members of the Swaraj Party. The De family of Beadon Street, for instance, were frequent contributors to the Party.[19] As landlords of several bustees, they did not carry out any improvement. To make matters worse, they served eviction notices to more than a hundred hut dwellers at once, asking them to leave within a week's time. This made tenants angry. They petitioned the Corporation, requesting Swarajists to intervene—to no avail.

Instead, the Swarajists came up with the idea of 'multipurpose Swaraj' to benefit loyalist landlords. Multipurpose Swaraj meant that the Corporation would carry out bustee improvements on behalf of the landlords.[20] C. R. Das had first put this idea forward at the Gaya Congress of 1922, arguing that to achieve self-government, the Swarajists had to organize workers and the urban poor alongside the middle and upper classes. He explained that organizing workers meant taking care of their needs and winning them over. To that end, the municipal commissioners promised to carry out improvements in the bustees on behalf of landowners.

Swarajist plans for a multipurpose Swaraj did not work, however. The state failed to transfer necessary funds to the Corporation. Without proper funds, improvement work remained stalled for months. Confused by the slow pace of improvements, bhadraloks accused the Swarajists of embezzling funds. In 1927, a Bengali periodical, *Svasthya Samacara*, published a cartoon that showed a Swarajist commissioner consuming 'Swaraj funds'. The cartoon (Figure 4.1) portrays the commissioner, bloated with pride, picking the fruit of a Swaraj fund from a tree. Instead of spending it properly, he consumes it. His open mouth and a monster-like creature inside his stomach represent his greed and

Figure 4.1 'The leader of the famine'. The image shows a Swarajist leader picking the fruit of a Swarajist Fund from a tree.

Source: Svasthya Samacara, vol. XVI (1927). Courtesy of CSSSC, originally from the Bangiya Sahitya Parishad.

A New Black Town

161

hunger. He holds a Congress flag and is dressed in *khadi*, but he does not care much about his country: on the ground behind him lies patriotism, hidden under a basket. A boat carrying education, health, and village improvement sails into the horizon like a distant hope. He does not care that the boat is sailing away. He stands on a footrest on which is written *humbora* (false pride) that detaches him from reality.

With the Swarajists unable to carry out reforms that they earlier promised, bhadralok fear of bustee dwellers deepened. A schoolteacher, Dhurjyoti Prasad, wrote to the Corporation that bustees of immigrant workers—Sikh taxi drivers and Madrasi labourers—were deteriorating the health of his para.[21] Another schoolteacher, Nripendra Gupta, hoped that the police would evict workers living near his house because they had different ethnicities—and for that reason did not understand hygiene.[22] In a deeply prejudiced and sweeping description of immigrant workers, Gupta ranked them on their cleanliness. He placed Bengalis at the top of his list, arguing that they were far cleaner than the immigrant Oriyas (immigrants from the state of Orissa), upcountrymen (villagers), and Mahomedans (Muslims), who were 'birds of passage with no idea of cleanliness'. He warned municipal authorities:

> The settlements [near his para] are inhabited by four groups of people: Bengalis, Oriyas, Upcountrymen and Mahomedans. I have placed them in order of their cleanliness. The lowest class domes, dosadhs, mehtars and Mahomedans are very dirty. Their bustees are quagmires of filth and foul-smelling sewage in which confusion stares in the face of the visitor. The majority Oriyas are temporary visitors. They are very dirty. They are birds of passage with no idea of cleanliness.

Gupta added to his list the dalits (class here overlapped caste) arguing that like the Muslims, they were 'very dirty' and that their bustees always gave off a strong and unpleasant smell. He deployed cleanliness as a category to create a hierarchy where he placed upper-caste Bengalis above all other city dwellers.

A pamphlet published in the Bengali health journal *Svasthya Samacara* in 1926 portrays a similar sentiment; it shows migrant workers as carriers of disease (Figure 4.2).[23]

The pamphlet, titled 'the depots of disease in the city', shows spaces where the immigrants worked as hubs of disease. It portrays the bodies of non-Bengali cooks, domestic helps, shopkeepers, beetle nut sellers, tea shop owners, and other vendors as infected. As the British had, the author of the pamphlet explained that epidemics like cholera and plague first infected the unclean bodies of immigrants from where these diseases spread to the rest of the city. Visuals of unhealthy immigrants spreading disease in the city's public spaces powered the larger bhadralok plea for segregating and controlling an 'unfit' *bustee* population.

Figure 4.2 'The depots of disease in the city', a pamphlet published in *Svasthya Samacara*.
Source: Svasthya Samacara, vol. XV (1926). Courtesy of CSSSC, originally from the Bangiya Sahitya Parishad.

A New Black Town 163

Adding to the stereotypes of unclean immigrants, Rakhal Das Bhowmick wrote an article for the *Svasthya Samacara* in 1926 in which he connected spatial to moral hygiene. He argued that individuals who lived in filthy conditions were capable of perpetrating the most unlawful acts.[24] For example, he showed that in the previous couple of years, bustees across the city had recorded extraordinary instances of crime. He cautioned that the Swarajists, ill-equipped to sanitize the city, were placing the lives of the city dwellers in great danger.

The racialization of hygiene that informed the discursive production of the black town in colonial health reports found its way into bhadralok descriptions of immigrant working-class neighbourhoods. While the British saw all Indian bodies as infected, bhadraloks described workers who belonged to different religions, castes, and ethnicities as diseased. Such portrayals were shaped by the threat the workers posed to the bhadralok project of crafting a Hindu-Bengali city-nation. With their diverse languages, religions, and caste practices, the workers called the normativity of a Hindu-Bengali nation into question. Bhadraloks responded to these threats by describing non-Bengali and non-Hindu neighbourhoods—in contrast to the normativity of Hindu paras—as bustees. As in colonial descriptions of the black town, bhadraloks argued that bustees were more than a planning issue: they were a social and health predicament.

Harijan Sevak Sangh and Spatial Shuddhi

Once the Swarajist Corporation made it clear that it did not have the necessary funds to improve bustees, bhadraloks took upon themselves the work of solving the health predicament they diagnosed in the bustees. They joined a Swarajist organization called the Harijan Sevak Sangh (HSS) (Association to serve the lowest caste) in 1933 that worked for the uplift of the lowest castes (*harijan*s).[25] In the early 1930s, two events had set the stage for the Sangh. The first was the Poona Pact of 1932. Signed between Gandhi and Ambedkar, the Pact declared 'amongst Hindus no one shall be regarded as an untouchable by reason of his birth and they will have the same rights in all the social institutions as the other Hindus have'.[26] The second was the caste Hindu resolution of 1933 to bring untouchability to an end. At a public meeting in Delhi, upper castes under nationalist leader Madan Mohan Malaviya formed the All India Untouchability League that was later renamed as the HSS. Although the Sangh worked for harijan 'uplift', it had a strong caste Hindu bias.[27] Ambedkar, earlier a member of the Sangh, left after experiencing caste Hindu biases within the Sangh.

The HSS had branches in all major cities of India, including Calcutta. It comprised a central board and a network of provincial boards under the supervision of the centre. At the head of the central board was the President, appointed from among the ranks of upper-caste volunteers. The President drafted laws and bye-laws and arranged for funds to carry out civic improvements. He also selected the head of the provincial boards, or the *pratinidhi*s. The pratinidhis ruled over smaller provincial boards, appointing volunteers or *pracharak*s.

In Calcutta, upper-caste, educated bhadraloks joined the HSS as pracharaks. The HSS gave them bicycles that they rode into the bustees, and thus came to be known as cycle-pracharaks.[28] The HSS advised the cycle-pracharaks to set personal examples through their improvement work. An ideal pracharak, it described, 'left bed at two-thirty in the morning, read the Gita, ran four miles and walked two, and then cleaned the street for an hour'.[29]

Convened for the uplift of harijans, the HSS, however, worked to maintain a status quo where upper castes watched over and supervised the dalits. Within the Sangh, any transgression of caste practices called for concern. Ramji Hansraj's writings on pracharak work in a bustee in Calcutta is an example of this concern. Hansraj, a Swarajist had travelled from Bombay to visit a bustee in Calcutta in 1935. He was much appalled by the pracharak work in that bustee.[30] Observing upper-caste pracharaks sanitize privies in lower-caste huts, he feared that the pracharaks would erase caste boundaries in their improvement work. He explained that the lowest castes, inherently unclean, should clean privies.

Quite contrary to what Hansraj thought, the pracharaks did not try to erase caste boundaries. Their improvement work reinforced caste expectations instead. The pracharaks agreed that street cleaning was indeed harijan work: they explained that the harijans had failed to do 'their work', that is, sanitize Calcutta's streets, privies, and huts. For that reason, the upper castes, who were more educated in hygiene, were instructing harijans on cleanliness. In such arguments, the pracharaks connected social to sanitary problems, explaining dirtiness as a caste disposition.

As cycle-pracharaks, bhadraloks surveyed bustees and undertook censuses. From their surveys, they compiled a list of behaviour common to all harijans. They labelled these as 'Harijan habits'.[31] As one enthusiastic pracharak of HSS, described, alcohol addiction, theft, immorality, violence, and laziness were common 'Harijan habits'.[32] He suggested other pracharaks to make sure that the harijans rid themselves of their habits by taking a bath everyday and

A New Black Town

keeping their houses clean. He also advised harijans to whitewash the interiors of their houses, start their day with prayers, and also follow a vegetarian diet. Clearly, the pracharaks used their list of 'Harijan habits' to intervene in the bustees and control the lives of its residents.

In the early days of the HSS, Gandhi's ideas of untouchability informed pracharak work in Calcutta. Gandhi had moved away from *sanatanist* (Hindu traditionalist) views that underscored the divine roots of untouchability; instead, he explained untouchability as 'a human manufacture', meaning that human agency produced untouchability.[33] This argument embroiled Gandhi in a debate with the sanatanists who believed in the divine origins of untouchability. Lawyer Basant Kumar Chatterjee, a sanatanist, for example, argued that ancient Hindu scriptures such as the Vedas referred to untouchability in defining groups like chandals and asprisyas.[34] Gandhi disagreed; he explained that asprisyas were not untouchables but morally impure.

Separating asprisyas from untouchables, Gandhi described untouchability as a 'law of sanitation' produced by 'the placement of human bodies in certain material conditions'.[35] The city, he explained, provided the material condition that produced untouchability. He described 'slums' as different from bustees— while urban filth shaped slums, 'bustees' were traditional Indian settlements in villages that were clean and hygienic. Gandhi argued that as the filth of the city produced unhygienic living conditions, harijans were not characteristically unclean; like all city dwellers, they deserved equal access to city spaces.

The cycle-pracharaks agreed with Gandhi on the human manufacture of untouchability, but rejected his view that harijans should have equal rights to the city. They explained that harijans, living in filth and excreta, if allowed to enter upper caste neighbourhoods, would only spread disease. For that reason, the pracharaks proposed 'spatial shuddhi' before granting harijans access to all city spaces. Spatial shuddhi involved a double wash: external and internal. For the external wash, the pracharaks sanitized streets, huts, and installed water stand posts in the bustees. Internal wash, on the other hand, involved the cleansing of the soul. This required bustee dwellers to chant Ramnam (the name of Hindu god Ram) and give up beef and alcohol.

The history of shuddhi can be traced back to the Arya Samaj, a militant Hindu-nationalist outfit. Under the supervision of their leader Dayanand Saraswati, the Arya Samaj initiated a movement called shuddhi or purification in April 1875. The shuddhi movement was premised on the idea that all Indians were Hindus and those that were not had to be converted. The Arya Samajists carried out *shuddhikaran*, purification rituals, to convert non-Hindus to Hinduism. The first recorded shuddhikaran took place in 1877, when a Muslim man was converted to Hinduism. In the early 1900s, a follower of Dayanand, Shraddhanand, worked on Sangathan, or uniting a Hindu group in north India. Over the next few years, shuddhi emerged as a powerful tool to consolidate Hindu ranks and galvanize the construction of a pan-Indian Hindu community.

Like the Arya Samajists, the pracharaks' shuddhi campaigns tried to establish a Hindu, upper caste hold over Calcutta by purging non-Hindu practices in the bustees. A nineteenth-century book, *Knights of the Broom*, by a civil servant, Richard Greeven, inspired the pracharaks in leading their shuddhi campaigns.[36] Greeven in his book had surveyed harijan sweeper slums of Benares. Analysing the street songs of the sweepers, Greeven argued that the Hindu god Nakul had created them to clean the stairway to heaven. Later, when the Muslims arrived, the harijan sweepers cleaned their camps and gave up their Hindu habits. The pracharaks borrowed from Greeven the idea that the harijans were Hindus; however, they rejected his argument that the harijans chose to renounce Hinduism—they pointed out instead that the Muslims had forced harijan sweepers to give up Hindu habits.

In addition to Greeven, the pracharaks drew inspiration from the work of Vindhya Babu, an HSS cycle-pracharak in Bihar, who in his sanitation drives took pride in converting groups of harijans to vegetarianism and teetotalism:

> Formerly they [harijans] were addicted to drink and took meat and fish. They lived in unclean surroundings and breed swine. They did not keep their bodies clean. Now they have given up flesh, fish and drinks. They wear Tulsi beads [Hindu prayer beads] and keep their houses and bodies clean.[37]

What Vindhya hoped to achieve in his pracharak work was a behavioural reform prior to initiating sanitary reforms in bustees. He described that a certain code of conduct—a vegetarian diet, the wearing of prayer beads, and abstinence from alcohol and meat-eating—could teach harijans self-discipline and keep their bustees clean. Inspired by Vindhya's work, cycle-pracharaks in Calcutta described their goal as 'establishing a permanent and close contact with them [harijans] and transforming their whole life'.[38] In addition, they warned, 'the Christian missionaries were already rushing to the scene [in the slums], doing nothing but providing a few amenities like a water pipe or a good road and making recipients declare they are Christians'.[39] Competing with missionaries in trying to influence harijans, the pracharaks saw in shuddhi a meaningful way to craft a Hindu-Bengali city.

A New Black Town

167

Spatial Shuddhi, a Process of Exchange

Naraindas Rattanmal Malkani, a member of the Swaraj Party, toured scavenger bustees in Benares in 1934.[40] He observed that the mud huts in these bustees violated building regulations. He also saw 'sickly dwellers covered in filth'.[41] The filth that covered their bodies troubled him: 'dirty and diseased', he explained, the bustee dwellers carried bamboo crates full of excreta on their heads, while their carts brimmed with liquid filth that let out noxious gases.[42] He described that the scavengers 'did not mind putting their hand into drums of night-soil' or 'carry the leaking crates of liquid excreta on their head'.[43] By the end of his tour, Malkani concluded that 'the bhangi (scavengers) caste plague society in not one, but multiple ways'.[44]

Malkani's descriptions of the scavenger bustee erased boundaries between the filth that the scavengers carried and their bodies. Covered in excreta, the scavengers gave a tangible form to filth. Malkani's understanding of the term 'bustee' was in fact similar to that of the British. His surveys of reeking huts and images of filth piling in the bustees was identical to what I described in Chapter 1 as the discursive production of a black town in colonial health surveys. But at the same time, he challenged sweeping generalizations implicit in colonial portrayals of dirty 'Indian neighbourhoods' and associated filth with working-class, lower-caste, non-Bengali inhabitants of bustees. Casteism echoed the colonial language of racism in his survey of bustee huts.

Malkani's description of bustees informed pracharak work in Calcutta. Satish Dasgupta, a chemist who quit his job at Bengal Chemicals to spend his time serving the nation led many bhadralok forays into bustees. He wrote about his experiences in the journal *Harijan*. Offering striking portrayals of filth, he tried to awaken caste Hindus to the dismal conditions in harijan bustees. Caste Hindu politicians of Bengal had earlier argued that untouchability did not exist in the region; they had refused to accept the Poona Pact. Dasgupta condemned this 'regrettable mentality of the caste Hindu councillors' arguing that 'untouchability is a greater curse in Bengal than in Madras'.[45] He camped in the bustees and invented new ways to observe, perceive, and intervene in the lives of the harijans.

Dasgupta's writings, however, reduced harijan bustees into receptacles of waste. He described slum streets heaped in filth and huts with 'broken window-panes stuffed with stinking rags and a fetid smell overpowering human senses'.[46] Like Malkani, he observed scavengers 'living like animals amidst shit and filth that covered the beds, tables, and kitchen corners, not to mention the pests that ate out of the plates'.[47] Far from describing these instances as extraordinary, he offered these as a general picture of unhygiene that plagued harijan bustees.

Dasgupta, similar to colonial health officers, argued that the proximity to waste had transformed bustee dwellers into groups outside the civilized space of society. He created categories of 'us' and 'them', setting apart bustee dwellers as insanitary and disorderly (them) from an otherwise sanitary city (us). At the heart of his writings were bustee dwellers who 'living in the bustees lost the sense that they were human beings'.[48] Vivid descriptions of filth that surrounded their huts showed that sitting in filth, they were incapable of self-government.

Dipesh Chakrabarty has argued that poverty gave the working classes a sense of identity; in their minds, they were 'poor people', different from those who seemed well-off.[49] For the pracharaks who surveyed bustees and forced their way into lower-caste huts, the working class residents of bustees were more than poor—they were harijans, an identity that made it easy for the pracharaks to make a case for their inherent dirtiness: they simply underlined lower castes as polluting and the upper castes as pure, an idea that was at the core of the caste system of India. Spatial shuddhi campaigns were thus predicated on a hygienic threat that the dalits posed to the Hindu nation.

In one of his routine visits to a bustee, Dasgupta met Chamaru, a dalit refuse cart driver.[50] He explained that Chamaru's hut, reeking and unclean, showed that he was unable to control the filth. The bustee lacked regular water supply. Neither Chamaru nor the other inhabitants of the bustee had approached the Calcutta Municipal Corporation for new water stand posts. Instead, he fetched water from stand posts in a different bustee. He used this water for drinking, cleaning utensils, and washing his clothes. This meant that the water often proved insufficient to clean his hut. For that reason, filth continued to accumulate in his hut and the adjoining streets. Dasgupta led the pracharaks in ignoring the problem of insufficient water supply and described that filth accumulated on the streets because Chamaru, a lower-caste cart driver, lacked a sense of hygiene.

Until the early twentieth century, the emerging discipline of public health had relied primarily on emergency measures, such as isolation of infected city dwellers. The state considered its success in eliminating periodic outbreaks of epidemics as a triumph of technological and scientific innovation. The pracharaks, on the other hand, saw in public health an effective way to persuade harijans to cede authority in them, rather than the state, in matters of sanitation. They explained that the spatial practices of the harijans carried on their lifestyles in the villages and was incompatible to the city—the harijans had to accept pracharaks as instructors of hygiene in the city.

A New Black Town

In an article titled 'The Denizens of Hell', Dasgupta explained that most harijans had migrated from villages and did not know how to keep their huts clean in the city.[51] He pointed to the case of Ramkhelan Dosad, a scavenger, who had moved from Bihar to Calcutta and lived in a small hut in a bustee that lacked water supply and modern privies. Human and animal excreta littered the streets near his hut. Dosad did not clean the streets. He soon fell sick and went back to his village where he died. In such descriptions of streets littered with excreta, and harijan indifference to it, the association of harijans and filth went hand in hand. Pracharaks explained that spatial shuddhi campaigns would dispel the 'deplorable ignorance of the bustee people like Chamaru'.[52]

Spatial shuddhi campaigns were steeped in mimesis: they re-enacted the colonial production of the black town. Colonial health officers had earlier seized on bustee filth to break into Bengali houses, sanitize their interiors, and instruct residents in hygiene. The pracharaks similarly described bustees overflowing with filth and excreta, and their residents unaware of hygiene. They employed examples of filth to produce and maintain the hegemony of the idyllic city space: the Hindu-Bengali paras. The more the pracharaks naturalized the otherness of the bustees, the more their paras enjoyed a subtle, elusive hegemony. Their ability to separate themselves from garbage, to expel it, was the marker of their modernity. In sharp contrast, the proximity of the non-Bengali, non-Hindu lower castes to garbage, waste, and filth marked their otherness, and turned their bustees into black towns.

In Chapter 1, I discussed late nineteenth-century public health campaigns that targeted the Marwari community of Calcutta. Health officials described Marwari houses, offices, and warehouses as filthy, and tried to demolish them. The Marwaris at the time controlled much of Calcutta's cotton trade. The British took to demolitions to displace this trade. When the HSS took up bustee reform in the 1930s, the Marwaris funded several spatial shuddhi campaigns. They saw these campaigns as occasions to demonstrate their awareness of hygiene. In addition, the campaigns assisted them to pass on the blame of unhygiene to a different group of city dwellers: the dalits. The leading entrepreneur of Calcutta, G. D. Birla, for example, opened schools and clinics for dalits, while also funding cleanliness campaigns that tied together caste, poverty, and unhygiene.[53] The campaigns built on the idea that the dalits were both poor and dirty.

Vasantalal Morarka, another Marwari businessman, advised pracharaks to focus on public health in their shuddhi campaigns. Under his supervision, the pracharaks opened schools in the *mehter* (scavenger) and *dome* (crematorium workers) bustees of Haribagan to instruct the residents in hygiene, linking the dirtiness of the bustee to the dirty habits of its inhabitants.[54] The pracharaks did little to improve sewers, conservancy, and water supply—they simply tried to clean bustees by 'reforming' dalit habits.

That the dalits were incapable of demonstrating cleanliness on their own informed Marwari work in the bustees. A group of young Marwari men established an association called Dalit Sudhar Society that opened day and night schools in Calcutta's bustees.[55] The students of these schools were dalit washers of tarred roads, sewer cleaners, sweepers, and cobblers. Keeping in tune with the nationalist argument that Hindi was the national language of India, the medium of instruction at the night schools was Hindi. Most students, however, spoke Urdu and Bengali and found it difficult to follow instructions at the school. Besides offering basic general education, the schools instructed them in cleaning privies. The school authorities also cooperated with societies that promoted vegetarianism to teach students the benefits of not eating meat (mostly spiritual benefits).[56] Instruction at the school was different from the lifeworld of the dalits, yet what attracted them to the school were the grain shops at the school premises that distributed rice at a subsidized rate.

Recent scholarship on caste has questioned earlier assumptions that Bengal demonstrated exceptionalism in matters of caste. While some scholars argue that there was a remarkable absence of caste-based mobilization in Bengal's electoral politics, others have shown that caste was always a socio-political reality.[57] As Partha Chatterjee pointed out, although electoral politics did not require caste mobilization, the upper castes exerted a unique hold over all public institutions and dominated public political life.[58] The upper castes benefitted from English education that gave them a higher class status and a voice that, as Dwaipayan Sen described, was the reason why 'all that upper-caste bhadralok saw in Dalits was fodder for their own ideologies'.[59] The gap between upper- and lower-caste aspirations kept growing from Namashudra revolts in late nineteenth century to the twentieth-century nationalist uprisings.[60] As Partha Chatterjee further explained, after provincial autonomy in Bengal in 1935, the centres of upper-caste Hindu dominance came under challenge from a rising Muslim middle class. The partition of India in 1947 solved this dilemma, re-instituting upper caste hold over public political life.[61]

Spatial shuddhi campaigns in the 1930s worked to extend upper caste hegemony over public spaces of Calcutta. These campaigns were part of a desperate effort that the bhadraloks had launched to eliminate all threats to the Hindu-Bengali city-nation. The campaigns involved bargains where

A New Black Town

bhadraloks guaranteed civic improvements in return of bustee dwellers' promises of giving up beef, alcohol, and other habits that the bhadraloks argued were not Hindu.

In May 1936, the pracharaks carried out spatial shuddhi in a bustee where lower-caste migrant rickshaw pullers from Bihar lived. Three people had died from smallpox in that bustee that year.[62] The rapid loss of lives worried the rickshaw pullers, who decided to pray to Sitala, the goddess of smallpox. On the day of worship, they assembled at a small field in the bustee and erected an adorned podium on which they placed the idol of Sitala. They decorated the nearby trees with lights and played loud music. All through the day, they engaged in rituals, offering gifts and flowers to the idol. The rituals ended with animal sacrifices. The butchers supplied them with cows, buffaloes, calves, goats, and rams. They put vermillion on the heads of these animals and slaughtered them in public.

At this point, the pracharaks intervened. They tried to stop the rickshaw pullers from slaughtering the cows.[63] Rather than pointing to the brutality of animal sacrifice, they argued that Hindu religion was against cow slaughter and that the rickshaw pullers—as Hindus—should abstain from it.

The rickshaw pullers resisted the pracharaks and rejected their advice. The next day, they brought in more cows and slaughtered them in broad daylight. The following morning, a young girl in the bustee contracted cholera. The pracharaks seized on this incident to strengthen their campaign against beef-eating. They argued that by consuming beef, the rickshaw pullers had angered Hindu gods, who had then inflicted cholera on the girl. Pracharaks explained to the rickshaw pullers that they could now promise clean streets, better sewers, water stand posts, and regular waste disposal only if the rickshaw pullers changed their conduct and took to a Hindu way of life.

Similarly, in the Muslim-majority bustee of Mehedibagan, pracharaks paved the streets and installed water pumps—but only once the residents agreed to give up alcohol and 'flesh' (meaning meat-eating).[64] The inhabitants of Mehedibagan bustee were Muslim sweepers who worked for the municipal corporation.[65] They were accustomed to consuming alcohol for a variety of reasons, including its curative powers. A glass of hadia, a local decoction brewed from fermented rice, energized their bodies after a long day's hard work. They consumed better varieties during festivals. Marriage ceremonies were, in fact, incomplete without alcohol. Though the Muslim sweepers did not consider alcohol to be a setback for their spirituality, the bhadraloks did.[66] As pracharaks, they argued that alcohol played havoc with the minds and bodies of the sweepers and could wreck the peace of their domestic lives.

Once the sweepers pledged to give up alcohol, the pracharaks carried out periodic surveys to check whether they had really given it up. In one such intervention, they planted *tulsi*, a tree considered holy by the Hindus, in the yards of the sweeper huts. This made the sweepers furious; they complained that the pracharaks were more interested in converting them to Hinduism than in cleaning the bustees and improving their hygiene.

The pracharaks celebrated 'Harijan Week' in May 1933. Caste Hindu organizations such as the Gujarat Shakahaari Mandal (Gujarat Vegetarian Association), the Arya Samaj Dalit Uddhar Samity (Arya Samaj Association for the Uplift of the Lower Caste), and the Calcutta Harijan Sabha (Calcutta Society for Improving Harijans) assisted pracharaks in organizing week-long activities in the bustees.[67] The week commenced with pracharaks cleaning the streets of the bustees while instructing its residents in Hindu hygiene and vegetarian diet. Sweeping the yards, they informed the hut dwellers of the evils of eating beef. While cleaning the interior of the huts, they explained how alcohol destroyed families.

The Harijan Week celebrations coincided with new schools that Swarajists opened in the bustees. The pracharaks paid chanda to run these schools.[68] They also worked as teachers. The curriculum at the schools included lectures on the lives and works of Hindu spiritual leaders. The teachers delivered speeches on Hindu deities and read passages from Hindu religious texts. They encouraged the students to worship the Hindu poet Tulisdas.[69] On the birth anniversaries of the Hindu gods Krishna and Ganesh, the students performed cultural programmes. In some schools, the teachers organized evening classes on hygiene. These classes instructed students in cleanliness, conveyed through the mythical tales of Hindu epics Ramayana and Purana.[70]

Other than classroom education, the schools also instructed students in a Hindu physical culture. The teachers encouraged mental, physical, social, and spiritual growth of the students, arguing that Hinduism mandated all-round growth. They invited Hindu scoutmasters, Pandit Sheo Nath Shukla and Baijanath Singh from Gujarat, to train students in Hindu martial arts: the use bows, arrows, spear, sword, and the lathi.[71]

The students who attended these schools were the children of sweepers and scavengers. Every morning they helped their parents clean the city. By the time they returned from work, their bustees had run out of water. When they reached school, dirt still covered their hands and clothes. The pracharaks rebuked the students for their 'inherent lack of hygiene' and explained that as Hindus, they were supposed to wash their bodies and wear clean clothes.

A New Black Town

After school, they visited the houses of the students to supervise the cleaning of their hands and feet.

The medium of instruction at these schools, unlike the night schools, was Bengali.[72] For students who did not speak Bengali, the schools did not have any alternate medium of instruction. This was a major problem in Muslim bustees where most residents spoke Urdu.[73] The parents informed the pracharaks that their children were facing difficulties at the schools and asked them to introduce Urdu as a medium of instruction. The pracharaks refused.

In September 1933, enrolment in the bustee schools suddenly dropped. The reason was a rumour that had circulated among the city's barbers.[74] The rumour was that in the name of recruiting students, the pracharaks were abducting children and silently killing them. The barbers claimed they had seen pracharaks taking children to a nearby bridge and pushing them off. Beating drums, they informed the inhabitants of bustees to take their children out of these schools.

When the pracharaks heard about these rumours, they organized awareness-raising campaigns to dispel the barbers' fears. Touring the bustees on their cycles, they advised the barbers to send their children back to the schools. Like the barbers, they also played drums to raise awareness of the good work they were doing in the schools. To attract students back to the schools, they opened grain stores in school compounds to sell it at subsidized rates.

Harijan Week also coincided with the annual celebrations of Durga Puja. The pracharaks introduced a new ritual of inter-caste mixing on the days of Pujas.[75] They encouraged para clubs to let the lower castes visit their Pujas and also made sure that they used the same entrance to the pandal. At night, the pracharaks took the upper castes on a tour of the bustees. They surveyed its spaces, planted flowering trees, and trimmed overgrown bushes. The next day, they allowed their children to play with the lower-caste children in neighbourhood parks.

The bustee dwellers, however, did not readily participate in these inter-caste mixing programmes. They pointed out that these interactions simply painted the lower castes as inherently dirty. When the pracharaks invited the residents of Tangra bustee to a Durga Puja in an upper caste neighbourhood, they declined. Instead, they organized a separate Puja in their own bustee.[76]

Spatial shuddhi campaigns worked to train the inhabitants of bustees as Hindu labouring subjects. The change brought about by these campaigns was not one of empowering and liberating bustee dwellers, but rather of controlling them and changing them narrowly in the framework of the bhadraloks'

174   A Hygienic City-Nation

thinking. Taking the para as the spatial unit of a Hindu-Bengali nation, the
bhadraloks offered a Hindu commentary on sanitation. They argued that
dalits, Muslims, and other bustee dwellers were far too uncivilized to enjoy
equal rights to the city. They tried to standardize Hindu-Bengali codes of
conduct as the form of behaviour that was acceptable in the city. Urbanity in
this respect was a misnomer; bhadraloks were grooming bustee dwellers as
Hindu city dwellers in preparation for an impending Hindu nation.

The World War, Famines, and a Red City

Intense factionalism kept the Swaraj Party divided after C. R. Das passed
away in 1925. Conflict centred on who would follow Das as the next mayor.
Between 1925 and 1930, urban landlords were a formidable group within the
party, and their power alienated politicians from the countryside. Meanwhile,
communalism divided the party as Muslim councillors questioned the party's
Hindu biases. A. K. Fazlul Huq was elected the first Muslim mayor of Calcutta
in 1935, but he resigned over religious differences. In 1937, with the support
of influential Muslim families, he launched an attack on the Corporation,
demanding communal awards or separate seats for the Muslims at the
electorate—a step that weakened the Congress's hold on the Corporation.
In 1940, with separate electorates, the Muslim League, a Muslim-majority
political party, was elected to lead the municipal corporation.

The Muslim League took up municipal work amidst wartime anxieties.
In 1942, the Japanese, who were allied with Germany in the ongoing world
war, defeated British soldiers in Burma and proceeded towards Calcutta.
The fear of an impending Japanese attack gripped the minds of Indians. In
December 1942, the Japanese bombed Calcutta. They tried to destroy the
famous Howrah Bridge and then targeted the port. Their goal was to cut off
Calcutta's connections with the rest of the country.

The bombing of the port killed three hundred dock workers. As Janam
Mukherjee has shown in a fascinating study of wartime Calcutta, the British
used the dead workers to make a case for tightening the city's defences, but once
their purpose was met, they disposed of the dead without even documenting
who they were.[77] These brutal, self-seeking policies of the British added to
the city's wartime anxieties. Perhaps the most ruthless of their policies was
stockpiling grain for soldiers who were already well supplied. The policy of
diverting grain supplies from the Bengal countryside to Britain resulted in a
horrific famine. In 1943, the famine destroyed the Bengal countryside, forcing

A New Black Town   175

farmers to flee their lands in search of food, shelter, and new work. They reached Calcutta and squatted on the street-sides.

Tanika Sarkar described the 1940s in Calcutta as 'a stormy decade'.[78] The war, together with widespread poverty, destitute villagers, hungry, and homeless people painted a picture of a wretched urban life. In January 1944, three hundred villagers from the famine-torn countryside reached Sealdah Railway Station in Calcutta. Upon arriving, they quickly made their way to relief shelters in the bustees. One group of farmers, who came from the district of Bagnan, reached a relief shelter in Barrabazaar bustee.[79] They hoped to live there for a few months while they sought work. But Seraj Mondol, who had been living at the shelter for months, warned that the shelter could not feed even half the bustee population.[80] Starving for days, his family joined *kangali micchil*s, processions of the starving, who marched in the streets, begging for food.

Calcutta's urban fabric was ripped apart in the 1940s by these kangali micchils begging passers-by for food, scouring trash bins, and fighting with stray dogs for the last crumbs of food from the bins. Their shadowy figures hovered like apparitions on the city's arterial streets and behind stylish storefronts. Their processions marched through the rich paras and knocked on the doors of the wealthy begging for *fyan* (a starchy residue of rice, usually discarded).[81] Their cries for fyan left an imprint in the Bengali psyche, finding their way into plays like *Nabanna*, written by Bijon Bhattachraya on the famine of 1943. The play centres on unfortunate events that take place in the life of a peasant, Pradhan Samaddar, as the famine develops in Bengal.

With kangali micchils and the fear of yet another Japanese attack, bhadraloks explained that the British were not their only enemy. The micchils had revealed two things. First, it was no longer possible to ignore global forces of fascism that had produced famines and destitution in India. Second, the Swarajist brand of nationalism was bourgeois; it served only the interests of the elites, leaving the poor without basic rights of food and shelter. Bhadraloks described that the war had unleashed fascist forces that affected everyday life in Calcutta; triggering violence and deepening poverty, the war made it necessary for Indians to redefine the nation as more than Hindu, as an anti-fascist community. Neither the Swarajist, nor Muslim League ideologies, however, were equipped to fight fascism.

Faced with the disastrous effects of the war, bhadraloks found the Communist ideologies of fighting global fascism more meaningful. The Communist Party had first taken shape in Kanpur in December 1925. In its initial years, it remained largely underground because the British banned all Communist activities in the country. World War II changed this scenario. When the Communists supported the British–Soviet wartime alliance in fighting Germany, the British softened their stance and, in 1942, lifted the prohibition on Communist activities.

The Communists saw themselves as internationalists, part of a larger, global community struggling against fascism. But given everyday colonial oppressions—the kangalis, the famine, and intense factionalism at the municipal corporation—local concerns coloured their global ambitions. They called for national unity, asking that the rich and poor and Hindus and Muslims join hands in the national work of fighting fascism. This fight, they argued, was both local and global. They explained, for example, that the municipal corporation was fascist and had for years promised urban improvements but carried none out. In coming together to fight fascism, the nation could pressure the Corporation to improve infrastructure, the state to reduce grain prices, and also lend their support to the Soviet Union in its antifascist war effort.

A substantial part of the Communist ideology centred on a critique of Congress nationalism. In 1925, M. N. Roy, an early Indian communist writer, claimed that Gandhian ideals of nationalism were not enough to free the country from colonial rule. He believed that the nationalist elites shared with imperial forces a fear of the working classes. He described the Indian intelligentsia as the 'child of the British Government'.[82] In his view, nationalism had created a space solely for bourgeois solidarity and self-aggrandizement. He predicted that 'there can be no doubt that the overthrow of British rule in India will be achieved by the combined efforts of the bourgeoisie and the masses, but we cannot say as yet what form their union will take'.[83]

In another article, Roy raised the question: *who will lead* (the masses)? In this article he compared the Swaraj Party to Russian cadets, arguing, after Lenin, that these were 'worms born out of the decayed carcass of Revolution'.[84] He wrote that Swarajist methods, their faith in passive resistance, had robbed the nationalist movement of its revolutionary goals, making it a program of bourgeois reforms. Quite like the Swarajist *Civitas Dei*, the Communists dreamed of a red city where workers and the urban poor would enjoy the same rights as all other city dwellers.

On the day Hitler attacked the Soviet Union, bhadraloks declared, 'we are the friends of the Soviet', and painted the city walls red, attached red flags to cars and buses, and plastered red posters on the walls of neighbourhood houses.[85] Their movement received further impetus when the celebrated Bengali poet,

A New Black Town   177

Rabindranath Tagore refused to endorse Japan's attacks on China. Japanese poet
Yone Noguchi had written to him asking for support. In a fiery letter, Tagore
castigated Japanese ideology, telling Noguchi, 'you are ascribing to humanity
a way of life which is not even inevitable among the animals'.[86] Bhadraloks
drew inspiration from Tagore's letter. They formed defence committees called
*janaraksha bahini*s (people's defence committees) in their paras that pledged
to fight fascism in all its forms. Similar to the pracharaks, volunteers of the
janaraksha bahini made inroads in bustees but expanded the earlier spatial
shuddhi campaigns to include an anti-fascist language.

Janaraksha Bahini and the Bustees

Although the Communists condemned Swarajists as bourgeois, their movement
to build a red city was similar to the Swarajist project of building a city-nation.
Like the Swarajists, the Communist movement centred on the everyday space
of the para and manifested itself by inscribing the para and bustee with distinct
cultural meanings that pitted one against the other. The Communists, like
the Swarajists, invested bhadraloks with the work of building the red city.
They held public meetings in parks and clubs in their para, where they read
proclamations (*istehar*s) congratulating the Red Army for saving Moscow from
the fascists and also discussed local concerns like the adverse effects of high
grain prices. They organized processions that walked the streets carrying red
flags (*lal jhanda*s) and shouting 'Soviet zindabad'—long live the Soviets. They
entered the bustees near their paras and carried out sanitation campaigns in
exchange for the bustee dwellers commitment to their antifascist movement.

The Strong organization (*songothon*) was at the heart of Calcutta's Communist
movement. Describing the state and all of its institutions as fascist, bhadraloks
argued that only a well-organized committee, janaraksha bahini, could shield
the para from fascist attacks. Each *bahini* comprised twenty members under
a leader (*dalapati*) who recruited the bahini volunteers from among the para's
men. The bahini met three times each week at a neighbourhood location
known as the party office. The party office was the centre of Communist
activities in the para. Like the para club, it was a room in the neighbourhood.
Here, the bahini received instruction in a global curriculum: Chinese history,
Indian history, Soviet guerrilla warfare, writing posters, military discipline,
and poetry and songs that celebrated antifascism.

The bahini worked as a propaganda squad in the para. It established close
ties with other para committees like the Durga Puja committee and the para

club. In many paras, the clubs doubled as party offices. Starting from the party office, the bahini led prabhat feri (groups that toured the para in the morning, singing antifascist songs), poster exhibits, daily *prachar* (publicizing Communist ideas), and collected signatures from the para's houses for their petitions. In the evenings, they met at the party offices to draft isthears or pamphlets that discussed both national and global concerns ranging from the high price of grain and Hindu–Muslim riots to Hitler's fascist ideologies. The bahini later pasted these istehars on the walls of the para's houses.[87] They held meetings or *sabha*s in the para demanding that the state quickly respond to their concerns.

In 1944, faced with high grain prices, the state opened ration stores in all wards of the city. Rationing fixed the quantity and price of grain in circulation. It promised to control further rises in the price of grain by determining who could buy grain, how much, and at what price. Those who were below the poverty line could buy grain at subsidized rates at the ration stores. Everyone who wanted to buy grain from ration stores had to register with the state, which issued ration cards that had to be produced when buying grain.

The state, however, mishandled the entire process of registering names and issuing cards. Some city dwellers complained they did not receive their cards in time, while others reported they did not receive their cards at all.[88] Bustee inhabitants said that they were not even asked to register their names for the cards. The administrative confusion in issuing ration cards dovetailed with a black market in grain that left ration stores understocked. Storekeepers sold the low-priced grain they got from the state at an inflated rate to black marketeers. The black marketeers, in turn, sold this grain at a higher price, resulting in skyrocketing grain prices in the city.

One of the earliest kinds of work that the bahini carried out was supervising ration stores in their para. Guarding the stores, they confirmed that store owners distributed the grain to para dwellers and not to the black marketeers. On the morning of 17 January 1945, neighbours in a south Calcutta para waited almost five hours for the ration store to open.[89] When the store still did not open, the bahini led them in confronting the store owner. While the store owner and the neighbours were caught up in loud exchanges, a truck stopped behind the store. A group of men got off the truck and started loading grain. When the neighbours realized that these men were black marketeers, they intervened and tried to stop them. A group of bahini volunteers rushed to the police, who refused to help. The bahini then decided to take matters in their own hands. They barricaded the ration store, not allowing the truck to leave. They made the truck driver and his associates return the grain back to the store.

A New Black Town

Although paras remained the centre of their activity, the bahini envisioned the bustee as the landscape of an antifascist united front. The bahinis' works in the bustees carved out an independent domain in which both the ability of the state and of landlords to intervene was limited. Instead, urban intellectuals—teachers, scientists, poets, and authors—who became members of the bahini raised subscriptions from their paras to design improvements to solve the plight of bustee dwellers. Like the Swarajist cycle-pracharaks, public health concerns cleared the way for the bahinis intervention in the bustees. They provided instructions to residents of bustees on how clean spaces and healthy bodies build a strong nation.[90] Between 13 and 20 June 1943, they arranged for a 'food week' to save the city from famine and epidemics. On these days, they sold rice at lower prices in the bustees. They not only tried to solve the food problem but also held lectures on public health and hygiene. In some bustees, the bahini established medical boards; they administered anti-cholera injections. With subscriptions raised from the para, they opened clinics and hired physicians.

One of the earliest campaigns that the bahini led was against malaria. The Municipal Corporation, then under the All-India Muslim League, had already declared that malaria was no longer a threat in Calcutta. The bahini, however, found numerous instances of the disease in the bustees they surveyed. In Narkeldanga Gas Company bustee, for example, they found a shoemaker dead of malaria. At the Kasai (butcher) bustee, a young boy named Hussain succumbed to the disease. [91] Worried about the health of the city, the bahinis carried out extensive cleansing of bustees at their own expense. Bahini volunteers cleaned the streets and sewers, doused disinfectants, and burnt piles of garbage.

On 25 November 1944, bahinis across Calcutta observed Malaria Nibaran Day (End Malaria Day). On that day, they opened red flag relief centres in bustees that worked as spaces both to educate bustee dwellers in hygiene and also to disseminate Communist ideologies.[92] Volunteers at the relief centres administered anti-malarial medicines while also training bustee dwellers to fight fascism. The red flag volunteers of Narkeldanga bustee led processions singing 'we will end malaria' while also chanting slogans of 'Soviet zindabad'. Mir Ahmed, who sold *surma* (kohl) and lived in the bustee brought together young boys to join the procession at the relief centre.[93] They complained that the Corporation was indifferent, that the ward councillor was always absent, and thanked the Communists for assisting them to fight a fascist Corporation.

At the red flag centres, the bahini formed smaller malaria prevention committees that appointed volunteers to sanitize bustees on a weekly basis. The Muslim League and the Congress both sent volunteers to work with the malaria prevention committees. Calcutta's *bidi* (a form of cheap cigarette), tram, and port workers unions also joined the relief centres.[94] Nevertheless, like the Swarajists, Communist improvement work in bustees conflated lower caste bustee dwellers with the space they inhabited. The sense of filth and disease in both Swarajist and Communist narratives remained a sociocultural construction that established social identity by reifying and reproducing social differences. The unhygienic quality of bustee streets was rapidly transferred to an image of the dirtiness of the lower castes who inhabited those spaces. While encouraging bustee dwellers to fight fascism, bhadralok surveys employed poverty and disease to argue that the residents of bustees lacked even the basic knowledge of how to clean themselves, which made it necessary for the bhadraloks to intervene in and control bustees.

The work of the bahini provided the ideological framework within which philosophies of a more inclusive nationalism were supposed to take shape. Expressing solidarity with Communist movements in Russia, the bahini envisioned a city that endorsed the principles of equality. Though their antifascist ideas embraced unity and equality, they did not consider bustee dwellers to be equal. For the bahini, bustees merely symbolized the failure of the bourgeoisie to address the needs of the people, and the inhabitants of bustees featured as individuals in need of guidance to become proper citizens.

In one of their surveys, when a bare-boned bustee dweller informed the bahini that government relief kitchens never had enough food, the bahini decided to open *longorkhanas* (soup kitchens). They did not petition the state for any help, convinced it would not respond. Instead, they raised *tarkari chanda* (subscriptions for cooking a vegetarian meal at the kitchens) in the para to open longorkhanas in the bustees.[95] With the money raised from the para, the bahini prepared *poori tarkari* (bread and potato-curry) for all bustee dwellers. Because the bhadraloks feared the sanitary situation in the bustees, the longorkhanas doubled as clinics. The bahinis administered vaccines to the destitute individuals who visited the longorkhana for a meal.

In the Dixon Lane longorkhana, a group of boys from the bustee refused to eat at the kitchen, complaining that the bahini 'pierce us with needles once we have eaten'. The bahini spent hours explaining that the needles were actually medicines that kept disease away. They told the boys that they were not aware of how much dirt stuck to their bodies and 'You are already starving. Now, if

A New Black Town   181

you fall sick ... imagine!'[96] After inoculating the bustee youth, the bahini told them stories about the greatness of India.[97] They instructed them in songs on the richness of their motherland and informed them as well about the ongoing war, forming them into squads of the antifascist movement.

The bahini had a separate wing to train the *kishore* (youth). This organization, the *kishore bahini* (youth brigade), issued membership cards. Its goal was to promote the dual spirit of nationalism and antifascism among the youth. Immediately after the Japanese bombing of the Calcutta dockyards, its organizers appealed to the youth to take up the work of saving bustees from further fascist attacks.[98] At three clubs across the city, youth received training to deal with bombs and firearms. One of the main grievances of the bustee dwellers was that even after the Japanese bombing, the state had not opened any shelter for them. The kishore bahini arranged for bustee dwellers to be housed in brick buildings when sirens went off and another bomb attack was expected.

Besides receiving instruction in armed fights, the kishore bahini also received training in sporting and cultural programmes that combined antifascist ideas with love for the motherland. Modelled after Marshal Tito's children's army, the kishore bahini engaged in sports to build strong bodies, useful for national work.[99] One of the games they played was called 'Burning Hitler's Train'. They pretended to be guerrilla soldiers who boarded a German train carrying fascists and then de-railed it.[100] In another game, they marched to the top of an imaginary hill, swords tied to their waist, and burned a Japanese camp.

Even with its broad appeal for national unity and Hindu-Muslim alliance, the janaraksha bahini had a strong Hindu bias. This bias was most visible in elaborate worships of Hindu deities like Saraswati that the kishore bahini organized. Saraswati is the Hindu goddess of wisdom and learning. The kishore bahini explained that as most of them were students, the worship of Saraswati made sense. Nevertheless, the puja was a way of celebrating the emergence of a Hindu nation united in its goal of fighting fascism. The kishore bahini raised subscriptions for the Puja in their para. They arranged for the Puja at the para club or in an open field under a canopy. In north Calcutta's Barrabazaar region, their invite read, 'the deity will impart truth and knowledge, which is most important for the nation'.[101] In Kalighat, the boys organized musical evenings on the day of the Puja and sang nationalist songs to entertain their para. The biggest Saraswati Puja, however, was in Priyanath Mallik Lane. The kishore bahini there fed three hundred people from bustees and distributed clothes. They also invited bustee families to share the *bhog*, the food offered to the deity.[102]

Bhadraloks drew inspiration from the antifascist movements of the Soviets in envisioning a red and equal city in Calcutta. Their work in the bustees, however, remained fraught with inequality. Far from egalitarian, bustees displayed the top–down application of normative rules and ideas articulated by the bhadraloks that established their dominance over the poor, non-Hindus, and lower castes. Meanwhile, bhadralok attempts to accommodate all local demands through an extended platform of discursive devices turned out to not to conform to goals of national unity. The manifold tensions that grew around bhadralok promises of equality and unity only tightened their hold over the bustee.

The bahinis celebrated 'national week' in the bustees to promote national unity. Volunteers from both the Congress and the Muslim League joined them to carry out bustee improvement work. In Natoon Bazaar in north Calcutta, the president of the local Congress led the bahini in his para.[103] Meanwhile, Debendranath Mukherjee, a ward councillor and leader of the Hindu Mahasabha, worked with Communist Kamal Basu to form a united front in relief work.[104] In addition to providing food and shelter, the committee planned to vaccinate bustee dwellers. A few days later, the Congress, Hindu Mahasabha, the Communists, Entally Arya Samajists, and Beleghata Jute Union workers together formed the Entally Central Relief Committee.

The various political parties joined hands to celebrate national week, yet they were far from united in their relief work. These were the years after the Government of India Act of 1935 provided for provincial autonomy and expanded the numbers of enfranchised people. The political parties took the opportunity of carrying out famine relief work to canvass the bustees. The Hindu Mahasabha and the Muslim League formed separate relief committees for the famine of 1943 that led to communal tensions. Dr Shyamaprasad Mukherjee of the Hindu Mahasabha spoke about Hinduism at the relief centres. But when Jinnah, who represented the Muslim League, organized a relief committee for Muslims only, Mukherjee blamed him for encouraging communalism.[105] The Communists, on the other hand, put up red flags on houses, lamp posts, and bustee walls. They encouraged bustee residents to wear red flag badges. Red flags were hoisted at the party offices for the occasion of the National Week. This sectarian behaviour undermined their promises of forming a united front with other political parties.[106]

The Communists used their influence on municipal infrastructure to bargain for votes in the bustees. A certain bhadralok, Somnath Lahiri, who was a leader of the Communist Party, oversaw bustee relief centres. He argued

A New Black Town

that the Corporation had failed to renovate bustees because it did not listen to the urban poor. Lahiri promised that the Communists would listen to the bustee dwellers when refurbishing bustees.

On Sunday, 19 March 1944, Somnath Lahiri and Ismail, two communists, agreed to run for municipal office. Their symbols were the cycle and the lock and key. Their chant to the gathering crowds in the bustees was 'Who will the workers vote for? The lock and key and cycle, who else?'[107] They sang and walked nearly forty miles of bustee lands, including Tiljala, Maniktala and Beleghata. Their campaigns familiarized bustee dwellers with worker movements across the world. On the one hand, they explained that they drew inspiration from workers and would represent their worldview, yet nationalism led them to add to the workers' demands. When they organized meetings of the bulb workers' union, for instance, they supplemented the workers' demands for better wages and better housing with demands for national unity and antifascism, making nationalism a key component of the workers struggle. They argued that the workers wanted higher wages to produce more as they had realized that producing more was their responsibility for their motherland.[108] Similarly, when they visited the tram workers' bustee to raise money for famine victims, they interlaced communism with nationalism, singing:

Lal jhanda tujh se kehta hay pukar bahiya majduro/deshke raksha karo sabhi bhaiya majduro

(The red flags are urging you to protect your country.)[109]

The war had devastated the Indian economy, and prices of commodities were high in the years after the famine of 1943. Yet the wages of workers did not increase at all. Siddhartha Guha Ray has described that the municipal corporation denied several requests of tram-workers to increase wages and offer bonuses at the time of festivals.[110] The bahini stepped in at this time, inviting tram workers to join them in fighting fascist forces globally, and in return promised to support the workers' demands of a wage-hike. But by the time of the elections of 1943, a certain Mr S. Varma, who represented workers and stood on behalf of the rickshaw-pullers' union had not carried out the improvements he had promised in the bustees. The bustees remained unsanitary, and the lack of water and light, combined with heavy corruption and high grain prices, worsened the situation of the workers.

Bhadralok control over bustees tried to set the terms under which other groups and classes had to operate. These interventions were important in creating social cohesion and a sense of in-group belonging among bhadraloks themselves. This sense of cohesion was heightened by the contrast between the para and bustee and the discourse of exclusion it shaped. Armed with a new language of hygiene and steered by the goal of crafting a nation, bhadraloks came to think of themselves as being in charge of the poor. Their knowledge of hygiene, together with their visions of nation building, assisted them in leading a movement to govern the poor. Their self-confidence and social polish made them project their own paras as aspirations for bustee dwellers, eliminating all differences and turning bustees into geographies that simply conformed to the normativity of the paras. In such efforts, bustees featured as a complex political terrain generated and characterized by the bhadraloks' changing visions of the nation. Whether driven by the religious concept of daridranarayan, the voluntarism of the cycle-pracharaks, or by Communist ideology, at different historical moments, space and specific bodies of the urban poor were tied together and publicly imagined to reinforce bhadralok control over Calcutta.

Conclusion

I have argued in this chapter that the bustee served as a colonial tool to represent filth and waste-ridden geographies in Calcutta. Initially, in colonial health reports, it was a ubiquitous term to mean Indian neighbourhoods in general. This changed with the Swarajist municipal administration, to which the modern origins of bustees can be traced. The cycle-pracharaks, working with the HSS, later exerted a level of autonomy in remoulding the space of the bustee. In their discourse on the bustee, they aligned the term with stereotypical notions of filth in harijan neighbourhoods. In these representations, descriptions of filth-ridden bustees displayed the lower castes as a sullied urban underclass. Spatial shuddhi, while promising to sanitize space, reproduced the figure of filth, redrawing the boundaries between respectable and non-respectable city dwellers. As with earlier colonial constructions of 'filthy' Bengalis, bhadraloks invoked the same metaphors of filth, disease, and ignorance, to differentiate their perception of their own respectability from the negative image of the lower castes.

Bhadraloks offered a kinetic commentary on filth to argue that bustee dwellers were far too uncivilized to enjoy equal rights to the city. They then took it upon themselves to survey bustees and supervise their cleanliness. As their sanitation campaigns reveal, they did not guarantee broad civil rights—

A New Black Town   185

entry into public places and use of public facilities—to the bustee dwellers. Instead, bustee dwellers had to live under strict bhadralok directives that tried to standardize behaviour fit for the city. Representations of bustee dwellers as unable to take care of themselves, further facilitated the triumphant assertion of bhadralok leadership in the city.

Notes

1. Government of India, *Annual report of the Sanitary Commissioner with the Government of India. Calcutta: Office of Superintendent of Government Printing, 1868* [NLA].
2. For an excellent visual archive of the famine, see Naresh Chandra Sourabh and Timo Myllyntaus, 'Famines in Late Nineteenth-Century India: Politics, Culture, and Environmental Justice', *Environment and Society Portal, Virtual Exhibitions* 2015, no. 2, Rachel Carson Center for Environment and Society, Munich.
3. Dawn Society, Calcutta, *Dawn and Dawn Society's Magazine* 10, no. 7 (1907): 146.
4. John H. Broomfield, *Elite Conflict in a Plural Society: Twentieth-Century Bengal* (Berkeley: University of California Press, 1968), 250.
5. Durba Ghosh, *Gentlemanly Terrorists: Political Violence and the Colonial State in India, 1919–1947* (Cambridge; New York: Cambridge University Press, 2017), 93.
6. Hemendranath Dasgupta, *Desbandhu Chittaranjan Das* (Delhi: Publications Division, Ministry of Information and Broadcasting, Government of India, 1960), 120.
7. B. C. Ghosh, 'Civitas Dei', *Calcutta Municipal Gazette* 3, 10 November 1925.
8. *The Times of India*, 6 September 1929.
9. Ibid., 5 July 1928.
10. Ibid., 2 October 1928.
11. David Douglas Cunningham, *Plagues and Pleasures of Life in Bengal* (London: John Murray, 1907).
12. W. J. Simpson, *A Note on the Sanitation of Calcutta and Other Papers*, 1894–1897 [KCA].
13. Bhairava Chandra Datta, *The Bengal Municipal Act, Being Act III. of 1884 with Notes and an Appendix Second Edition, Revised and Enlarged* (Calcutta: Rai M.C. Sarkar Bahadur & Sons, 1916) [TBLA].
14. Amar Nath Saha, *The Bengal Municipal Act, 1932 (Bengal Act XV of 1932), Corrected Up-to-date* (Calcutta: Eastern Book Agency, 1974).

186   A Hygienic City-Nation

15. 'Minutes of the Proceedings of Corporation of Calcutta, November 23, Resolution No 1242', in *Reports on the Municipal Administration of Calcutta* (Calcutta: Government Publication, 1900) [TBLA].
16. Ibid.
17. 'Barada Prosad Roy Chowdhury vs Corporation of Calcutta', in *Report on the Municipal Administration of Calcutta* (Calcutta: Government Publication, 1926) [TBLA].
18. *The Times of India*, 18 August 1929.
19. *Janayuddha*, 5 August 1942.
20. Dasgupta, *Desbandhu Chittaranjan Das*, 12.
21. Dhurjyoti Prasad, 'Calcutta Has No Character', *Calcutta Municipal Gazette*, July 1927.
22. Nripendra Kumar Gupta, 'Soul of a City', *Calcutta Municipal Gazette*, April 1925.
23. 'Sohore Rog Songrakramoner Depot', *Svasthya Samacara*, vol. XV (1926).
24. Rakhal Das Bhowmick, 'Moral education in Health', *Svasthya Samacara*, vol. XV (1926): 233–5.
25. I would like to note here that although *dalit*s (broken) is a more fitting term, I have used the word *harijan* in this chapter to convey the inequity attached to the term and describe the way the bhadraloks used it to secure caste hierarchy, while calling to abolish caste prejudice.
26. D. C. Ahir, *Poona Pact of 1932* (New Delhi: Blumoon Books, 1999), xv.
27. Anupama Rao, *The Caste Question: Dalits and the Politics of Modern India* (Berkeley: University of California Press, 2009), 333.
28. Harijan Sevak Sangh, *Annual Report of the Harijan Sevak Sangh*, October 1932–September 1933, Delhi [NYPL].
29. *Harijan*, 5 December 1936.
30. Ibid., 15 July 1933.
31. Harijan Sevak Sangh, *Annual Report of the Harijan Sevak Sangh*, October 1933–September 1934, Delhi [NYPL].
32. *Harjian*, 16 March 1934.
33. Ibid., 27 October 1933.
34. Ibid., 29 July 1933.
35. Ibid., 2 December 1933.
36. Richard Greeven, *Knights of the Broom* (Benares: Medical Hall Press, 1894).
37. Ibid.
38. *Harijan*, 27 April 1935.
39. *The Statesman*, 4 April 1936.
40. I use the word 'scavenger' to convey the discrimination built into the term and show how widely it was used in the twentieth century by the upper castes.

A New Black Town 187

41. Naraindas Rattanmal Malkani, *Clean People and an Unclean Country* (Delhi: Harijan Sevak Sangh, 1965), 32–5.
42. Ibid., 37.
43. Ibid., 57.
44. Ibid., 56.
45. *Harijan*, 18 March 1933.
46. Ibid., 9 April 1934.
47. Ibid.
48. Ibid., 12 August 1933.
49. Dipesh Chakrabarty, *Rethinking Working-Class History: Bengal 1890–1940* (Princeton: Princeton University Press, 2018).
50. *Harijan*, 19 August 1933.
51. Ibid., 12 August 1933.
52. Ibid., 19 August 1933.
53. *The Times of India*, 9 April 1937.
54. *Harijan*, 18 February 1933.
55. Harijan Sevak Sangh, *Annual Report of the Harijan Sevak Sangh*, October 1937–Septemebr 1940.
56. *Harijan*, 14 October 1933.
57. For debates on caste in Bengal, see Praskanva Sinha Roy, 'A New Politics of Caste', *Economic and Political Weekly* 47, no. 34 (25 August 2012): 26–7. See the response to this article in Kenneth Bo Nielsen and Uday Chandra, 'The Importance of Caste in Bengal', *Economic and Political Weekly* 47, no. 44 (3 November 2012): 55–6. Also see the excellent anthology of essays on cast in Uday Chandra, Geir Heierstad, and Kenneth Bo Nielsen, *The Politics of Caste in West Bengal* (New Delhi: Routledge India, 2017).
58. Chatterjee, Partha, 'Historicising Caste in Bengal Politics', *Economic and Political Weekly* 15 December 2012.
59. Dwaipayan Sen, *The Decline of the Caste Question: Jogendranath Mandal and the Defeat of Dalit Politics in Bengal* (Cambridge; New York: Cambridge University Press, 2018), 12.
60. Sekhar Bandyopadhyay, *Caste, Culture and Hegemony: Social Dominance in Colonial Bengal* (New Delhi; Thousand Oaks; London: Sage Publications India, 2004).
61. Chatterjee, 'Historicising Caste in Bengal Politics.'
62. *Harijan*, 20 May 1933.
63. Ibid.
64. *Harijan*, 29 April 1933.
65. Badruddin Khan, 'Letter from Badruddin Tyabji to the Corporation', *Calcutta Municipal Gazette*, March 1935.
66. *Harijan*, May 1933.

67. *The Times of India*, 3 May 1933.
68. *Harijan*, 21 June 1938.
69. Ibid., December 1938.
70. Ibid., January 1939.
71. Harijan Sevak Sangh, *Annual Report of the Harijan Sevak Sangh*, September–October 1934, Delhi.
72. Ibid.
73. Ibid.
74. Ibid.
75. *Harijan*, August 1938.
76. *The Times of India*, 23 April 1938.
77. Janam Mukherjee, *Hungry Bengal: War, Famine and the End of Empire* (New York: Oxford University Press, 2015), 153.
78. Tanika Sarkar and Sekhar Bandyopadhyay, *Calcutta: The Stormy Decades* (London: Routledge, 2018).
79. *Janayuddha*, 26 January 1944.
80. Ibid., 28 November 1944.
81. Ibid.
82. M. N. Roy, *Political Letters* (Zurich: Vanguard Bookshop, 1924).
83. Ibid.
84. M. N. Roy, 'Who Will Lead? Class Differentiation in the Indian National Movement', *Communist International* 11 (1925): 55–65.
85. *Janayuddha*, 2 February 1944.
86. Ibid., 10 November 1943.
87. Ibid., 23 June 1943.
88. Ibid., 3 January 1943.
89. Ibid., 20 January 1943.
90. Ibid., 8 September 1943.
91. Ibid., 6 December 1944.
92. Ibid.
93. Ibid., 20 December 1944.
94. Ibid., 6 December 1944.
95. Ibid., 29 September 1943.
96. Ibid., 5 October 1943.
97. Ibid., 25 August 1943.
98. Ibid., 13 January 1943.
99. Ibid., 1 May 1944.
100. Ibid., 28 June 1944.
101. Ibid., 9 February 1944.
102. Ibid.
103. Ibid., 27 October 1947.

104. Ibid., 27 October 1943.
105. Ibid., 15 September 1943.
106. Ibid., 2 February 1944.
107. Ibid., 29 March 1944.
108. Ibid., 5 May 1943.
109. Ibid., 1 May 1944.
110. Siddhartha Guha Ray, 'Protest and Politics: Story of Calcutta Tram Workers: 1940–1947', in *Calcutta: The Stormy Decades*, ed. Tanika Sarkar and Sekhar Bandyopadhyay, 151–76 (Abingdon; New York: Routledge, 2018).

Epilogue

In 1903, a Bengali playwright, Beharilal Adhya, wrote *Adbhut Durgotsabh* (A Strange Durga Puja Festival), a play that explored the impact of English education on the minds of Bengalis.[1] Shyam, the protagonist of the play, is a wealthy, English-educated Bengali man who leaves his ancestral home in Calcutta's black town to live in the white town. His Bengali neighbours do not approve of his decision—they fear that living with the British, he would copy their habits and forget what his caste forbade him to do. Worried by the neighbours' concerns, his father makes several requests for him to return. Shyam finally returns, but with a heavy heart and 'against his will'.[2]

Once back in the black town, Shyam explains that the reason he left the neighbourhood was its poor sanitation. He describes the vicinities of his ancestral house as '*dirty place, dirty locality, everything dirty*'.[3] The play, in fact, opens with Shyam bewailing:

> The *native quarter* will not suit me. The sanitation here is not up to date. Who said a Bengali has to live in Bengali-tola (tola means locality)? *Foolish idea, illiterates do not know how to keep health*. Dad says people will badmouth if I live in Chowringhee. Do I care? *Life is precious and to promote longevity, it is indispensably necessary to live in an airy house*.[4]

Shyam's friends and neighbours find his behaviour confusing. They do not understand why he thinks his neighbourhood as unfit for human habitation. When his friend Akhil asks him this question, Shyam replies, 'How would you understand? *You have no idea of sanitation; you don't know how to keep up health; how to maintain longevity*'. When an elderly neighbour asks him the same question, Shyam snaps back: 'mister, a *major portion* of the bigha [nearly six thousand square metres] is used up in dalaan and uthhon. The rooms are now like *pigeonholes. Indians need lessons in house building as much as they do in shipbuilding*.'[5]

Neither Shyam's neighbour nor his friend Akhil agrees with him—they do not find their neighbourhoods unsanitary or houses improperly built.

Epilogue 191

Representing a Bengali psyche heavily influenced by British sensibilities, Shyam symbolizes a British voice in the play. He speaks like late nineteenth-century health officers who described Indians as clueless about sanitation and their houses as unsanitary structures.

In Chapter 1, I pointed to the inconsistencies in British town improvement plans for Calcutta. While the British emphasized the need for open spaces, they also forced the Bengalis to cover *uthhon*s and *dalaan*s that were open spaces inside their house. Health officers explained uthhons as spaces where Indians dumped filth. Shyam believed the same. He described uthhons and dalaans as spaces where dirt piled and remained unattended for days. He also pointed out that uthhons occupied too much space, leaving other rooms of the house a lot smaller.

In this book, I have argued that colonial practices of metaphoring filth—inscribing filth with meanings that linked dirtiness to spaces and their inhabitants—triggered late nineteenth-century town 'improvements'. I have also argued that the metaphoring of filth produced responses that went beyond simple categories of (British) force and (Indian) resistance, and generated a plethora of reactions, outlooks, and judgements among city dwellers that established *bhadralok* control over their *para*s and adjoining *bustee*s. In Chapter 1, I discussed that the British, faced with an impermeable cultural geography of Calcutta, retaliated by shaping a black town in their surveys of the city. They painted images of Indian houses seething in filth that they linked to the habits of Indians. Blackness implied more than the darkness produced by filth; it indicated the unhealthy habits of an entire race. In Chapter 4, I discussed how upper-caste Bengalis appropriated the colonial practices of metaphoring filth to trace dirtiness to the poor, lower caste, non-Hindu, and non-Bengali working-class neighbourhoods or bustees. Bhadraloks described bustees or informal settlements in exactly the same way the British described Indian neighbourhoods in need of civilization. Like the British, they employed metaphors of filth to connect bodies to waste to rationalize oppressive schemes that segregated their paras from nearby bustees and justified their ambitions of controlling the lives of the lower castes.

Analysing Victorian journalist Henry Mayhew's writings on London, Sabine Schulting described the association of dirt with bodies of the urban poor in the wake of the industrial revolution: living near dirt, the poor embodied the dirt. As the connection between human bodies and the filth grew stronger through the nineteenth century, Schulting writes that the rich also saw the poor as bearers of disease. Cholera, for instance, came to be known as 'a lower-class filth disease'. In the 1830s, British health officers in Calcutta drew similar connections between filth and human bodies, establishing a cultural association between whiteness and cleanliness. As Chapter 1 described, the spatial binaries of white/black town went beyond extending the economic and political domination of the colonizing society to authenticate the British as hygienic and civilized.

By the early twentieth century, global movements to control infectious diseases had marked scientific and technological advances that built the foundations of present-day medical surveillance and control systems. In North America, contagion control measures saw the discovery of antibiotics and a surge in vaccination programmes.[6] Public health measures in Europe included provisions for clean water and the creation of a public bath movement to instruct the poor on the benefits of cleanliness.[7] In India, public health reforms furthered colonial ambitions of domination and control. The state proposed a single standard of hygiene that failed to incorporate the multitude of concerns that informed spatial practices of the diverse population of India.

A single standard of hygiene applicable to all meant that Indians were forced to give up their caste and religious practices. Unfortunately, in this oppressive climate, even forgoing caste and religion, and a strict adherence to the new standards of hygiene, did not guarantee freedom from the stigma of being categorized as filthy; Chapter 2 pointed out that in the early twentieth century, improvement committees demolished Indian houses with the goal of evicting Indians from the centrally located parts of the city. In such efforts, the colonial construct of a 'black town' built on descriptions of Indian unhygiene facilitated authoritarian schemes of demolition and control.

We can situate the power imbalances and knowledge hierarchy of present-day developmentalism—the West's 'discovery' of poverty in the global south and suggestions of market reforms that only serves to recast the superiority of the West even in postcolonial times—in the colonial dyad of white/black town. Conceptualized as a set of epistemic/ideological systems, with the global (mostly Western) knowledge at the top and the local (local or regional) knowledge at the bottom, developmentalism works through the production of binaries similar to the colonial crafting of the white/black towns that enfolded the categories of civilized/uncivilized. Similar to the colonial plans for town improvement, the global knowledge of development (urban and economic growth), in the form of the neo-liberal paradigm, claims universal applicability. It declares the efficacy of free markets to maximize economic growth and reduce poverty. When the local fails to match up, the global knowledge

Epilogue 193

describes it as a failure of policy and advocates the need to open economies to the influence of global market forces. The supporters of developmentalism usually trace policy failure to a 'backward' government and calls for a new government that is more democratic, transparent, efficient, and non-corrupt: in a word, more Western. In such proclamations, the authors of global knowledge pay little regard to historical records that show the failure of planting ideas and practices on different cultural landscapes. Instead, they describe a single strand of development applicable to all landscapes. This idea of universal applicability conditions the ways in which they view the world and the policies that they follow, even when empirical evidence points to the contrary.

* * *

I have argued that public health concerns did not simply work to advance colonialism but embodied a rich history of appropriation of colonial ideas. As Chapter 3 describes, the Swarajists shared with the British concerns of public health. Bhadraloks, agents of the Swarajist ideas in the paras, offered their zealous support to public health campaigns. Their commitments to cleanliness and hygiene marked them as different from other city dwellers. Their obsession with hygiene transformed them into urban sanitarians and also informed their management of city space. At the heart of bhadralok management of space were codes of Hindu spatial and bodily hygiene that formed the mainstay of their government in the para.

In their pedagogic efforts to improve hygiene in their paras, bhadraloks advanced new standards of behaviour in the city. Chapters 3 and 4 argue that ideas of development in bhadralok sanitation campaigns manifested as interventions in conduct. Bhadralok campaigns included a wide variety of bodily practices such as fitness, exercise, and diet together with instructions in conduct. The campaigns therefore extended bhadralok authority to all aspects of personal and public life: they recruited men from the para to oversee and reform the hygienic habits of their neighbours. 'Watching over' the health of their neighbours, these men also entered bustees that adjoined paras and advised residents on behaviour fit for the Hindu nation.

Chapter 3 describes that the entrenchment of the bhadralok social rule echoed in several other aspects of urban life: it configured new identities, including those of women and youth. The domestic roles of women, nurturing and improving the health of their families, were central to enforcing the 'bhadralok values' of personal and domestic hygiene. Bhadralok fixation on hygiene also influenced the role they assigned to the para's youth. In routines of physical exercises at the park, and scout training camps, bhadraloks instructed young boys to follow orders and improve their physical strength. These instructions were couched in medical, social, and political terms: the boys were taught to exercise and behave in particular ways because it was good for their bodies, created social order, and also because the bhadraloks said so. The association between schooling and cleaning was so well established in the bhadralok government that it extended their authority to every aspect of everyday life.

In addition to individual cleanliness and hygiene, bhadraloks also emphasized the need to improve the moral fitness of paras. This meant that they did not simply condemn filth for spreading disease but also offered a critique of 'filthy bodies' for infecting the moral health of the para. Bhadralok goals of improving moral fitness sustained their discriminations against the lower castes who they argued were the exact opposites of respectable city dwellers. At the same time, new ideas of respectability resulted in bhadraloks redrawing boundaries of their *para*, marking its spaces as different from bustees. As Chapter 4 describes, bhadraloks actively managed urban space to display the divides between *bhadra* (respectable) residents of the para and dirty lower-caste inhabitants of bustees. By the 1930s, bhadraloks had used hygiene as the code to translate bustees as undesirable city-spaces. Their control of bustees was not simply discursive—they invaded bustees to make its spaces desirable. They schooled 'unclean' and 'corrupt' lower-caste and non-Hindu residents of bustees in Hindu hygiene. In such efforts, they subjected dalit inhabitants of bustees in a discipline similar to what the colonial state had earlier enforced upon them.

In the early twentieth century, bhadralok fascination with hygiene mirrored similar efforts of the English middle classes, but also departed from them in significant ways. Similar to Calcutta, epidemics had ravaged London at the turn of the twentieth century. City administrators responded by sanitizing the city: they built sewers and published literature that instructed city dwellers on ways to maintain good health.[8] Added to this, the English middle classes transformed their manners, emphasizing bodily hygiene, restraint, and self-control.[9] These 'manners' of the English middle classes distinguished them from the common and 'offensive' lower classes. To some degree, bhadralok interventions in the bustees was similar to the English middle-class efforts to portray cleanliness as a class disposition; however, ideas of sanitation that they encouraged also tried to transform the city into a microcosm of a Hindu-Bengali nation. For that reason, religion and caste practices overlaid principles of hygiene and mandated a certain order of space.

Epilogue

The spatial shuddhi campaigns that bhadraloks led in the bustees further tried to establish Hindu practices of sanitation as normative in the city. The overtly Hindu tone of these campaigns implied that the dalits had to give up practices that either contrasted with the Hindu principles of hygiene or borrowed from Islamic rituals. Bhadralok campaigns in the bustees were in fact similar to the Americanization movement of North America where reformers used instructions in hygiene to convert European working-class immigrants into Americans. In this movement, maintenance of social order was contingent on the maintenance of high standards of hygiene, based on perceived manners of the Americans.[10] Nevertheless, unlike cities in Europe and North America, Bengali demands for autonomy matched colonial goals to overwrite the norms of spatial hygiene. While improvement commissioners argued that the sewers and filtered water supply could civilize the city, bhadraloks resisted these improvements by inventing a new code of Hindu hygiene. Inscribing hygiene with spiritual values, they argued that their 'civilization' was different from that of the British. They described hygiene and cleanliness as their 'virtue', an asset unique to them, while also drawing on Hindu religion to explain that their hygiene was different from what the British preached. These assertions facilitated the meteoric rise of the bhadraloks as pioneers of Hindu hygiene; their houses, bodies, speech, and lifestyles reflected their cleanliness.

At the same time, bhadralok clubs in their para evolved as centres of cultural diffusion that shaped a regional Bengali identity. As Chapter 3 describes, discussions of literature and music at the para clubs cemented the bonds of a Bengali nation. Strengthening the kinship-like ties of the para, these clubs, however, were far from the space of civil society. Ideally, the civil society is the non-state voluntary organization constituted by people who have power to influence the state. It includes a wide range of organizations, networks, associations, groups, and movements independent of the state that come together to advance their common interests through collective action. In that sense, civil society provides a way for the people to cope with a larger, more bureaucratized society.[11] It provides people with power within the impersonal structures of modern society: the government and corporate business. By bringing together the people on a relatively local scale, civil society then allows ordinary people to voice and solve their common problems. In studies of European civil societies, this concept is therefore coupled with the idea of popular democracy.[12] Scholars have described voluntary associations, ranging from communes to neighbourhood associations as harbingers of democratic transitions.[13]

196   Epilogue

Although clubs brought together ordinary people of the para to advance common interests, these were far from democratic spaces. The clubs did not offer a social space between the family and the state; instead, rooted in kin-like ties, it was an extension of the family, as well as an alternative to the state. The association of bhadraloks in the clubs, rather than facilitating the democratic transition of the para, configured it to reinforce their growing authority. In such efforts, their meetings at the club resisted state intervention while also forcing their neighbours to behave in ways that they deemed proper.

International organizations such as the World Bank and the United Nations have, over the years, actively promoted the idea of civil society as a development tool for 'third world' countries. They have argued that these countries do not have experience of freedom, democracy, or economic well-being, and civil societies can usher in democratic transitions. These organizations therefore see the emergence of civil society as a mechanism to counterbalance the autocracy that reigns in these 'traditional' societies. Yet empirical evidence shows that in these countries, a very different historical condition had brought together associations of people with common interests. Within the framework of colonialism, their aspirations, however, remained very different and their methods far from democratic. More than democratic transitions, the goals of these associations were driven towards trying to adapt to changes—urban, economic, and cultural—that colonialism had forced on them. In these efforts, the associations crafted new identities through means that were not always democratic. These new identities, nevertheless, helped the people to survive the colonial city and its discipline(s).

*   *   *

This book has moved beyond the study of the built environment to focus on everyday urban life in the colonial city. Both social history and postcolonial scholarship on cities describe urbanization as a structural intervention. Exploring maps and town plans, scholars have analysed streets, buildings, and facades to explore an urbanity rooted in physical space. Scholarship on spaces that cannot be mapped is not enough; also missing are accounts of hierarchies within the black town itself. This book has addressed these gaps in the historiography of global colonial cities. I have narrated hidden stories of a city that was born in the minds of the people who lived in its spaces.

One of my main goals in writing this book was to examine regional identities that are born in urban space and to show how everyday life in the city shape these identities. To that end, I have explored strategies that city dwellers employed in their daily life to resist colonial town planning and the broad

Epilogue

homogenizing forces of Indian nationalism as well. I have argued that cultural events at bhadralok clubs fuelled a regional Bengali identity that contrasted with the ideas of cohesion that Indian nationalists, like Gandhi, projected. In Chapters 3 and 4, I have explained how bhadraloks crafted new identities as a response to colonial indifference to their caste and religious practices. Armed with this new Bengali identity that was both Hindu and upper caste, bhadraloks transformed their paras into spatial units of a Hindu-Bengali nation.

The study of the everyday in this book goes beyond surveying the work of municipal authorities, nationalists, and town planners and instead focuses on the lived experiences of the people. Calcutta's urban transitions, however, took shape in the backdrop of colonialism; I have therefore explored an everyday that unfolded in the shadow of colonialism. The para forms a lens to examine how broad historical forces like imperialism and nationalism played out in everyday spaces of the colonial city, moulding its spaces, and was, in turn, moulded by the city. This book also describes new spaces, social organizations, associations, and exchanges between people that only an analysis of ground-level urbanization can reveal. I have pointed to new forms of power, social and moral disciplines, and redefinitions of the public and private that informed everyday urban formation in colonial Calcutta, and remain relevant till date. Most importantly, paras as autonomous communities with aspects of self-rule took shape much before India achieved formal independence in 1947. Although threatened by the army of flats that have over the years occupied much of Calcutta, paras still continue to remain sovereign spatial units in the city.

Notes

1. Beharilal Adhya, *Adbhut Durgotsabh Ba Samaj Kalanka* (Calcutta: Jogendranath Sadhu, 1903).
2. Adhya, *Adbhut Durgotsabh*, 3.
3. Ibid. I have used italics for those words that are in English in the play.
4. Adhya, *Adbhut Durgotsabh*, 1.
5. Ibid., 6.
6. James Colgrove, *State of Immunity: The Politics of Vaccination in Twentieth-Century America* (Berkeley; Los Angeles; London: University of California Press, 2006).
7. Marilyn Thornton Williams, *Washing 'the Great Unwashed' Public Baths in Urban America, 1840–1920* (Columbus: Ohio State University Press, 1991).

8. Ryan Johnson and Amna Khalid, *Public Health in the British Empire: Intermediaries, Subordinates, and the Practice of Public Health, 1850–1960* (New York; Abingdon: Routledge, 2012), 89.
9. Ibid., 92.
10. Mel Van Elteren, *Americanism and Americanization: A Critical History of Domestic and Global Influence* (North Carolina: McFarland and Company, 2006).
11. Michael Edwards, *Civil Society* (Cambridge; Malden: Polity Press, 2014).
12. Tymen J. van der Ploeg, Wino J. M. van Veen, and Cornelia R. M. Versteegh, *Civil Society in Europe* (Cambridge; New York: Cambridge University Press, 2017).
13. Hillel Schmid, *Neighborhood Self-Management: Experiments in Civil Society* (New York: Springer Science & Business Media, 2001).

Glossary

adda	informal conversation
atithisala	boarding house
bhog/prasad	food cooked and offered first to the deity and then to devotees
bastubhita	ancestral house
bazaar(s)	market(s)
bhadralok(s)	English-educated, salaried, Bengali men
bustee	makeshift settlement/housing
chanda	subscription
chattra	public centre of charity, donation, and distribution
chawl	tenement like row houses
chawk	a quadrangle surrounded by apartments
cottah	unit of area used for measuring land parts; a *cottah* is roughly 1/32 of one acre
cutcherry	office to collect revenues
dalaan	a verandah or open hall for receiving visitors
dalit	the lowest in the caste hierarchy
dana	religious gift/charity
danda	stave
debutter	property invested in the deity
dwondo	punishment
ghat	embankments where pilgrims gather to take holy dip in the river
haat	seasonal markets
jaat	caste; also, can mean religion
jamaat	council of elderly Muslim men
karkhana	factories
kutcha	mud-built
*mantra*s	hymns
mehtranee(s)	women cleaners
mlechhachar	any practice that violates caste
mofussil	satellite town

moholla	neighbourhoods, usually not Bengali
nagorik	citizen
pala	turn
pandal	decorated canopy
para	neighbourhood community
pukka	brick built
samaj	precolonial Hindu community
sangha	community
sarbojonin	public
shuddhi	purification
sevak	volunteer
swaraj	self-government
tickawalah	inoculator
thakurbari	temple, a place where the Thakur (deity) resides
uthhon	courtyard
waqf	religious endowment made by a Muslim

Bibliography

Primary Sources

Unpublished Government Reports

Bengal Civil Judicial Proceedings, 1818. [TBLA]
Bengal Judicial Criminal Proceedings, 1822. [TBLA]
Bengal Judicial Proceedings, 1833. [TBLA]
Bengal Municipal Proceedings and Consultations of the Government of India and of its Presidencies and Provinces, July 1913. [TBLA]
General Department, Sanitation Branch. [WBSA]
General Department Medical Branch. [WBSA]
General Department, Miscellaneous Branch. [WBSA]
General Department, Sanitation Branch. [WBSA]
Political Department, Medical Branch. [WBSA]
Municipal Department, Sanitation Branch. [WBSA]
Municipal Department, Medical Branch. [WBSA]

Published Reports

Ahir, D. C. *Poona Pact of 1932*. New Delhi: Blumoon Books, 1999.
Agnew, William Fischer and M. Krishnamachariar. *The Law of Trusts in British India*. Calcutta: Thacker, Spink & Co., 1920.
Arthur, Phillips and Ernest John Trevelyan. *The Law Relating to Hindu Wills, Second Edition Revised by Sir E. J. Trevelyan*. London; Calcutta: W. Thacker & Co.; Thacker, Spink & Co., 1914.
Ashesh, Ashna and Arun K. Thiruvengadam. *Report on Citizenship Law: India*. GLOBALCIT. Badia Fiesolana, Italy: European University Institute, 2017.
Bellew, H. W. *The History of Cholera in India from 1862 to 1881: Being A Descriptive and Statistical Account of the Disease: As Derived from the Published Official Reports of the Several Provincial Governments During that Period and Mainly in Illustration of the Relation Between Cholera Activity and Climatic Conditions: Together with Original Observations on the Causes and Nature of Cholera*. London: Trubner & Co., 1885.
Bengal (India) Sanitary Commission. *First Annual Report of the Sanitary Commission for Bengal*. London, 1866.

202 Bibliography

Bengal Drainage Committee and London School of Hygiene and Tropical Medicine. *Report of the Drainage Committee, Bengal.* Calcutta: Bengal Secretariat Press, 1907.

Bengal (India), Calcutta Rent Enquiry Committee. *Report of the Committee Appointed to Enquire into Land Values and Rents in Calcutta.* Calcutta, 1920.

Beverley, H. *Report of the Commission Appointed under Section 28 of Act IV (B.C.) of 1876 to Enquire into Certain Matters Connected with the Sanitation of the Town of Calcutta.* Calcutta: Printed at the Bengal Secretariat Press, 1885.

Bright, W. R. *Report of the Epidemics of Plague in Calcutta during the Years 1898–99, 1899–1900 and up to 30th June, 1900–1901.* Calcutta: E. D'Rozario at the Municipal Press, 1900.

Calcutta Building Commission. *Annual Reports, 1897–1898.*

Calcutta (India), Plague Department. *Report on Plague in Calcutta, 1904.*

Calcutta Domiciled Committee. Enquiry Committee. *Report of the Calcutta Domiciled Committee 1918–1919.* Calcutta: The Bengal Secretariat Press, 1920.

Chief Executive Officer. *Chairman's (Chief Executive Officer's) Report on the Municipal Administration of Calcutta for the Year 1925.* Calcutta, 1925.

Calcutta Improvement Trust. *Annual Report on the Operations of the Calcutta Improvement Trust for the Years* [1912–1940].

———. *The Calcutta Improvement Act, 1911 & Allied Matters.* Calcutta, 1912.

Calcutta Municipal Corporation. 'The Drainage of Calcutta [A Letter from the Commissioners for the Improvement of Calcutta on the Subject of a Proposed New System of Drainage of That City with the Report of Messrs. M. and G. Rendel, and Observations Thereon by W. Clark and A. M. Dowleans]'. Calcutta, 1859.

Clark, William. 'A Collection of Papers Relating to the Drainage System of Calcutta Carried Out by W. Clark, 1869'. Minutes of Proceedings of the Institution of Civil Engineers, Vol. 63. London, 1869.

Clarke, Richard. *Digest, or Consolidated Arrangement, of the Regulations and Acts of the Bengal Government, from 1793 to 1854.* London: Printed by J. & H. Cox, 1855.

Clemow, F. G. and W. C. Hossack. *Report upon the Sanitary Condition of Ward VII (Burra Bazaar).* Calcutta: Caledonian Steam Printing Press, 1899.

Crake, H. M. *The Calcutta Plague 1896–1907.* Calcutta: Criterion Printing Works, 1908.

Deb, Binay Krishna. *The Early History and Growth of Calcutta.* Calcutta: Romesh Chandra Ghose, 1905.

Engineers Department of Calcutta Corporation. 'Aughore Moni Bewah versus Calcutta Corporation'. In *Annual Report on the Municipal Administration of Calcutta, 1897.*

———. 'Doorgah Money Bewah versus the Calcutta Corporation'. In *Annual Report on the Municipal Administration of Calcutta, 1897.*

Bibliography

Geddes, Patrick. *Barrabazaar Improvement: A Report to the Corporation of Calcutta.* Calcutta: Calcutta Corporation Press, 1919.

Ghose, Jogendra Chunder. *The Law of Impartible Property: Rajas, Chieftainships, Zemindaries, Taluks, Tekaiti-Gadis, Military and Other Service Tenures, Polliems, Ghatwalis, Digwaris, Vatans, Inams, Tarwads &c.* Calcutta: R. Cambray & Co., 1916.

Ghosh, Abinaschandra. *The Laws of Improvement and Acquisition in Calcutta: With Complete Commentaries and Forms.* Calcutta: Eastern Law House, 1919.

Government of Bengal Proceedings, Local Self Government, Municipalities Branch, 1922 and 1927.

Gupta, M. N. *Land Acquisition Acts and Principles of Valuation.* Calcutta: S. C. Sarkar & Sons Ltd., 1939.

Hamilton, Walter. *The East India Gazetteer; Containing Particular Descriptions of the Empires, Kingdoms, Principalities, Provinces, Cities, Towns, Districts, Fortresses, Harbours, Rivers, Lakes, &c. of Hindostan, and the Adjacent Countries, India beyond the Ganges, and the Eastern Archipelago; Together with Sketches of the Manners, Customs, Institutions, Agriculture, Commerce, Manufactures, Revenues, Population, Castes, Religion, History, &c. of Their Various Inhabitants.* London: Printed for J. Murray by Dove, 1815.

Indian Plague Commission. *Minutes of Evidence Taken by the Indian Plague Commission with Appendices.* London: Printed for H.M.S.O. by Eyre and Spottiswoode, 1900–1901.

Kanjilal, Manindranath. *The Calcutta Rent Act, Bengal Act III Of 1920, Annotated, etc.* Calcutta, 1920.

Lal, Nathuni and Gupta, Rajesh. *Lal's Commentary on the Societies Registration Act, 1860 (Act No. 21 of 1860): States Amendments, State Rules, Model Forms along with Allied Laws.* New Delhi: Delhi Law House, 2016.

Lanchester, H. V. 'Calcutta Improvement Trust: Precis of Mr. E. P. Richards Report on the City of Calcutta Part II'. *The Town Planning Review* 5, no. 3, October 1914.

Lawyer's Companion Office (ed.). *High Court Reports; Being a Re-Print of All the Decisions of the Privy Council on Appeals from India and of the Various High Courts and Other Superior Courts in India Reported Both in the Official and Non-Official Reports from 1862 to 1875.* Trichinopoly and Madras: T. A. Venkasawmy Row and T. S. Krishnasawmy Row, 1915.

Maden James and Albert de Bois Shrosbree. *City and Suburban Main Road Projects, Joint Report, 1st July 1913.* Calcutta: Calcutta Improvement Trust, 1913.

Moreno, H. W. B. *Anglo-Indians and the Housing Problem.* Calcutta: Central Press, 1917.

Pearse, T. Frederick, edited by W. C. Hossack. *Report on Plague in Calcutta for the Year Ending 30th June 1910.* Calcutta: Bengal Secretariat Press, 1910.

Pearse, T. Frederick. *Report on Plague in Calcutta for the Year Ending 30th June 1908.* Calcutta: Bengal Secretariat Press, 1908.

Pettifer, E. C. 'A Report on Plague in Calcutta'. In W. R. Bright, *Report of the Epidemics of Plague in Calcutta During the Years 1898–1999, 1899–1900 and up to 30th June, 1900–1901.* Calcutta: E. D'Rozario at the Municipal Press, 1900.

Report on the Municipal Administration of Calcutta for the years, 1875; 1887–1888; 1899; 1900; 1901; 1910; 1916; 1926.

Revenue Department, Bengal. *Report on the Administration of Bengal.* Calcutta: Bengal Government Press, 1872–1873.

Richards, E. P. *Report by Request of the Trust on the Condition, Improvement and Town Planning of the City of Calcutta and Contiguous Areas: The Richards Report.* Ware, Hertfordshire, 1914.

Risley, Hebert Hope. *The Tribes and Castes of Bengal: Ethnographic Glossary.* Calcutta: Bengal Secretariat Press, 1892.

Robinson, Charles Mulford. *The Improvement of Towns and Cities; or, The Practical Basis of Civic Aesthetics.* New York: G. P. Putnam's Sons, 1901.

Royal College of Surgeons of England. 'Report on Cholera in Alipore Jail, 1864'. In *Measures for the Prevention of Cholera among European Troops in Northern India.* Calcutta: Printed at the Alipore Jail Press, 1864.

Sanitary Commissioner, Government of India. *Annual Report of the Sanitary Commissioner with the Government of India.* Calcutta: Office of Superintendent of Government Printing, 1868.

Simpson, W. J. *Report of the Health Officer of the Town on Calcutta, and the Resolutions of commissioners Thereon: 1886.* Calcutta: Municipal Print Office, 1887.

Smith, David Boyes. *Report on the Drainage and Conservancy of Calcutta.* Calcutta: Bengal Secretariat Press, 1869.

Strachey, J. 'The Second and Third Sections of the Report of the Commissioners Appointed to Inquire into the Cholera Epidemic of 1861 in Northern India'. In *Report of the Commission to Inquire into the Cholera Epidemic.* Calcutta: Cutter, 1864.

Sutherland, D. *The Regulations of the Bengal Code, in Force in September 1862 with a List of Titles and Index.* Calcutta: Bengal Printing Co., 1862.

Trevelyan, Ernest John. 'Answers by Babu Satish Chandra Ghosh and Okhil Chandra Ray to the Building commission'. In *Calcutta Building Commission Reports, May 1897.*

———. 'Answers by Babu Dinendra Narain Roy to the Building Commission'. In *Calcutta Building Commission Reports, May 1897.*

———. 'The Case of Bama Bewah and Shama Bewah'. In *Report of the Calcutta Building Commission, 1897.*

———. 'Papers Related to the Erection of a Building at 31 Dhurrumtollah Lane'. In *Report of the Calcutta Building Commission, 1897.*

Bibliography

———. 'Extract of a Letter from James A. Lowson to H. H. Risley'. In *Report of the Calcutta Building Commission, 1897*.

———. 'Answers by Mr. Braunfield to James A. Lowson'. In *Report of the Calcutta Building Commission, 1897*.

———. 'Answers by Babu Jadunath Sen to the Building Commission'. In *Report of the Calcutta Building Commission, 1897*.

———. 'Answers by Babu Kanayee Lall Mukherjee'. In *Report of the Calcutta Building Commission, 1897*.

———. 'Speech of Babu Priya Nath Mullick'. In *Report of the Calcutta Building Commission, 1898*.

———. 'Bheemraj Jhoonjhoonwala, 33 Ezra Street versus the Calcutta Corporation'. In *Report of the Calcutta Building Commission, 1898*.

———. 'Papers on Kali Prasad Dutt Street'. In *Report of the Calcutta Building Commission, 1898*.

———. 'Papers on 1, Bysack Lane'. In *Report of the Calcutta Building Commission, 1898*.

Maps and Paintings

Calcutta in the Olden Time—Its Localities. From the Calcutta Review ... Map of Calcutta, 1792–3. By A. Upjohn. [With a Plate.], 1852.

Hindoo *Mutt* (temple) in the Chitpore Bazaar. Sir Charles D'Oyly's Twenty-eight 'Views of Calcutta and its Environs'. [Object no. R2566-24]. Image Credit: Victoria Memorial Hall Archives, Kolkata.

Europeans Visiting a Princely Home in Calcutta to Witness Durga Puja. A Painting by Alexis Soltykoff (1859). Image Source: Catalogue of the exhibit 'Puja and Piety: Hindu, Jain, and Buddhist art from the Indian subcontinent' By Susan S. Tai in collaboration with Pratapaditya Pal, Santa Barbara Museum of Art, April 17– July 31 2016.

Publications in English

A Member of the Family. *An Account of the Late Govindram Mitter and of His Descendants in Calcutta and Benares*. Calcutta: National Press, 1869.

Abdul Ali, A. M. F. 'Lotteries in Calcutta in Days of John Company', *Calcutta Municipal Gazette*, January 1929, 82.

Agarwal, Om Prakash. *Compulsory Acquisition of Land in India and Pakistan, Being an Exhaustive, Critical and Analytical Commentary on the Acquisition Land Act I of 1894 and Other Allied Acts*. Allahabad: University Book Agency, 1950.

Banerjee, Sukanya. *Becoming Imperial Citizens Indians in the Late-Victorian Empire*. Durham, NC: Duke University Press, 2013.

206   Bibliography

Chatterjee, Dinabandhu. *A Short Sketch of Rajah Rajendro Mullick Bahadur and His Family.* Calcutta: G. C. Day, 1917.

Cunningham, David Douglas. *Plagues and Pleasures of Life in Bengal.* London: John Murray, 1907.

Dasgupta, Hemendranath. *Desbandhu Chittaranjan Das.* Delhi: Publications Division Ministry of Information & Broadcasting, 2017 (reprint).

Datta, Bhairava Chandra. *The Bengal Municipal Act, Being Act III. of 1884 with Notes and an Appendix, Second Edition, Revised and Enlarged.* Calcutta: Rai M.C. Sarkar Bahadur & Sons, 1916.

Duff, Alexander. *A Description of the Durga and Kali Festivals, Celebrated in Calcutta, at an Expense of Three Millions of Dollars.* Troy, NY: C. Wright, 1846.

Dutt, Haradhan. *Dutt Family of Wellington Square.* Calcutta: Haradhan Dutt, 1995 (reprint).

Siddha, Mohana Mitra. *Indian Problems.* London: J. Murray, 1908.

Ghosha, Lokanātha. *The Modern History of the Indian Chiefs, Rajas, Zamindars, &C.* Calcutta: J. N. Ghose, 1881.

Greeven, Richard. *Knights of the Broom.* Benares: Medical Hall Press, 1894.

Harijan Sevak Sangh. *Annual Report of the Harijan Sevak Sangh.* Delhi: Harijan Sevak Sangh.

Malkani, Naraindas Rattanmal. *Clean People and an Unclean Country.* Delhi: Harijan Sevak Sangh, 1965 (reprint).

Mukerjee, Radhakamal. *Principles of Comparative Economics.* London: P. S. King & Son, 1921–1922.

Saha, Amar Nath. *The Bengal Municipal Act, 1932 (Bengal Act XV of 1932), Corrected Up-to-date.* Calcutta: Eastern Book Agency, 1974.

Sinha, Kaliprasanna and Swarup Roy. *The Observant Owl: Hootum's Vignettes of Nineteenth-Century Calcutta: Kaliprasanna Sinha's Hootum Pyanchar Naksha.* Ranikhet; New Delhi: Rupa & Co., 2008 (reprint).

van der Ploeg, Tymen J., Wino J. M. van Veen, and Cornelia R. M. Versteegh. *Civil Society in Europe.* Cambridge; New York: Cambridge University Press, 2017.

Williams, Marilyn Thornton. *Washing 'the Great Unwashed' Public Baths in Urban America, 1840–1920.* Columbus: Ohio State University Press, 1991.

Wilson, Charles Robert. *The Early Annals of the English in Bengal: Being the Bengal Public Consultations for the First Half of the Eighteenth Century, Summarised, Extracted, and Ed., with Introductions and Illustrative Addenda.* London: W. Thacker, 1895–1911.

English Periodicals

Calcutta Journal: or, Political, Commercial and Literary Gazette, 1819 and 1821.
Calcutta Journal of Medicine, 1906.

Bibliography

Calcutta Municipal Gazette, 1923–1940.
Amrita Bazar Patrika, 2 September 1918.
Amrita Bazar Patrika, 5 September 1941.
Dawn Society, Calcutta, *Dawn and Dawn Society's Magazine* X, no. 7 (1907).
Harijan, 1933–1950.
The Statesman, 12 October 1921.
The Statesman, 29 June 1922.
The Statesman, 30 January 1918.
The Times of India, 14 May 1915.

Club Archives

Sanat Ganguly and Ashok Das. *Simla Byayam Samiti O Sarbojonin Durgotsover Sonkhipto Itibritto, 1926–2000.* Calcutta: Published by Simla Byayam Samiti, 2000.
Interview with Sandip Chakravarty, General Secretary of the Badamtola Ashar Sangha Club, 21 May 2012.
Interview with Sridhar Kundu, Associate of the Simla Byayam Samiti, 30 May 2012.

Bengali Sources

Adhya, Beharilal. *Adbhut Durgotsabh Ba Samaj Kalanka.* Calcutta: Jogendranath Sadhu, 1903.
Basu, Amrita Krishna. *Plaguetottwo.* Calcutta: Taruni Press, 1899.
Basu, Buddhadeb. *Amar Joubon.* Calcutta: M. C. Sarkar and Sons, 1977.
Datta, Kiranacandra. *Bāgabājāra: Atipurātana Nahe, Madhya o Bartamāna Yugera Citra.* Kalakātā: Bāṃlāra Mukha Prakāśana; Mukhya Prāptisthāna De'ja, 2009.
Dutta, Mahendranath. *Kalikatar Puratan Kahini O Pratha.* Calcutta: Mahendra Publishing Committee, 1973.
Mitra, Bipinbihari. *Kalikatastha Sobhabajara-Nibasi Maharaja Nabakrsna Deba Bahadurerea Jibana-Carita.* Calcutta: Stanhope Press, 1879.
Mukhopadhyay, Bhubanchandra. *Bangarahasya (Nutan Naksa).* Calcutta: Upendranath Mukhopadhyay. Printed by Basumati Electro Press by Purnachandra Mukhopadhyay, 1904.
Pakshi, Rupchand. 'Dhonyo Sohor Kolkata'. Reproduced in Benoy Ghosh, ed., *Samayikpatre Banglar Samajchitra*, Vol. 4 (Calcutta: Papyrus, 1966), 957.
Rāya Caudhurī, Bhabānī. *Baṅgīẏa Sābarṇa Kathā, Kālīkshetra Kalikātā: Ekaṭi Itibṛtta.* Kalakātā: Mānnā Pābalikeśana, 2006.
Seth, Nagendranath. *Kalikatastha Tantu Banik Jatir Itihas.* Calcutta: A. K. Basaka, 1950.

Bengali Periodicals

Svasthyo, 1899–1902.
Svasthya Samacara, 1912–1927.
Basantak, 1874–1875.
Samachar Darpan, 5 October 1832.
Janayuddha, 1942.

Secondary Sources

Adhikary, Sayantani. 'The Bratachari Movement and the Invention of a "Folk Tradition"'. *South Asia: Journal of South Asian Studies* 38, no. 4 (2 October 2015): 656–70.

Ahmed, Waquar, Amitabh Kundu, and Richard Peet. *India's New Economic Policy: A Critical Analysis*. New York; London: Routledge, 2010.

Alter, Joseph S. *The Wrestler's Body: Identity and Ideology in North India*. Berkeley: University of California Press, 1992.

Anderson, Warwick. 'Excremental Colonialism: Public Health and the Poetics of Pollution'. *Critical Inquiry* 21, no. 3 (1995): 640–69.

Appadurai, Arjun. *Modernity at Large: Cultural Dimensions of Globalization*. Minneapolis: University of Minnesota Press, 1996.

Archer, John. 'Paras, Palaces, Pathogens: Frameworks for the Growth of Calcutta, 1800–1850'. *City & Society* 12, no. 1 (1 June 2000): 19–54.

Arnold, David. *Colonizing the Body: State Medicine and Epidemic Disease in Nineteenth-Century India*. Berkeley: University of California Press, 1993.

———. *Science, Technology and Medicine in Colonial India*. Cambridge: Cambridge University Press, 2000.

Arnold, David John. *The Tropics and the Traveling Gaze: India, Landscape, and Science, 1800–1856*. London; Seattle: University of Washington Press, 2015.

Bandyopadhyay, Sekhar. *Caste, Culture and Hegemony: Social Dominance in Colonial Bengal*. New Delhi; Thousand Oaks; London: Sage Publications India, 2004.

Bayly, C. A. *Rulers, Townsmen, and Bazaars: North Indian Society in the Age of British Expansion, 1770–1870*. Cambridge; New York: Cambridge University Press, 1983.

Behar, Cem. *A Neighborhood in Ottoman Istanbul: Fruit Vendors and Civil Servants in the Kasap İlyas Mahalle*. Albany: State University of New York Press, 2003.

Bhadra, Gautam. 'The Mentality of Subalternity: Kantanama or Rajdharma', CSSSC Occasional Paper No. 104. CSSSC, Calcutta, August 1988.

Bhattacharya, Neeladri. 'Notes towards a Conception of the Colonial Public'. In *Civil Society, Public Sphere, and Citizenship: Dialogues and Perceptions*, 130–56. New Delhi: Sage Publications, 2005.

Bhattacharya, Sabyasachi. *The Defining Moments in Bengal, 1920–1947*. New Delhi: Oxford University Press, 2014.

Bibliography

Bhattacharya, Tithi. *The Sentinels of Culture: Class, Education, and the Colonial Intellectual in Bengal*. New Delhi; Oxford; New York: Oxford University Press, 2005.

Beverley, Eric Lewis. *Hyderabad, British India, and the World*. Cambridge: Cambridge University Press, 2015.

Bidyaratna, Bhabataran. 'Shastriyo Svasthya Kotha'. *Svasthya Samacara* 1 (1912): 328–29.

Bigon, Liora. *Garden Cities and Colonial Planning*. Manchester: Manchester University Press, 2017.

Bissell, William Cunningham. *Urban Design, Chaos, and Colonial Power in Zanzibar*. Bloomington: Indiana University Press, 2011.

Bose, Nirmal Kumar. *Calcutta, 1964: A Social Survey*. Bombay: Lalvani Publishing House, 1968.

Breeze, Gerald. *Urbanization in Newly Developing Countries*. New Delhi: Prentice-Hall of India, 1969.

Bremner, G. A. *Architecture and Urbanism in the British Empire*. Oxford, New York: Oxford University Press, 2016.

Brennan, James R., Andrew Burton, and Yusuf Lawi, eds. *Dar Es Salaam Histories from an Emerging African Metropolis*. Dar Es Salaam; Nairobi: Mkuki na Nyota Publishers; The British Institute in Eastern Africa, 2007.

Broomfield, J. H., John H. Broomfield, and Nicholas Broomfield. *Elite Conflict in a Plural Society: Twentieth-Century Bengal*. Berkeley; Los Angeles: University of California Press, 1968.

Çelik, Zeynep. *Urban Forms and Colonial Confrontations: Algiers under French Rule*. Berkeley; Los Angeles: University of California Press, 1997.

Certeau, Michel de. *The Practice of Everyday Life*. Berkeley: University of California Press, 2008.

Chakrabarty, Dipesh. *Rethinking Working-Class History: Bengal 1890–1940*. Princeton: Princeton University Press, 2018.

Chandavarkar, Rajnarayan. *The Origins of Industrial Capitalism in India: Business Strategies and the Working Classes in Bombay, 1900–1940*. Cambridge: Cambridge University Press, 2003.

Chang, Jiat-Hwee. *A Genealogy of Tropical Architecture: Colonial Networks, Nature and Technoscience*. London; New York: Routledge, 2016.

Chaudhuri, Nupur. 'Clash of Cultures: Gender and Colonialism in South and Southeast Asia'. In *A Companion to Gender History*, ed. Teresa A. Meade, 430–3. Oxford, UK: Blackwell Publishing Ltd, 2008.

Chaudhuri, Supriya. 'Remembering the Para: Towards a Spatial History of Our Times'. In *Strangely Beloved: Writings on Calcutta*, ed. Nilanjana Gupta, 118–25. New Delhi: Rupa Publications, 2014.

Chaudhury, Sushil. *Companies, Commerce and Merchants: Bengal in the Pre-Colonial Era*. London: Routledge, Taylor & Francis, 2017.

Chaudhary, Zahid R. *Afterimage of Empire: Photography in Nineteenth-Century India.* Minneapolis: University of Minnesota Press, 2012.

Chatterjee, Anasua. *Margins of Citizenship: Muslim Experiences in Urban India.* London: Taylor & Francis, 2017.

Chatterjee, Partha. *Nationalist Thought and the Colonial World: A Derivative Discourse.* London: Zed Books, 1993.

———. *The Black Hole of Empire: History of a Global Practice of Power.* Princeton: Princeton University Press, 2012.

———. *The Nation and Its Fragments: Colonial and Postcolonial Histories.* Princeton: Princeton University Press, 1993.

Chatterji, Joya. *Bengal Divided: Hindu Communalism and Partition, 1932–1947.* Cambridge: Cambridge University Press, 2002.

Chattopadhyay, Swati. *Representing Calcutta: Modernity, Nationalism, and the Colonial Uncanny.* London; New York: Routledge, 2005.

Chakrabarty, Dipesh. 'Of Garbage, Modernity and the Citizen's Gaze'. *Economic and Political Weekly* 27, no. 10/11 (1992): 541–7.

Chandra, Uday. 'The Importance of Caste in Bengal'. *Economic and Political Weekly* 47, no. 44 (November 3, 2012): 55–6.

Chandra, Uday, Heierstad Geir, and Bo Nielsen Kenneth. *The Politics of Caste in West Bengal.* New Delhi: Routledge India, 2017.

Chaudhuri, K. N. *Trade and Civilisation in the Indian Ocean: An Economic History from the Rise of Islam to 1750.* Cambridge: Cambridge University Press, 2008.

Chopra, Preeti. *A Joint Enterprise: Indian Elites and the Making of British Bombay.* Minneapolis; London: University of Minnesota Press, 2011.

Cohen, William A. and Ryan Johnson. *Filth: Dirt, Disgust, and Modern Life.* Minneapolis: University of Minnesota Press, 2005.

Colgrove, James. *State of Immunity: The Politics of Vaccination in Twentieth-Century America.* Berkeley; Los Angeles; London: University of California Press, 2006.

Cooper, Frederick. *Citizenship between Empire and Nation: Remaking France and French Africa, 1945–1960.* Princeton: Princeton University Press, 2016.

Dasgupta, Hemendranath. *Desbandhu Chittaranjan Das.* Delhi: Publications Division, Ministry of Information and Broadcasting, Government of India, 1960.

Dasgupta, Keya. 'Mapping the Places of Minorities: Calcutta through the Last Century'. In *Calcutta Mosaic: Essays and Interviews on the Minority Communities of Calcutta,* ed. Himadri Banerjee, Nilanjana Gupta, and Sipra Mukherjee, 23–70. Cambridge: Cambridge University Press, 2009.

Datta, Partho. *Planning the City: Urbanization and Reform in Calcutta; c. 1800–c. 1940.* New Delhi: Tulika Books, 2012.

———. 'Ranald Martin's Medical Topography'. In *The Social History of Health and Medicine in Colonial India,* ed. Biswamoy Pati and Mark Harrison, 15–31. Delhi: Primus Books, 2015.

Bibliography

Daunton, M. J. *Wealth and Welfare: An Economic and Social History of Britain, 1851–1951*. Oxford; New York: Oxford University Press, 2007.

Demissie, Fassil. *Colonial Architecture and Urbanism in Africa: Intertwined and Contested Histories*. Surrey, UK: Ashgate, 2012.

Devine, Thomas Martin. *Glasgow*. Manchester: Manchester University Press, 1995.

Dirks, N. B. *Castes of Mind: Colonialism and the Making of Modern India*. Princeton, NJ: Princeton University Press, 2011.

Donner, Henrike. 'The Politics of Gender, Class and Community in a Central Calcutta Neighborhood'. In *The Meaning of the Local: Politics of Place in Urban India*, ed. Geert de Neve and Henrike Donner, 141–58. London; New York: Routledge, 2006.

Drysdale, John. *Singapore: Struggle for Success*. Singapore: Times Book International, 1984.

Edensor, Tim and Mark Jayne. *Urban Theory Beyond the West: A World of Cities*. London: Routledge, 2012.

Edwards, Michael. *Civil Society*. Cambridge; Malden: Polity Press, 2014.

Elias, Norbert. *The Civilizing Process: Sociogenetic and Psychogenetic Investigations*. Oxford; Malden, MA: Blackwell Publishing, 2000.

Elteren, Mel Van. *Americanism and Americanization: A Critical History of Domestic and Global Influence*. Jefferson, NC: McFarland and Company, 2006.

Erens, Bob, Laura Mitchell, Jim Orford, Kerry Sproston, and Clarissa White. *Gambling and Problem Gambling in Britain*. Hove; New York: Brunner Routledge, Taylor and Francis, 2003.

Escobar, Arturo. *Encountering Development: The Making and Unmaking of the Third World*. Princeton; Oxford: Princeton University Press, 2012.

Freitag, Sandria B. *Collective Action and Community: Public Arenas and the Emergence of Communalism in North India*. Berkeley: University of California Press, 1989.

Frost, Joe L. *A History of Children's Play and Play Environments: Toward a Contemporary Child-Saving Movement*. New York: Routledge, 2012.

Furedy, Christine. '"New Men" Political Clubs in Calcutta in the 1870's and 1880's: A Colonial Mix of Self-Interest and Ideology'. *Indian Journal of Politics* 13, nos 1 and 2 (August 1979): 63–73.

Gallagher, John and Ronald Robinson. 'The Imperialism of Free Trade'. *The Economic History Review* 6, no. 1 (1953): 1–15.

Gangrade, K. D. *Social Legislation in India*. Delhi: Concept Publishing, 1978.

Garber, Nicholas J. and Lester A. Hoel. *Traffic and Highway Engineering*. Stamford: Cengage Learning, 2014.

Ghosh, Anindita. *Claiming the City: Protest, Crime, and Scandals in Colonial Calcutta, c. 1860–1920*. New Delhi, India: Oxford University Press, 2016.

Ghosh, Anjan. 'Spaces of Recognition: Puja and Power in Contemporary Calcutta'. *Journal of Southern African Studies* 26, no. 2 (2000): 289–99.

Ghosh, Durba. *Gentlemanly Terrorists: Political Violence and the Colonial State in India, 1919–1947.* Cambridge; New York: Cambridge University Press, 2017.

Glover, William J. *Making Lahore Modern: Constructing and Imagining a Colonial City.* Karachi Division (Pakistan): Oxford University Press, 2011.

Gorman, Daniel. *Imperial Citizenship: Empire and the Question of Belonging.* Manchester; New York: Manchester University Press, 2013.

Guha Thakurta, Tapati. *In the Name of the Goddess: The Durga Pujas of Contemporary Kolkata.* Delhi: Primus Books, 2015.

———. 'Demands and Dilemmas of Durga Puja "Art": Notes on a Contemporary Festival Aesthetics'. In *Bloomsbury Research Book of Indian Aesthetics and Philosophy of Art,* ed. Arindam Chakrabarti, 317–53. London: Bloomsbury Academic, 2016.

Guha Ray, Siddhartha. 'Protest and Politics: Story of Calcutta Tram Workers: 1940–1947'. In *Calcutta: The Stormy Decades,* ed. Tanika Sarkar and Sekhar Bandyopadhyay, 151–76. Abingdon; New York: Routledge, 2018.

Gupta, Narayani. *Delhi between Two Empires, 1803–1931: Society, Government and Urban Growth.* Delhi: Oxford University Press, 1997.

Gupta, Swarupa. *Notions of Nationhood in Bengal: Perspectives on Samaj, C. 1867–1905.* Leiden: Brill, 2009.

Habermas, Jürgen. *The Structural Transformation of the Public Sphere: An Inquiry into a Category of Bourgeois Society.* Cambridge, MA: Polity Press, 2011.

Habib, Irfan. *Essays in Indian History: Towards a Marxist Perception.* New Delhi: Tulika, 2015.

Harrison, Mark. *Public Health in British India: Anglo-Indian Preventive Medicine, 1859–1914* Cambridge: Cambridge University Press, 1994.

Harvey, David. *Social Justice and the City.* Baltimore: The Johns Hopkins University Press, 1973.

———. *Paris, Capital of Modernity.* New York: Routledge, 2006.

Hazareesingh, Sandip. *Colonial City and the Challenge of Modernity: Urban Hegemonies and Civic Contestations in Bombay, 1900–1925.* Bombay: Orient Longman, 2006.

Haynes, Douglas E. *Rhetoric and Ritual in Colonial India: The Shaping of a Public Culture in Surat City, 1852–1928.* Delhi; New York: Oxford University Press, 1992.

Heber, Reginald. *The Life and Writings of Bishop Heber the Great Missionary to Calcutta, the Scholar, the Poet, and the Christian.* Boston: Albert Colby & Company, 1861.

Hempel, Sandra. *The Medical Detective: John Snow, Cholera and the Mystery of the Broad Street Pump.* Granta Books, 2014.

Home, Robert K. *Of Planting and Planning: The Making of British Colonial Cities.* London: Spon, 1997.

Hosagrahar, Jyoti. *Indigenous Modernities: Negotiating Architecture and Urbanism.* London: Routledge, 2009.

Bibliography

Hutnyk, John. *The Rumour of Calcutta: Tourism, Charity, and the Poverty of Representation*. London; New Jersey: Zed Books, 1996.

Jayal, Niraja Gopal. *Citizenship and Its Discontents: An Indian History*. Cambridge, MA: Harvard University Press, 2013.

Jacobs, Jane. *The Death and Life of Great American Cities*. New York: Vintage, 1992.

Johnson, Ryan and Amna Khalid. *Public Health in the British Empire: Intermediaries, Subordinates, and the Practice of Public Health, 1850–1960*. New York; Abingdon: Routledge, 2012.

Karim, Farhan. *Of Greater Dignity than Riches: Austerity and Housing Design in India*. Pittsburgh: University of Pittsburgh Press, 2019.

Kaviraj, Sudipta. 'Filth and the Public Sphere: Concepts and Practices about Space in Calcutta'. *Public Culture: Bulletin of the Project for Transnational Cultural Studies* 10, no. 1 (1997): 83–113.

Kelley, Victoria. *Soap and Water: Cleanliness, Dirt and the Working Classes in Victorian and Edwardian Britain*. London; New York: I.B. Tauris, 2010.

Kennedy, Liam. *Race and Urban Space in Contemporary American Culture*. Edinburgh: Edinburgh University Press, 2000.

Kidambi, Prashant. *The Making of an Indian Metropolis: Colonial Governance and Public Culture in Bombay, 1890–1920*. Burlington, VT: Ashgate Publishing Company, 2007.

King, Anthony D. *Colonial Urban Development: Culture, Social Power and Environment*. London: Routledge, 2010.

King, Blair B. 'Entreprenurship and Regional Identity in Bengal'. In *Bengal Regional Identity*, ed. David Kopf, with contributions by Edward C. Dimock, Jr. East Lansing, MI: Asian Studies Center, 1969.

Kopf, David. 'Editor's Preface'. In *Bengal Regional Identity*, ed. David Kopf, with contributions by Edward C. Dimock, Jr, 1–2. East Lansing, MI: Michigan State University, 1969.

Landes, Joan B. *Feminism, the Public and the Private*. Oxford: Oxford University Press, 1998.

Laporte, Dominique. *History of Shit*. Cambridge, MA: MIT, 2002.

Lefebvre, Henri. *The Production of Space*. Oxford; Cambridge, MA: Blackwell, 1991.

Legg, Stephen. 'A Pre-Partitioned City? Anti-Colonial and Communal Mohallas in Inter-War Delhi'. *South Asia: Journal of South Asian Studies* 42, no. 1 (2 January 2019): 170–87.

Masselos, Jim. *The City in Action: Bombay Struggles for Power*. New Delhi: Oxford University Press, 2007.

McAuslan, Patrick. *Land Law Reform in East Africa: Traditional or Transformative?* New York: Routledge, 2015.

McDermott, Rachel Fell. *Revelry, Rivalry, and Longing for the Goddesses of Bengal: The Fortunes of Hindu Festivals*. New York: Columbia University Press, 2011.

Mehta, Uday Singh. *Liberalism and Empire: A Study in Nineteenth-Century British Liberal Thought*. Chicago: The University of Chicago Press, 1999.

Meter, Rachel R. Van. 'Bankimcandra's View on the Role of Bengal in Indian Civilization'. In *Bengal Regional Identity*, ed. David Kopf, with contributions by Edward C. Dimock, Jr, 61–74. East Lansing, MI: Michigan State University, 1969.

Mills, Sarah. '"An Instruction in Good Citizenship": Scouting and the Historical Geographies of Citizenship Education'. *Transactions of the Institute of British Geographers* 38, no. 1 (1 January 2013): 120–34.

Minoru, Mio. 'Community of Retrospect: Spirit Cults and Locality in an Old City of Rajasthan'. In *Cities in South Asia*, ed. Minoru Mio and Crispin Bates, 210–27. New York: Routledge, 2015.

Mitchell, Timothy. *Colonising Egypt*. Cambridge: Cambridge University Press, 2007.

Mukharji, Projit Bihari. *Nationalizing the Body: The Medical Market, Print, and Daktari Medicine*. London; New York: Anthem Press, 2009.

Mukherjee, Janam. *Hungry Bengal War, Famine and the End of Empire*. New York, NY: Oxford University Press, 2016.

Mukherjee, Madhuja. 'Football in Asia: History, Culture and Business'. In *Football in Asia: History, Culture and Business*, ed. Younghan Cho, 74–92. New York: Routledge, 2016.

Mukherjee, S. N. *Calcutta: Myths and History*. Calcutta: Subarnarekha, 1977.

Nair, Janaki. 'Beyond Nationalism: Modernity, Governance and a New Urban History for India'. *Urban History* 36, no. 2 (August 2009): 327–41.

Nakazato, Nariaki. 'The Role of Colonial Administration, "Riot Systems" and Local Networks during the Calcutta Disturbances of August 1946'. In *Calcutta: The Stormy Decades*, Tanika Sarkar and Sekhar Bandyopadhyay, 267–319. New York: Routledge, 2018.

Nandy, Ashis. *An Ambiguous Journey to the City: The Village and Other Odd Ruins of the Self in the Indian Imagination*. New Delhi: Oxford University Press, 2007, New edition.

Neve, Geert de and Henrike Donner. *The Meaning of the Local*. London: Routledge, 2010.

Nightingale, Carl H. *Segregation: A Global History of Divided Cities*. Chicago; London: University of Chicago Press, 2012.

Njoh, Ambe J. *Planning Power: Town Planning and Social Control in Colonial Africa*. London; New York: UCL Press, 2007.

Nuttall, Sarah and Achille Mbembe. *Johannesburg: The Elusive Metropolis*. Durham; London: Duke University Press, 2008.

Oldenburg, Veena Talwar. *The Making of Colonial Lucknow, 1856–1877*. Princeton: Princeton University Press, 2014.

Bibliography

Orsini, Francesca. *The Hindi Public Sphere 1920–1940: Language and Literature in the Age of Nationalism*. Delhi; Oxford: Oxford University Press, 2009.

Palit, Chittabrata and Tinni Goswami. 'Sanitation, Empire, Environment: Bengal (1880–1920)'. *Proceedings of the Indian History Congress* 68 (2007): 731–44.

Pande, Ishita. *Medicine, Race and Liberalism in British Bengal: Symptoms of Empire*. London: Routledge, 2012.

Pandey, Gyanendra. *The Construction of Communalism in Colonial North India*. Delhi; New York: Oxford University Press, 1900.

———. 'The Subaltern as Subaltern Citizen'. *Economic and Political Weekly* 41, no. 46 (2006): 4735–41.

Parsons, Timothy. *Race, Resistance, and the Boy Scout Movement in British Colonial Africa*. Athens, OH: Ohio University Press, 2004.

Peckham, Robert. 'Introduction: Panic: Reading the Signs'. In *Empires of Panic: Epidemics and Colonial Anxieites*, 1–22. Hong Kong: Hong Kong University Press, 2015.

Picker, Giovanni. *Racial Cities: Governance and the Segregation of Romani People in Urban Europe*. London; New York: Routledge, 2019.

Pinney, Christopher. *Camera Indica: The Social Life of Indian Photographs*. London: Reaktion, 1997.

Prashad, Vijay. 'The Technology of Sanitation in Colonial Delhi'. *Modern Asian Studies* 35, no. 1 (2001): 113–55.

Prakash, Gyan. *Mumbai Fables*. Princeton; Oxford: Princeton University Press, 2011.

Prestel, Joseph Ben. *Emotional Cities: Debates on Urban Change in Berlin and Cairo, 1860–1910*. Oxford: Oxford University Press, 2017.

Ranajit, Guha. 'A Colonial City and Its Time(s)'. *The Indian Economic and Social History Review* 45, no. 3 (September 2008): 329–51.

Rao, Anupama. *The Caste Question: Dalits and the Politics of Modern India*. Berkeley: University of California Press, 2009.

Rao, Nikhil. *House, but No Garden. Apartment Living in Bombay's Suburbs, 1898–1964*. Minneapolis: University of Minnesota Press, 2013.

Ray, A. K. *A Short History of Calcutta, Town and Suburbs*. Calcutta: Riddhi India, 1982.

Ray, Rajat Kanta. *Urban Roots of Indian Nationalism*. New Delhi: Vikas Publishing House Pvt Ltd, 1980.

Raychaudhuri, Tapan. *Europe Reconsidered: Perceptions of the West in Nineteenth-Century Bengal*. Delhi: Oxford University Press, 1998.

———. 'Mother of the Universe, Motherland'. *The Rite Stuff* 1, no. 4 of *The Little Magazine*.

Robinson, Cedric J. and Robin D. G. Kelley. *Black Marxism: The Making of the Black Radical Tradition*. Chapel Hill, NC: The University of North Carolina Press, 2000.

Rogaski, Ruth. *Hygienic Modernity*. Berkeley, CA: University of California Press, 2014.

Roy, M. N. *Political Letters*. Zurich: Vanguard Bookshop, 1924.

———. 'Who Will Lead? Class Differentiation in the Indian National Movement'. *Communist International* 11 (1925): 55–65.

Roy, Praskanva Sinha. 'A New Politics of Caste'. *Economic and Political Weekly* 47, no. 34 (25 August 2012): 26–7.

Ryan, James R. *Picturing Empire: Photography and the Visualization of the British Empire*. London: Reaktion, 1997.

Sarkar, Sumit. *Writing Social History*. New Delhi: Oxford University Press, 2009.

Sarkar, Tanika and Śekhara Bandyopadhyay. *Calcutta: The Stormy Decades*. London: Routledge, 2018.

Schmid, Hillel. *Neighborhood Self-Management: Experiments in Civil Society*. New York: Springer Science & Business Media, 2001.

Seal, Anil. *The Emergence of Indian Nationalism: Competition and Collaboration in the Later Nineteenth Century*. Cambridge: Cambridge University Press, 1971.

Sen, Asok. *Iswar Chandra Vidyasagar and His Elusive Milestones*. Calcutta: Riddhi-India, 1977.

Sen, Dwaipayan. *The Decline of the Caste Question: Jogendranath Mandal and the Defeat of Dalit Politics in Bengal*. Cambridge; New York: Cambridge University Press, 2018.

Sen, Jai. 'The Unintended City'. In 'Life and Living'. *Seminar 200*, 1976.

Sen, Ranjit. *Birth of a Colonial City: Calcutta*. New York: Routledge, Taylor & Francis, 2019.

Sennett, Richard. *The Fall of Public Man*. New York; London: W. W. Norton & Company, 1992.

Sengupta, Kaustubh Mani. 'Community and Neighbourhood in a Colonial City: Calcutta's Para'. *South Asia Research* 38, no. 1 (February 1, 2018): 40–56.

Sett, Nagendranath. *Kalikatastha TantuBanik Jatir Itihas*. Calcutta: A. K. Basaka, 1950.

Singh, Abhay Kumar. *Modern World System and Indian Proto-Industrialization: Bengal 1650–1800*. New Delhi: Northern Book Centre, 2006.

Sinha, Mrinalini. *Colonial Masculinity: The 'Manly Englishman' and the Effeminate Bengali in the Late Nineteenth Century*. New Delhi: Kali for Women, 1997.

Sinha, Pradip. *Calcutta in Urban History*. Calcutta: Firma KLM, 1978.

Sircar, Jawhar. 'Durga Pujas as Expressions of "Urban Folk Culture"'. *The Times of India*, 23 October 2011.

Smith, Neil. *Uneven Development: Nature, Capital and the Production of Space*. Oxford: Blackwell, 1984.

Sourabh, Naresh Chandra, and Timo Myllyntaus. 'Famines in Late Nineteenth-Century India: Politics, Culture, and Environmental Justice'. *Environment*

Bibliography

and Society Portal, Virtual Exhibitions 2015, no. 2. Rachel Carson Center for Environment and Society, Munich.

Spodek, Howard. 'City Planning in India Under British Rule'. *Economic and Political Weekly* 48, no. 4 (2013): 53–61.

Stokes, Eric. *The English Utilitarians and India*. Delhi; New York: Oxford University Press, 1990.

Subramaniam, Banu. *Holy Science: The Biopolitics of Hindu Nationalism*. Seattle: University of Washington Press, 2019.

Streets, Heather. *Martial Races: The Military, Race and Masculinity in British Imperial Culture, 1857–1914*. Manchester: Manchester University Press, 2011.

Subramanian, Lakshmi. *Three Merchants of Bombay: Trawadi Arjunji Nathji, Jamsetjee Jeejeebhoy, and Premchand Roychand: Doing Business in Times of Change*. New Delhi: Allen Lane, 2012.

Subrahmanyam, Sanjay. *Improvising Empire: Portuguese Trade and Settlement in the Bay of Bengal, 1500–1700*. Oxford: Oxford University Press, 1990.

Weightman, Gavin. *London's Thames: The River That Shaped a City and Its History*. Macmillan, 2005.

Wright, G. *The Politics of Design in French Colonial Urbanism*. Chicago: University of Chicago Press, 1991.

Yeoh, Brenda S.A. *Contesting Space in Colonial Singapore: Power Relations and the Urban Built Environment*. Singapore: Singapore University Press, 2003.

Zeheter, Michael. *Epidemics, Empire, and Environments: Cholera in Madras and Quebec City, 1818–1910*. Pittsburgh: University of Pittsburgh Press, 2016.

Index

Ahiritola Street, dispute in, 91
Ahmed, Sultan, 96
*akhara*s (gymnasiums), 132, 137
All India Untouchability League, 163
All-India Muslim League, 179
Ambedkar, 163–164
American colonialism, 35
American playground movement, 132
Amherst Street, 30
Amin, Shaik Moniruddin, 96
Amrita Bazar Patrika, 80
ancestral house (*bastubhita*s), 76–7, 82, 86, 88, 90, 107, 190
Anderson, Warwick, 35
Anglo-Indian
    collaboration, 120
    economic partnership, 120
    trade, 114, 116
annachattra, 118, 141–2
anti-cholera campaign, 130–1, 179
anti-colonial nationalism, 4
anti-plague measures, 56
anti-spitting campaign, 131
Appadurai, Arjun, 14, 110
Arnold, David, 16, 35
Arya Samaj, 165–6, 172, 182
Arya Samaj Dalit Uddhar Samity, 172
Arya Samajists, 165–6, 182
Asiatic Journal and Monthly Register, 32
atomization, 42
awqaf (plural of waqf), 95
Ayurveda, 5

Baghbazaar Amateur Theatre group, 138
Baghbazaar Sarbojonin Club, 142
Baghbazaar Sarbojonin Durgotsav, 141

Baghbazaar, 117
Balak Sangha, 132–40
Ballygunge
    New, 83
    Old, 82–3
    Railway Station, 78
Banerjee, S. N., 80
Bangiya Sābarna Kathā, 146n23
baroyaari (organized by twelve friends), 140–1
Barrabazaar, 41, 55, 75–80, 83, 175, 181
Battle of Plassey (1757), 3
Bayly, C. A., 120
Behar, Cem, 14
Bellew, H. W., 65n71
Bengal Legislative Council, 81
Bengal Muslim league, 96
Bengal Regulation I of 1824, 73
Bengali
    consciousness, 4
    intellectuals, 4
    nationalism, 6, 19, 108, 139
Bengali city dwellers, resistance to
    waterworks, 26–7
bhadralok(s) (gentlemen), 5, 131, 139–41, 144,
        145n4, 151n105, 154–6, 160–1, 163–4,
        167, 170–1, 173–7, 180, 182–3, 191,
        193–7
    assisted local health associations, 128
    associations, 149n79
    borrowed colonial categories, 16
    campaign to sanitize bustees, 20
    challenged wealth-based authority, 123
    civilizing process, 17
    clubs, 195–7
    constituted health promotion societies,
        129

Index

fitness exercises in neighbourhood parks, 132

encouraged cultural programmes, 138

focus on shaping social perceptions, 127

Hindu-Bengali, 19

kinetic commentary on filth, 184–5

led process of spatial *shuddhi*, 17–18

meaning of, 4, 21n13

not allowing women at para clubs, 137

origin of, 122

professions, 6

promoted agenda and character of Hindu nationalism, 143

sanitarians, 127, 137

supervision of paras, 126–7

surveys conducted by, 108

swarajists collaboration with, 107

urbanists, 13–14, 17, 128

voluntary association of, 4, 125–6

Bhattacharya, Sabyasachi, 4, 124

Bhattachraya, Bijon, 175

Birla, G. D., 169

Bissell, William Cunningham, 8, 11

Bombay *chawl*s, 83

Bompas, C. H., 96

Bose, Subhas Chandra, 139, 142

Boulton, Matthew, 33

Bow Street tenements, 84

Brahmachari, U. N.

advised Bengalis for exercise, 142–3

discovered treatment for kala-zaar in 1922, 142

Breeze, Gerald, 7

Breeze's theory, 7

Bremner, G. A., 20n6

Brien, Dr. G., 40, 42

British East India Company, 28, 53, 119–20

British health maps, 38

British Nationality and Status of Aliens Act of 1914, 51

British urbanism in India, 3

buddhir koushol process, 25

bustee, 16–20, 49, 95, 129, 144, 154–75, 177–85, 191, 193–5

Calcutta Building Commission, 46–52

Calcutta Domiciled Committee 1918–1919, 103n54

Calcutta Harijan Sabha (Calcutta Society for Improving Harijans), 172

Calcutta Improvement Trust, 9–13, 18, 68–76, 78–80, 87, 107

requirement of land, 80–5

Tribunal decisions between 1922 and 1926, 85–7

Calcutta Journal, 30

Calcutta Municipal Act of 1876, 158

Calcutta Municipal Amendment Act of 1899, 158

Calcutta Municipal Corporation, 49, 70, 74, 81, 85, 124, 133, 156, 168

Calcutta Municipal Gazette, 124

caste, 2–3, 7, 11, 13–14, 26, 35, 49, 52, 70–1, 98, 108, 110, 123, 138, 141, 145n4, 146n14, 154, 163, 186n25, 190, 192, 194

-based familiarity, 20n5

-based mobilization in Bengal, 170

-based paras, 5, 19, 112

choices, 129

identities, 128

inter-, 173

lines, 98

lower, 5–6, 15–16, 18, 51, 109, 116, 135, 155, 168–9, 171, 180, 182, 184

-marked socio-spatial entity, 17

overlapped, 161

upper-, 4, 12, 18, 34, 51, 53, 75, 84, 107, 111–13, 116, 135, 156, 161, 164–6, 173, 186n40, 191, 197

Central Avenue, 73, 76–8, 82, 86

Chang, Jiat Hwee, 11

Chattopadhyay, Swati, 7–8, 38

cholera, 37–8, 40–1, 130–1, 161, 171

broke out in 1875, 39, 46

lower-class filth disease, 191

Chopra, Preeti, 3, 7

Chowdhury, Barada Prasad, 159

city nation, 5–6, 107, 123, 140, 154, 156, 163, 170, 177

city space, 109–11
civicization, 125
Civil Disobedience movement, 123
civilizing process, 5
civitas dei (city of god), 156–7, 176
Clark, William, 26, 33
clubs, 76, 82, 106, 108, 119, 121, 133–5, 137–43, 177–8, 181, 196 (see also *para*[s])
Cohen, William, 38
College Street, 29
colonial city
    as a joint enterprise between British colonizers and Indian traders, 3
    Kolkata/Calcutta as a, 6–9
colonial Improvement Trusts, 11–12, 18
colonial Zanzibar, 8
colonization of bodies, 16
communalism, 4, 174, 182
Communist Party of India, 155, 175, 182
Cook, J. Nield, 45
Cornwallis Street, 29, 95
courtyard, 38–9, 45, 47–8, 58, 84, 90–1, 138
    building commission refusal in Indian houses, 59
    meaning of, 106
    of neighbourhood houses, 85
    receptacles of filth and kutcha huts, 35
    refuse-filled, 37
    use by Bengalis for worship and social gatherings, 34
cultural imperialism, 34
Cunningham, D. D., 157–8
cycle-*pracharak*s, 164–6, 179, 184

*daktar*s, 6
*dalit*s (lowest caste), 13–14, 19, 161, 164, 168–70, 174, 186n25, 194–5
dana, 113–23
daridranarayan, 156–7, 184
Das, C. R., 123
Dasgupta, Satish, 167–9
Datta, Partho, 11, 32
debutter, 12, 69
    estate, 93
    private, 91

property, 69, 87–95
    public, 91
de Certeau, Michel, 13, 113
Deb, Binay Krishna, 29
Dighi, Lal, 6
dirtiness, 6, 14, 37, 168, 191
    of bustee, 170
    as caste disposition, 164
    deterioration of public health, 158
    of Indian, 38
    of lower castes, 180
    as racial disposition, 38
    selective representation, 38
disciplinary power, concept of, 8
discursive
    black town, 8
    production, 8, 35–6, 59, 155, 163, 167
Donner, Henrike, 110
Doorgah Money Bewah
Drainage Committee, 64n43
Durga Puja, 106–8, 119–22, 126, 140–3, 145n3, 149n66, 153n124, 173, 177–8, 190

economic boycott movement in 1905, 108
Edensor, Tim, 13
Egypt, British colonialism in, 8
Elliot Road, 29
endowment deed (*waqfnamaah*), 95
enframes space, 8
Ernest John Trevelyan, 63n41–42, 66n82–85, n88–89, n98–99, 67n119–120
Escobar, Arturo, 9
European modernity, 12

fascism, 155–6, 175–7, 179–81
filth/filthy, 8, 10, 18, 26–7, 35–8, 41–2, 44, 47, 57, 60n2, 72, 75, 95, 144, 155, 158, 161, 163, 165, 167–9, 180, 191–2
    accumulation of, 157
    bodies, 194
    British portrayals of Bengalis, 45–6
    of native privies, 40
    -ridden bustees, 17, 184
    -ridden spaces, 17

Index

221

fitness programmes, 17, 108, 124, 129, 132, 134–5, 143

flat dwellers, 83, 90

flats, 11, 30, 75, 82–4, 90, 98, 101n21, 197

follow the leader, 135

Foucault, Michel, 8

Ganpati festival, 153n124

Geddes, Patrick, 76–7, 101n23

germ theory, 37

German Cholera Commission, 63n36

*ghat*s (bathing platforms), 31, 117

Ghosh, B. C., 124

Ghosh, Chandra Kanta, 86–7, 93

Ghosh, Durba, 156

Glasgow Improvement Trust of 1866, 72, 100n10

Glover, William, 3, 7

Government of India Act of 1935

Guha, Ranajit, 14, 111

Gupta, Swarupa, 3

Habermas, Jurgen, 109
  public sphere, 15

Haffkine's vaccine, 49

Harijan Sevak Sangh (HSS), 163–6

Harijans (lowest caste), 163–9, 184, 186n25

Harijan Week (May 1933), 172–3

Harvey, David, 10

Haussmann, Georges-Eugène, 78

health association, 6, 127–32, 140, 143

Hindu-Bengali nation, 4, 14, 19–20, 108, 111, 122, 131–2, 140, 143, 163, 174, 194, 197

Hindu Bengali nationalists, 145n4

Hindu hygiene, 6, 19, 127, 129, 140, 155, 172, 194–5

Hindu Mahasabha, 182

Hindu merchants
  and *dana*s, 113–23
  worshipped deity in private recesses, 106

Home, Robert, 10

Hosagrahar, Jyoti, 7

Hossack, W. C., 66n97

hygiene, 1, 5, 37, 69, 71–2, 75, 77–8, 80, 126–8, 131, 139, 144, 156–7, 161, 164, 168–70, 179, 184, 192–4
  Calcutta, 98
  Hindu, 6, 14, 19, 129–30, 140, 155, 172, 195
  moral, 163
  personal, 6
  racialization of, 163
  science of, 56
  and urban modernity, 15–18
  Victorian notions of, 68
  Western, 99n2

Hussain, Hedayat, 96

Hutnyk, John, 9

immigrants, 6, 7

Indian National Congress, 2, 96, 123

indigenous modernity, 7–8

James Watt & Company, 26, 33

Jayal, Niraja Gopal, 51

Jayne, Mark, 13

jhupdi (shack), 96

Jorabagaan, 40–1, 49

Justices of the Peace, 31, 57

Kahar, Bhundoo, 41

*kangali micchil*s, 175

Kar, S. K., 133

Karim, Farhan, 84

Kennedy, Liam, 10

Kidambi, Prashant, 11, 14

King, Anthony D., 7, 27, 114

kinship-like ties, 4, 15, 107, 110–11, 113, 116, 119, 125, 195

kishore bahini, 181

Knights of the Broom, 166

kutcha, 43–4
  houses, 42
  huts, 33, 35, 38, 48–9
  structures, 42, 45

Lanchester, H. V., 84

Land Acquisition Act of 1894, 71, 74

landscapes, colonial, 28–36

Laporte, Dominique, 38
lathi khela (game of staves), 133, 135–6, 140–1
Lefebvre, Henri, 2, 10
Left radicalism, 124
libraries, 126, 138–40
Lottery Committee, 29–32, 62n24, 68

Maden, J. M., 73
*madrasa*s (schools), 95
*mahalle*s in Istanbul, 14
Mahatma Gandhi, 123, 156, 163, 197
   boycott of British products, 108
   Civil Disobedience Movement, 140
   on filth of the city, 165
   ideas of untouchability, 165
   nationalism, 108, 176
   Non-Cooperation movement, 124
   Non-violence, 139
Malkani, Naraindas Rattanmal, 167
Marwari Chamber of Commerce, 75
Marwari, 18, 34, 39–40, 71, 75–7, 86, 169–70
marzul-maut, 97
Masselos, Jim, 14
Mbembe, Achille, 13
Mehedibagan, 171
Mill, John Stuart, 29, 32
Mitchell, Timothy, 8, 27
modernization, 7
*mofussil*s (satellite towns), 4
moholla, 14, 20n5, 110, 146n14, 152
monumental space, 2
Moorghyhatta Road, 30
Moreno, H. B., 84
Moulavi Fazal Ul Haq, 96
Mukerjee, Radhakamal, 125
Mukharji, Projit Bihari, 6, 37
Mullick, Madubram, 31
Mullick, Nilmani, 117
Mullick, Ramchunder, 31
Mullick, Saratchandra, 58
multipurpose Swaraj, 160
Municipal Act of 1923, 159
Muslim League, 96, 174–5, 179–80, 182
Muslim rule in Bengal and threat to Hindus, 2

Nair, Janaki, 12
Nandy, Ashis, 15
Nehru, Motilal, 123
neighbourhoods, Bengali, 36
Neve, Geert De, 110
Nightingale, Carl, 10
*nagorik*s (citizens), 28, 51
   Hindu in colonial city, 52–9
   refashion their own identities, 59–60
Non-Cooperation movement, 123–4
Nuttall, Sarah, 13

Orsini, Francesca, 4

Pakshi, Rupchand, 25
Pal, Bipin Chandra, 123, 125
*pandal*s (decorated canopies), 106, 140–1, 173
Pande, Ishita, 17
Pandey, Gyanendra, 4, 52
para(s), 6, 12–15, 98–9, 111, 133–4, 137–8, 140, 142, 144, 145n5, 147n25, 151n105, 155–6, 161, 163, 174–75, 177, 179–82, 184, 191, 193–7
   Bhat-, 112
   caste-based, 5, 19, 112
   clubs, 4, 125–7, 135, 143, 149n80, 173
   committees, 177–8
   cultural life of, 2
   Das-, 112
   Dhali-, 112
   Duley-, 112–13
   dwellers, 108, 178
   earliest Calcutta, 3
   early, 113–23
   Goyal-, 112
   health association, 6, 127–32, 140, 143
   Hindu-Bengali, 154, 169
   Jeley-, 112
   Kulin-, 113
   Kumar-, 112
   Kumor-, 113
   meaning of, 2, 106–7
   middle-class, 16
   Muchi-, 112–13
   offering fertile grounds for Bengali nation, 4

Index

providing space for nationalists, 111
Sabarna-, 112–13
urbanization in, 2
urban life in, 113
Park Street, 82, 90
parks, 93, 98, 106, 109, 132–7, 140, 143, 173, 177, 194
Permanent Settlement (1793), 80
physical fitness, 133–4
Picker, Giovanni, 10
Pinney, Christopher, 8
plague, 10, 36–8, 41, 48–9, 55–6, 68, 71, 75–6, 158, 161–2, 167–8
playground movement, 132–40
pukka (or brick-built houses), 33–4, 42, 44, 48
Pultah, 25–6, 33

*qabristan*s (graveyards), 95

racial capitalism, 9–10
rajasik, concept of, 124
rajdharma, 54–6
Rashbehari Avenue, 82–3
Ray, Subhas Chandra, 78
Raychaudhuri, Tapan, 4
regional community-based identity construction, 4
Richards, E.P., 72, 101*n*35
Risley, Herbert, 70–1
Robinson, Cedric, 9–10
Rogaski, Ruth, 16
Rouf, Abdur, 96
Roy, M. N., 176
Russa Road, 78–9, 87–90
Russel Street, 40
Rutland, Ted, 10
Ryan, James, 8

samaj(es), 2–4, 111–14, 116–18, 146*n*24
samaj-ik, 138
sarbojonin (public) (*see* Durga Puja)
sattwik, concept of, 124
selective representation
colonial strategy of, 9, 38
meaning of, 27, 40
Sen, Jai, 15

Sen, Mathur Mohun, 92–3
Sengupta, Kaustubh Mani, 14
*sevak*s (volunteers), 128–30
Simla Byayam Samiti, 141–2
Simpson, William John Ritchie, 42–6, 158
Singapore Improvement Trust, 11
Smith, Neil, 10
Social Darwinist theory, 10
Societies Registration Act, 1860 74, 149*n*80
south suburban municipality, 75–80, 82
spatial *shuddhi,* 17–18, 155
benefits of, 184
campaigns, 177, 195
external, 165
internal, 165
process of exchange, 167–74
Swadeshi
activism, 71
economic boycott movement, 108, 154
factories, 154
movement, 70
products, 156
Swaraj in Calcutta paras, 123–5
Swarajist Corporation, 129, 133, 163–4
Swarajists (members of Swaraj Party), 19–20, 123, 141–3, 155–6, 161, 163, 175–7, 179–80, 184, 193
adopted from Mukerjee idea of civicization, 125
Bengali, 108
as city administrators, 156
cleanliness means control in 1930, 131
collaboration with *bhadralok*s, 107–8
commissioned a special playground committee, 132–3
divided city into blocks, 128
efforts to transform paras into Hindu-Bengali city-nation units, 154
employed hygiene, 127
encourage flowering of Bengali nationalism, 139
Harijan Week celebrations in bustees, 172
municipal rule, 14, 111
on nation and nationalism, 124
plan for multipurpose Swaraj, 160

samajes fired envision of nation, 4–5
separatism with Gandhian nationalism, 108
sponsored maternity and health week for
women, 137
targeted para, 111
two-pronged policy in bustees, 159
urban improvement initiatives, 131
vision of street-level institutes, 125
won municipal elections in Calcutta, 124
worked with clubs and libraries, 139
Swaraj party
defeated British in municipal elections in
1923, 1
Strachey, John, 26
Strachey, John, 26, 63*n*38
Strand Road, 29
Svasthya, Bengali health periodicals, 51

tamasik, concept of, 124
Tarun Sangha, 20, 23, 132–40
town(s)
black, 1–3, 7–10, 15, 17–19, 22*n*20, 27,
35–46, 59–60, 68, 114–15, 155,
163, 167, 169, 191–2, 196

white, 1, 7–9, 17, 22n20, 27, 114–15, 190,
192

Upjohn, A., 62*n*21
urban modernity, 15–18
uthhon, 34

ventilation, in Bengali houses, 34
Virastami festival, 142

waqf, 69
and public purpose, 95–8
*waqif*s (settlers), 95
Ward Institution Lane, 83–4
Wellesley Street, 30
Wellington Street, 30
Western categories of hygiene, 16
Westernization, 7

*yatimkhana*s (orphanages), 95
Yeoh, Brenda S. A., 11, 66*n*81

zamindari (tax collecting) rights, 6
Zeheter, Michael, 37